Banana Republicans

Also by Sheldon Rampton and John Stauber

WEAPONS OF MASS DECEPTION

TRUST US, WE'RE EXPERTS!

TOXIC SLUDGE IS GOOD FOR YOU!

MAD COW U.S.A.

Banana Republicans

How the Right Wing Is Turning America
Into a One-Party State

SHELDON RAMPTON
and **JOHN STAUBER**

JEREMY P. TARCHER / PENGUIN
A MEMBER OF PENGUIN GROUP (USA) INC.
NEW YORK

Most Tarcher/Penguin books are available at special quantity discounts for bulk purchase for sales promotions, premiums, fund-raising, and educational needs. Special books or book excerpts also can be created to fit specific needs. For details, write Penguin Group (USA) Inc. Special Markets, 375 Hudson Street, New York, NY 10014.

Jeremy P. Tarcher/Penguin
a member of
Penguin Group (USA) Inc.
375 Hudson Street
New York, NY 10014
www.penguin.com

Library of Congress Cataloging-in-Publication Data

Rampton, Sheldon, date.
    Banana republicans: how the right wing is turning America into
a one-party state / by Sheldon Rampton and John Stauber.
        p. cm.
    Includes index.
    ISBN 1-58542-342-4
        1. Republican Party (U.S. : 1854–) 2. Business and politics—
United States. 3. United States—Politics and government—2001–
I. Stauber, John C. (John Clyde), date.   II. Title.
JK2356.R26   2004   2004046015
324.2734—dc22

Printed in the United States of America
10 9 8 7 6 5 4 3 2 1

This book is printed on acid-free paper. ∞

BOOK DESIGN BY LOVEDOG STUDIO

Contents

Acknowledgments

We thank our employer, the nonprofit educational organization Center for Media & Democracy, and the individuals and nonprofit foundations that have supported its work since 1993. This book is part of the center's unique mission of investigating propaganda as corporations and governments use it. For information on the center, visit its website at www.prwatch.org, or contact its office: 520 University Avenue, Suite 227, Madison, Wisconsin 53703; phone (608) 260-9713.

Many thanks to our wonderful colleagues Bob Burton, Diane Farsetta, Kristian Knutsen and Laura Miller, and especially to Diane, whose research and writing contributed substantially to Chapters Four, Five, and Six of this book.

Thanks especially to our editor, Mitch Horowitz, for his patience, insight and ability to find order in the chaos of our first drafts. Thanks also to publisher Joel Fotinos of Tarcher/Penguin for the opportunity to write it. We thank Tarcher/Penguin publicists Ken Siman and Kelly Groves, and Tom Grady, our wise agent and adviser.

The following organizations and individuals have helped us with ideas, comments, research and other support: Grant Abert, Harriet Barlow, Benno, Laura Berger, Jenny Clark, Jon Cracknell, Deer Creek Foundation, the Disinfopedia Community (www. disinfopedia.org), Christian Ettinger, Linda and Gene Farley, Jonathan Frieman, Ross Gelbspan, Lynn Haanen, Dan Hind, HKH Foundation, Linda Jameson, Rob Levine, Donna Balkan Litowitz, Art and Sue Lloyd, William Lutz, Marianne Manilov, Bob McChesney, Joe Mendelson, David Merritt, Chris Micklos, Ellen Miller, Michael Picker, Scott Robbe, Debra Schwarze, Louis Slesin, Paul Alan Smith, Gerson Smoger, John H. Stauber, Stephen Viederman, Ted Welch, Sean Wilentz and Walda Wood.

Finally, Sheldon would like to dedicate this book to the memory of his uncle, Roger Marchant, whose life exemplified the virtues of thoughtful, informed citizenship, love of family and basic human decency—the real resources from which democracy draws its strength.

The War at Home

"I'm a uniter, not a divider," said candidate George W. Bush during his 2000 campaign for president. "I refuse to play the politics of putting people into groups and pitting one group against another."[1] This promise to be a "uniter, not a divider" was a recurrent theme throughout Bush's campaign, repeated verbatim in media interviews, fund-raising letters, campaign stump speeches and debates.

As Bush neared the end of his first term, however, evidence suggested that he had been just the opposite. The Pew Research Center for the People and the Press conducts periodic opinion polls that compare the attitudes of Republican and Democratic voters. "National unity was the initial response to the calamitous events of Sept. 11, 2001," noted its November 2003 update, "but that spirit has dissolved amid rising political polarization and anger. In fact, a year before the presidential election, American voters are once again seeing things largely through a partisan prism. . . . The Pew Research Center's longitudinal measures of basic political, economic and social values, which date back to 1987, show that political polarization is now as great as it was prior to the 1994 midterm elections that ended four decades of Democratic control in Congress."[2]

The reasons for these deepening divisions are not hard to find. The voting system that brought Bush into office was seriously flawed, and he presided over an unsteady economy, soaring budget deficits, tax cuts that primarily benefit the wealthy, some of the worst business scandals in U.S. history and a devastating terrorist attack. As Bush prepared to run for re-election, fears of future terrorism continued to grip the nation, which had become embroiled in two overseas guerrilla wars with no end in sight. Outside its own borders, moreover, the administration's aggressive foreign policy made the United States hated and feared as never before. These conditions might seem to have presented an opportune moment for serious reconsideration of America's course and future direction in the early 21st century, and yet during the first three years of the Bush presidency, little serious public debate could be heard.

These conditions reflected the highly effective political organizing strategy of the conservative coalition that brought the Bush administration to power. The Republican party's hard right—"movement conservatives," as they like to call themselves—hold views and long-term objectives that are considerably to the right of mainstream public opinion, but they had managed to maneuver themselves into a position of control over nearly every branch of the American government. As we will explore, politics for them is not a debate. It is, quite literally, a "war by other means."

Intellectual Ammunition

During the 2000 presidential and congressional elections, every Republican member of the U.S. Congress received a free pamphlet, compliments of Congressman Tom DeLay, the party's majority whip. Written by conservative activist David Horowitz, the pamphlet was called *The Art of Political War: How Republicans Can Fight to Win*. It came with an endorsement on the cover by Karl Rove, the senior adviser to then-candidate George W. Bush. According to Rove, *The Art of Political War* was "a perfect pocket guide to winning on the political battlefield from an experienced warrior." In addition to DeLay's gift to members of Congress, the Heritage Foundation, one of the leading conservative think tanks in Washington, found Horowitz's advice so impressive that it sent another 2,300 copies to conservative activists around the country.[3]

True to its title, *The Art of Political War* argues that "Politics is war conducted by other means. In political warfare you do not fight just to prevail in an argument, but to destroy the enemy's fighting ability. . . . In political wars, the aggressor usually prevails." Moreover, "Politics is a war of position. In war there are two sides: friends and enemies. Your task is to define yourself as the friend of as large a constituency as possible compatible with your principles, while defining your opponent as the enemy whenever you can. The act of defining combatants is analogous to the military concept of choosing the terrain of battle. Choose the terrain that makes the fight as easy for you as possible."[4]

This concept of politics as warfare is intimately connected to Horowitz's personal political roots. In the 1960s, he was a militant Marxist and editor of *Ramparts*, one of the most radical leftist magazines in the United States. He also lent his vocal support to the Black Panther Party, which advocated and practiced armed "self-defense" against what it viewed as the "foreign occupying force" of racist white police. After becoming disillusioned with the Panthers, Horowitz took a hard swing to the right, thereby winning the admiration of the conservatives he used to denounce. His memoir of the 1960s, *Destructive Generation*, was one of three books that Karl Rove recommended to George W. Bush in 1993 as Rove began grooming Bush for the presidency.[5] Horowitz has visited Bush personally on several occasions to offer advice, beginning with Bush's days as governor of Texas and continuing during his presidency.[6]

Of course, Horowitz is not the only disillusioned leftist from the sixties. What makes him significant is that his militancy has remained constant, even as his worldview has changed. In a strange way, he remains a Leninist, right down to his appearance (balding, with a Lenin-like goatee). He even continues to offer Lenin's words as advice. "You cannot cripple an opponent by outwitting him in a political debate," he explains in *The Art of Political War*. "You can do it only by following Lenin's injunction: 'In political conflicts, the goal is not to refute your opponent's argument, but to wipe him from the face of the earth.'"[7]

Field Marshall Norquist

Grover Norquist is another prominent leader in the conservative movement's political war. "I would call him our field marshal," said Horace Cooper, a former aide to House majority leader Dick Armey.[8] Norquist helped the Heritage Foundation write Newt Gingrich's "Contract with America." His most important contribution, however, has been coalition building. Since 1992, he has hosted Wednesday morning meetings in the Washington, D.C., office of his organization, Americans for Tax Reform. The Wednesday meeting pulls together the heads of leading conservative organizations to coordinate activities and strategy. "The meeting functions as the weekly checklist so that everybody knows what's up, what to do," says Kellyanne Fitzpatrick, a conservative pollster and regular attendee.[9]

George W. Bush began sending a representative to the Wednesday meeting even before he formally announced his candidacy for president. "Now a White House aide attends each week," reported *USA Today* in June 2001. "Vice President Cheney sends his own representative. So do GOP congressional leaders, right-leaning think tanks, conservative advocacy groups and some like-minded K Street lobbyists. The meeting has been valuable to the White House because it is the political equivalent of one-stop shopping. By making a single pitch, the administration can generate pressure on members of Congress, calls to radio talk shows and political buzz from dozens of grassroots organizations."[10]

Norquist's coalition advocates abolishing taxes, especially estate taxes and capital-gains taxes. Regulations they want abolished include minimum-wage laws, affirmative action, health and safety regulations for workers, environmental laws and gun controls. They also support cutting or eliminating a variety of government programs including student loans, state pension funds, welfare, Americorps, the National Endowment for the Arts, farm subsidies and research and policy initiatives on global warming. Even well entrenched and popular programs such as Medicare, Social Security and education are targeted for rollbacks, beginning with privatization. Most members of the coalition are anti-gay and anti-abortion, although Norquist has made an effort to recruit gay and pro-choice Republicans.[11]

Norquist's political leanings were cemented in his youth by reading anti-communist tracts such as *Masters of Deceit* by J. Edgar Hoover and *Witness* by Whittaker Chambers.[12] During the 1980s, he visited battlegrounds in the Third World to support anti-Soviet guerrilla armies. In Africa, he assisted guerrilla movements backed by South Africa's apartheid regime — Mozambique's RENAMO and Jonas Savimbi's UNITA in Angola, for which he worked as a lobbyist in the 1990s.[13] Among the memorabilia in his Washington office, a prominent photograph shows Norquist holding an AK-47 in Afghanistan — a memento, not of the recent war, but of the 1980s when he and other Reagan conservatives backed the mujahideen in their guerrilla war against the occupying Soviet army.[14] If it troubles him that the mujahideen went on to become the organizing base for Al Qaeda, he has never said so publicly.

The connecting thread between these foreign adventures and the conservative movement's domestic issues is the idea, also born in the Cold War, that all government is somehow like the Soviet bureaucracy and that government programs aimed at promoting the general welfare are therefore "creeping socialism" that must be fought with the same ferocity with which the cold warriors countered revolution in countries like Angola or Mozambique. Norquist has declared that his goal is "to cut government in half in twenty-five years, to get it down to the size where we can drown it in the bathtub."[15]

This is also the logic behind the name of Norquist's group, Americans for Tax Reform. "It's not just because taxes are irritating and unpopular and all that," says journalist Elizabeth Drew, who profiled Norquist extensively in her book, *Whatever It Takes*:

The Real Struggle for Political Power in America. "He has a long-term view, which is the lower the revenues that the government takes in, the less spending it will be able to do, the less money will go to the groups that he sees as the base of the Democratic party and its power—the teachers' unions, welfare workers, municipal workers and so on. This is a big, long-term war. It's total. It's Armageddon. And I have to say that the people on the right, I think, have thought this through much more than their opponents on the other side who really don't much know what they do and how the opposition thinks and are just waking up to it."[16]

The Debate Club

Whereas Republicans see politics as a war, strategists for the Democratic Party tend to see politics as a debate. And at that level, they think they have been doing pretty well. According to Stanley Greenberg, who was Bill Clinton's pollster, the Democratic and Republican parties have been trapped in "the politics of parity" ever since Eisenhower's election in 1952 ended Democratic dominance and began "a half century that no party would dominate."[17] As an example of this parity, Greenberg points to the 2000 presidential election, in which voters split almost evenly between George W. Bush and Al Gore, with Gore actually winning a narrow majority in the popular vote. "The loyalties of American voters," Greenberg concludes, "are now almost perfectly divided between the Democrats and Republicans. . . . The two parties are so evenly matched that the slightest shift in the political winds could blow the balance."[18]

Other Democratic strategists, notably John B. Judis and Ruy

Teixeira, see bright prospects for the party's political future. Their 2002 book, *The Emerging Democratic Majority*, looked at the growing influence of Democratic-leaning voter blocs—minority voters, women and educated professionals—and predicted that "Democrats are likely to become the majority party of the early twenty-first century."[19]

Some of this analysis is valid. Over a period of decades, for example, polls have regularly shown that a majority of the American people support the U.S. Supreme Court's 1973 Roe v. Wade decision, which left the choice on whether to have an abortion up to a woman and her doctor.[20] On the environment, more than 70 percent of the American people believe that the burning of coal, oil and other fuels is responsible for global warming, and roughly the same majority supports the Kyoto Protocol and other international agreements to limit greenhouse gas emissions.[21] In a 2002 Gallup poll, more than half of respondents said they were concerned about water, soil and air pollution, damage to the earth's ozone layer and the loss of tropical rain forests.[22] Majorities of 70 to 80 percent support higher emissions and pollutions standards for industry, spending more government money on developing solar and wind power and stronger enforcement of environmental regulations.[23] Although terrorism and the war in Iraq have recently become significant public concerns, by far the most enduring concerns expressed in opinion polls are the economy and jobs, followed usually by health care, education and national defense. On the issue of health in particular, Democrats enjoy a clear advantage over Republicans. Surveys consistently show that most Americans want an *expanded* government, in the form of a tax-financed universal health-care program—an idea that Republicans consistently oppose and that liberal Democrats have supported.[24]

If politics were simply a matter of debate over policies, therefore, Democrats would appear well-positioned to defeat their Republican rivals.

The Fight Club

Whatever advantages the Democrats might enjoy in theory, Republicans have achieved victory upon victory in practice. The 2000 elections gave the Republican Party the White House, a razor-thin majority in the U.S. House of Representatives and a 50–50 split in the U.S. Senate. By 2002, the GOP was able to consolidate its control of the House and achieve a majority in the Senate. It already controlled the Supreme Court, with Republican appointees comprising seven of the nine justices who sit on the court. This gave the Republican Party majority control of every branch of the federal government for the first time since 1932.

The situation for Democrats didn't look any better at the state level. The 2002 elections, noted *Denver Post* reporter James Aloysius Farrell, "marked a tectonic and largely unheralded shift in the American political landscape. For the past half-century, Democrats dominated the state legislatures—in the mid-1970s by 2-to-1 ratios in the number of overall legislative seats. But when the dust settled after the 2002 elections, Republicans had emerged on top."[25] Norquist celebrated this victory by telling Farrell, "We are trying to change the tones in the state capitals —and turn them toward bitter nastiness and partisanship." He added, "Bipartisanship is another name for date rape" (an axiom that he attributed to one his mentors, former U.S. House Speaker Newt Gingrich).[26]

At the end of 2003, Republicans held a 28–22 majority of state governorships. They also controlled more state legislatures than Democrats. In 22 states, Republicans controlled both the state Senate and state House of Representatives. Democrats enjoyed similar control in only 16 states, with control split between the two parties in 12 others—the first time that Republicans have had a significant advantage in state legislatures since 1952.[27] According to conservative writer Bruce Walker, the shift of power at the state level reflected a long-term "disintegration of Democrat power in state legislatures. Twenty or thirty years ago, 'Republican state legislative strength' was an oxymoron. While Republicans won national elections and even controlled the Senate for six years under Reagan, Democrats totally dominated state legislatures."[28]

Republican domination of all these political institutions has created secondary synergistic effects that further strengthen the party's hold on power. Its dominance in the U.S. Supreme Court and its control of the Florida governor's mansion helped give George W. Bush the White House in 2000, even though Al Gore received a majority of the popular vote and irregularities dogged the Florida recount. Increased power at the state level has also enabled Republicans to push through electoral redistricting in several states, further solidifying the party's power at the national level. "In crafting its agenda for economic reform," Norquist wrote in June 2003, "the Bush administration has the luxury of being able to think and plan over a full eight years. . . . This guarantee of united Republican government has allowed the Bush administration to work and think long-term."[29] Republicans, he predicted, "are looking at decades of dominance in the House and Senate, and having the presidency with some regularity."[30]

The shift to Republican control has also extended the party's fund-raising advantage, and as former California State Assembly Speaker Jesse Unruh once observed, "money is the mother's milk of politics." To give just one example of how funding trends have shifted, tobacco industry contributions to politicians prior to 1990 were split evenly between Democrats and Republicans. As Republicans have increasingly dominated traditionally tobacco-friendly states in the South, industry funding has swung accordingly. From 1991 to 1994, Republicans received 62 percent of the industry's political contributions; from 1995 to 2000, they received 82 percent.[31] Similar trends have occurred in other business sectors. In 1990, agribusiness gave 56 percent of its contributions to Republicans. By 2002, that figure had climbed to 72 percent. During the same period, contributions to Republicans from the defense industry went from 60 to 69 percent; from construction, 53 to 65 percent; energy and natural resource extraction, 53 to 65 percent; finance, insurance and real estate, 48 to 58 percent; health care, 48 to 65 percent; transportation, 53 to 71 percent; other businesses, 59 to 65 percent. The only business sector to buck the trend was communications and electronics, which increased its giving to Democrats slightly, from 58 to 61 percent.[32]

One-party dominance has also muted political debates that would have otherwise greeted many of the actions of President George W. Bush. The presidential administrations of Ronald Reagan, the first George Bush and Bill Clinton all had to contend with opposition from at least one other branch of government, and the resulting hearings in the House of Representatives or the Senate fueled controversy and media coverage. With the same party controlling all branches of government, there has been minimal public debate over the policies of the current Bush administration, even as it has launched two wars, reversed long-standing policies on worker safety and the environment and cut taxes for the rich while 2.7 million private-sector jobs have been lost and the number of unemployed Americans has increased by more than 45 percent under its watch.

Although Republicans frequently complain about the "liberal bias" of the news media—the so-called fourth branch of government—the reality is that conservatives have become increasingly influential within the media, with overwhelming domination of talk radio and a preponderant advantage on cable television, if not on the broadcast networks. In November 2003, conservatives demonstrated their power to influence the media agenda when they mounted an organized outcry that succeeded in killing the CBS network's broadcast of a docudrama about the presidency of Ronald Reagan. CBS yielded, according to conservative *U.S. News & World Report* columnist John Leo, because "the conservative media world is now good at gang tackling. From Matt Drudge's *Drudge Report* (which framed the issue of the miniseries) to Fox, the bloggers, talk-radio hosts and the columnists, everybody piled on."[33] A couple of weeks later, by contrast, there was no comparable outcry when the History Channel marked the 40th anniversary of the assassination of John F. Kennedy by airing a documentary which speculated that Lyndon B. Johnson had helped plot the assassination. The documentary drew angry condemnation from Johnson's family and former staff members, but otherwise there were virtually no public objections to its broadcast.[34]

The Permanent Warfare State

The Republican Party's successes have not come quickly or easily. For more than four decades, conservatives have worked to build a network of grassroots organizations and think tanks that formulate and promote conservative ideas—a process that we describe in Chapter One, "The Marketplace of Ideas." Conservatives are now enjoying the fruits of this long-term investment. Unhappy with what they regard as the "liberal bias" of the news media, they have attacked from both the outside and the inside, building their own, unabashedly conservative media such as talk radio and Fox News at the same time that they have systematically set about promoting the careers of conservatives *within* the mainstream media—a strategy that we explore in Chapter Two, "The Echo Chamber." They have built ideological alliances between industry, government and regulatory agencies, further blurring the lines between each, with consequences that we examine in Chapter Three, "The One-Party State." And although the entertainment industry may be more liberal than, say, the tobacco or construction industries, Republicans have been more effective than Democrats at capitalizing on the ways entertainment has transformed politics—the 2003 election of Arnold Schwarzenegger being a recent case in point, as we shall see in Chapter Four, "Pumping Irony." But they have also understood that politics involves more than dominating the news cycle or influencing public opinion, and they have not hesitated to use hardball tactics in pursuit of power. Blacks and other minorities consistently vote Democrat, so in response—as we show in Chapter Five, "Block the Vote"—Republicans have developed techniques for suppressing voter turnout in minority communities or have used old-fashioned gerrymandering to effectively marginalize minority votes. Notwithstanding their stated aversion to "big government," now that they have *become* the government they have not hesitated to expand its powers in precisely those areas that are most threatening to individual freedoms, through the USA Patriot Act and other measures that authorize spying on citizens and detentions without trial. The likelihood that those powers will be abused has increased, moreover, as the conservative movement accuses its ideological adversaries of "treason," "terrorism" and "un-Americanism," threatening long-standing traditions of tolerance and diversity. We discuss these trends in Chapter Six, "Traitor Baiters." In sum, the direction in which forces in the GOP are moving looks—at times absurdly, at times ominously—similar to the "banana republics" of Latin America: nations dominated by narrow corporate elites, which use the pretext of national security to violate the rights of their citizens.

David Horowitz's notion that politics is "war conducted by other means" inverts a statement originally made in 1832 by the German military theorist Carl von Clausewitz. Clausewitz stated that "war is merely the continuation of politics by other means." In this original formulation, war was one among multiple methods by which competing nations might resolve their differences. Clausewitz's original statement allowed for the possibility that differences could also be resolved peaceably, which of course he preferred. Without a political purpose, moreover, war becomes "pointless and devoid of sense." Accordingly, Clausewitz wrote, "No one starts a war—or rather, no one in his senses ought to do so—without first being clear in his mind what he intends to achieve by that war and how he intends to conduct it."[35]

Standing Clausewitz on his head, as the Republican right has done, leads to radically different and dangerous conclusions. If *politics* is merely the continuation of *war*, then war becomes the norm, and peaceful politicking becomes simply a temporary maneuver aimed at gaining battlefield advantage. The political arts of compromise, negotiation, dialogue and debate—even culture itself—become mere weapons with which to destroy your enemies. And since war is the norm, there is no need to worry about *whether* to start one. War already exists, and the point is simply to win or at least keep fighting. (Understanding this mentality may help explain why the Bush administration showed so much enthusiasm for initiating war in Iraq as part of a broader "war on terrorism," while displaying little interest in exit strategies or clarity about what it intended to achieve.)

When one party is able to impose its will without consulting others, the temptation is to run roughshod over the opposition—especially when it sees politics as a form of warfare. During late 2003, for example, the GOP developed a proposal for Medicare reform, which included the most sweeping changes since the program's establishment in 1965. Drug companies and private health care plans—strong financial backers of the party—stood to benefit financially from the reform proposal, and the Republican leadership simply ignored opposing viewpoints. House Democrats were excluded from the conference committee reconciling the House and Senate versions of the Medicare bill. When the House vote on the bill began on November 22, 2003, it faced defeat by a two-vote margin, as a number of the Republican Party's own congressmen refused to support its $400 billion price tag. Desperate to win, the GOP leaders held open the vote (normally a 15-minute procedure) for nearly three hours, the longest House roll call ever.

In what has been called "the most efficient party whip operation in congressional history,"[36] GOP Majority Leader Tom DeLay, Speaker Dennis Hastert, Health and Human Services Secretary Tommy Thompson and even President Bush used the prolonged roll call—from 3:00 a.m. to almost 6:00 a.m.—to persuade dissenting Republicans to change their votes. According to outgoing Michigan congressman Nick Smith, the "persuasion" included offers of assistance (by some accounts, including $100,000 in contributions) for his son's upcoming campaign. When Smith refused to change his vote, fellow Republicans taunted him, saying his son was "dead meat."[37]

The metaphors that guide politics have consequences that affect us all. The notion that politics is a process by which a community governs itself leads to radically different consequences than the notion that politics is a form of war. One assumption leads to civil debate, negotiation and compromise, while the other leads to incivility and a no-holds-barred approach that shreds moral restraints and institutional safeguards. Treating politics as war may be an effective way to win power, but it has rarely succeeded as a philosophy for wise governance.

CHAPTER ONE

The Marketplace of Ideas

"It was like hell had opened up," said Danny Smalley, as he testified in court about the death of his 17-year-old daughter, Danielle, on August 24, 1996.[1]

Danielle had been packing for college at her home near Lively, Texas, a small town southeast of Dallas, when her friend Jason Stone, also 17, stopped by to help plan her farewell party. They noticed the odor of butane gas about the same time that dozens of other people in the neighborhood began to notice it as well. "We had twenty-one nine-one-one calls in this area from the fumes so terrible that they were scared to turn their lights on, scared to leave, start their cars," recalled an emergency worker summoned to the scene.

Because the Smalley family did not have a phone, Danielle and Jason offered to go alert county emergency workers. Danny Smalley watched them get in the family pickup truck and drive off. Later, he said, he wished he had known how dangerous it was to operate a vehicle amid flammable vapors. "We would have run," he said. "I'm ignorant—I blame myself. Why didn't I get into the truck?"[2]

A few moments later, he heard the explosion. The road had taken Danielle and Jason into a low-lying area where the leaking gas had collected, causing their truck to stall. When they attempted to restart the engine, the ignition spark was like a match dropped in a 16-acre puddle of fuel. The explosion blew out the back windshield of the truck and sent a 150-foot fireball shooting from the ground at the spot where a high-pressure butane pipeline had rusted through. Despite rainfall that evening, the fireball continued to rage through the night, spewing smoke into the air and leaving a swath of more than 15 scorched acres looking as though they had been hit with napalm.

"I was hoping it wasn't my daughter, that it was something else," Danny Smalley recalled. "And then I seen the truck, and I knew that my baby had been killed."[3]

The pipeline belonged to Koch Industries, a company that operates one of the largest pipeline systems in the United States. Residents in the Smalleys' neighborhood said Koch had not told them about the pipeline's history of corrosion problems (which dated almost to the minute it was put into the ground) or that the electrical system intended to inhibit corrosion was not working properly.[4] Most residents had no idea that there was even a pipeline next to their homes.

It was not the first time that Koch Industries had operated a pipeline known to have problems. Just two years previously, corrosion in one of its oil pipelines had contributed to a 90,000-gallon oil spill that fouled miles of shoreline along the Texas Gulf Coast. In fact, Koch Industries is one of America's most notorious polluters. During the 1990s, its faulty pipelines were responsible for more than 300 oil spills in six states, prompting a landmark EPA penalty of $35 million.[5] In Minnesota, it was fined an additional $8 million for discharging oil into streams. During the months leading up to the 2000 presidential elections, the company faced even more liability, in the form of a 97-count federal indictment charging it with concealing illegal releases of 91 metric tons of benzene, a known carcinogen, from its refinery in Corpus Christi, Texas. If convicted, the company faced fines of up to $352 million, plus possible jail time for company executives.[6] That's more than small change even for a company the size of Koch Industries, the nation's second largest privately held company, with annual revenues of more than $25 billion.

Fortunately for Koch, it also had a cozy relationship with America's future ruling party. During the 2000 election campaign, Koch Industries and its employees donated more than $1 million to political campaigns, 90 percent of which went to Republicans.[7] Shortly after Bush's election, his Justice Department announced a deal with Koch, dropping all outstanding environmental charges against the company in exchange for a one-time fine of $20 million—about 5 percent of its potential liability if the case had gone to trial.[8] In addition, the administration also launched several policy initiatives to gut the Clean Air Act, the Clean Water Act and other environmental laws, thus opening the way for corporate polluters to dump toxins into the environment without fear of fines or prosecution. Of course, Koch was not the only company that gave big to Republicans and got a boost from

Bush's policies. During the 2000 elections, the oil and gas industries overall gave 77 percent of their $14 million in contributions to Republicans.[9] (The biggest single energy-industry contributor was Enron.)

The money that Koch gives to political candidates, however, is only a small part of the role that it has played in influencing politics. It has also played a key role for decades in financing the *ideas* that have driven the rise of the conservative movement. The company is owned by brothers Charles G. and David H. Koch, each of whom has a net worth of $4 billion, earning them separate spots in the *Forbes* list of the 50 richest people in America.[10] Like their father, Fred Koch, an oil-and-gas entrepreneur who was a founding member of the far-right John Birch Society in 1958,[11] they have used their wealth in concert with a handful of other extraordinarily wealthy individuals to build a political machine that spreads their ideas about law, culture, politics and economics throughout the political and media establishment. The Kochs are part of a network of conservative benefactors that support industry-friendly think tanks, experts and subsidized media that repeat, embellish and reinforce their core message that corporations are good while government regulations, labor unions, environmentalists, liberal Democrats and anything else that might restrict corporate behavior are bad.

A Million for Your Thoughts

The Koch brothers began actively funding conservative political causes in the 1970s through the Koch Family Foundations, which consist of the David H. Koch Charitable Foundation, the

Charles G. Koch Charitable Foundation, and the Claude R. Lambe Charitable Foundation. Since then, they have lavished tens of millions of dollars on "free market" advocacy in and around Washington. According to their filings with the Internal Revenue Service, they gave away more than $9 million in 2001 alone, almost all of it to conservative groups such as the libertarian Cato Institute (which Charles co-founded in 1977), Citizens for a Sound Economy (which David helped launch in 1986), the American Legislative Exchange Council, the Reason Foundation, Heritage Foundation, Landmark Legal Foundation and Young America's Foundation.[12]

Like the Koch brothers, another conservative billionaire, Richard Mellon Scaife—a member of the Mellon banking and oil family—also began giving heavily to conservative causes in the 1970s. According to former *Wall Street Journal* reporter Karen Rothmyer, Scaife was "the biggest funder of the New Right, spending millions of dollars a year to help establish the Heritage Foundation and a host of other think tanks focused on marketing conservative ideas both to Congress and to the public."[13] Since then, he has continued to be a prodigious funder of the right. After Republicans won a majority in Congress in the 1994 elections, political science professor Thomas Ferguson commented that Scaife "had as much to do with the Gingrich revolution as Gingrich himself."[14] By 1999, the *Washington Post* reported that Scaife's foundations—the Sarah Mellon Scaife Foundation, the Carthage Foundation, the Allegheny Foundation and the Scaife Family Foundation—had given $340 million over a period of four decades to conservative causes and institutions.[15] By 2002, they held more than $230 million in assets, and in that year alone they gave away more than $22 million.[16]

Other leading conservative funders include the following:

- The Milwaukee-based Lynde and Harry Bradley Foundation, with assets exceeding $532 million,[17] was founded by brothers Lynde and Harry Bradley, who made their fortunes producing electronic and radio components. Harry Bradley was an early financial supporter of the John Birch Society and a contributor to William F. Buckley's *National Review.*[18] The foundation gives away more than $25 million a year to promote the deregulation of business, privatization of public education, the rollback of social welfare programs and the privatization of government services. Bradley money supports major conservative groups such as the American Enterprise Institute and the Heritage Foundation.

- The John M. Olin Foundation, which grew out of a family manufacturing business in chemicals and munitions, had assets of approximately $90 million in 1998. Since the year 2000, however, it has begun spending down its endowment at a rate of about $20 million per year, with the goal of putting itself out of business by the end of the year 2005.[19] This policy reflects the wishes of John Olin, who selected politically like-minded colleagues to manage the fund upon his death and who wanted to make sure that following *their* deaths, the fund would not pass into the hands of people with contrary views.

- The Adolph Coors Foundation, funded by the family that owns the Adolph Coors brewery, earned notoriety in the 1970s and 1980s for its anti-union, anti-gay, anti-minority stance. Recipients of its funding have included Paul Weyrich's Free Congress Foundation, which has filed legal briefs opposing gay marriage, calling it "an infamous crime against nature." It also helped fund publication of Catholic priest Enrique Rueda's books, *The Homosexual Network* and *Gays, AIDS and You*, which refer ominously to "the evil nature" of homosexuality. It has also funded the Heritage Foundation, which opposes gays and lesbians serving in the military and other actions that "advance the goals of homosexual activists."[20] Other recipients of Coors funding have included anti-feminist icon Phyllis Schlafly's Eagle Forum and Stop ERA campaign, the John Birch Society and a variety of organizations affiliated with the religious right. In the 1990s, however, the Coors company launched an aggressive public relations campaign to repair its image with supporters of gay rights who were boycotting Coors beer. It offered money to gay and lesbian rights groups and became one of the first companies in the United States to offer marriage benefits to employees in same-sex relationships.[21] It hired Mary Cheney, the openly lesbian daughter of current vice president Dick Cheney, as its "corporate relations manager for the gay and lesbian market" and signed a marketing contract with Witeck-Combs Communications, a public relations firm that specializes in niche marketing to the gay community.[22] The Coors family also took steps to distance the Coors name from its political activities. In 1993, it established the Castle Rock Foundation with a $36.6 million endowment from the Coors Foundation.[23] Under the family's direction, Castle Rock continues to pour $2 to $3 million of Coors profits each year into anti-gay and other conservative causes,[24] but the company itself is officially gay-friendly.

- Other significant conservative foundations include: the Smith Richardson Foundation, financed by the Vicks VapoRub fortune, with assets of about $250 million, which gives grants totaling more than $20 million per year; the Michigan-based Earhart Foundation, which gives away about $5 million annually, including grants and fellowships to help conservative college students; and the JM Foundation and Philip M. McKenna Foundation, each of which gives away more than $1 million annually.

As conservative groups point out when their finances are scrutinized, theirs is only a tiny slice of the money that foundations give away every year in the United States. The foundations listed above give a total of approximately $110 million each year, which is only one-third of one percent of the $30.5 billion that foundations of all types—left, right, center and apolitical—gave in 2001. The assets held by conservative foundations are also tiny compared to the $24.1 billion held by the Bill & Melinda Gates Foundation, the Ford Foundation's $9.3 billion, or the Rockefeller Foundation's $2.6 billion. The Gates Foundation gives hundreds of millions of dollars to the National Institutes of Health, the Children's Hospital Foundation, KnowledgeWorks Foundation, the Seattle Art Museum, Mexico's public libraries—recipients that reflect their interest in education and global health. The Ford and Rockefeller foundations concentrate on projects like economic development, human rights and eliminating hunger. Most foundations spend their money on "brick and mortar" philanthropy—hospitals, museums, universities and symphonies. Many foundations have progressive intentions that they express by funding food banks, housing for the homeless and other direct services to the poor, disabled or disadvantaged. What makes conservative foundations different is that they are remarkably unencumbered by these sorts of distractions, enabling them to focus in a disciplined way on achieving their direct political goals. Whereas other foundations mostly try to change the world by offering *services*, the conservative foundations have prioritized influencing *ideas* and *policies*.

Philanthropy Roundtable

Conservative funders also work cooperatively. They share information and strategies for giving through the Philanthropy Roundtable, a clearinghouse for conservative donors that arose in the late 1970s and whose activities exemplify the seriousness with which the conservative movement focuses on coordinating its activities. It holds annual and regional conferences, advises individual donors and grant-making foundations and publishes papers and books with titles like *Strategic Investment in Ideas* aimed at helping conservatives maximize the political impact of their grant-making. They have a long-term strategic vision forged through several decades of political organizing.

"Things take time. It takes at least ten years for a radical new idea to emerge from obscurity," said Christopher DeMuth of the American Enterprise Institute, who spoke at a conference organized by the Philanthropy Roundtable in 2002. Speaking as one of the panelists in a discussion titled "Philanthropy, Think Tanks, and the Importance of Ideas," DeMuth pointed out that ideas like school vouchers and Social Security privatization were considered radical when first proposed but have now entered public discourse. Other ideas championed by conservative foundations were also considered radical at their inception but have already become accepted as conventional wisdom, such as the notion that welfare causes poverty or that antitrust enforcement backfires — ideas that conservative foundations pushed into the mainstream by funding and publicizing the ideas of once obscure academics and jurists like Charles Murray and Robert Bork.[25]

"You get huge leverage for your dollars," said Roger Hertog, a wealthy donor who sat alongside DeMuth on the same panel, as did the heads of three other leading conservative think tanks: Ed Crane of the Cato Institute, Edwin Feulner of the Heritage Foundation, and Larry Mone of the Manhattan Institute for Public Policy Research.[26]

American Prospect columnist Robert Kuttner attended the Philanthropy Roundtable's event as, in his words, a "token liberal." He came away impressed by the right's realization that ideas matter in politics. "What was impressively revealed here was precisely the right's movement consciousness," Kuttner observed. "When I was young, the people who spoke of 'the movement' and who used 'radical' as an affirmative word were progressive. The movement, at first, referred to the civil-rights movement; by the mid-1960s, it referred to a generalized movement for social justice. 'Movement people' boycotted nonunion grapes, worked on voter registration, opposed the war in Vietnam. Today, one hears the phrase 'movement conservatism.' The right's think tanks and philanthropists alike understand that the enterprise is — above all — political." As an indicator of the power of this approach, Kuttner noted, "It has been a while since a progressive idea, per se, transformed politics. A generation ago, activists in the streets were energized by books such as Betty Friedan's *The Feminist Mystique*, Rachel Carson's

Silent Spring, Ralph Nader's *Unsafe at Any Speed,* and Mike Harrington's *The Other America.* These in turn transformed national policy.... It was breathtaking to see the policy strategists of the other side preen for the edification of their steadfast funders—the culmination of a 25-year strategic alliance between organized business, ideological conservatism, advocacy research, and the Republican Party. Hertog was right: $70 million a year is chump change to the American elite, but invested strategically in the battle of ideas, it yields a bountiful political harvest."[27]

From Ideas to Finished Products

In 1997, Sally Covington of the National Committee for Responsive Philanthropy—a progressive counterpart to the Philanthropy Roundtable, although it has less than half of the Roundtable's funding—conducted a study titled "Moving a Public Policy Agenda: The Strategic Philanthropy of Conservative Foundations."[28] Covington looked closely at the giving activities of 12 leading conservative foundations during the period from 1992 to 1994. The foundations she reviewed controlled more than $1.1 billion in assets and awarded $300 million in grants during the period of her study, of which $210 million went to support conservative policy objectives. The funding was targeted to serve three main objectives:

- *Developing ideas that serve conservative goals:* $88.9 million went to support conservative scholarship and programs at universities such as Harvard, Yale and the University of Chicago, with the purpose of training conservative thinkers and activists while challenging progressive curricula and policy trends on college and university campuses.

- *Translating those goals into specific policy proposals:* $79.2 million went to support think tanks and advocacy groups such as the Heritage Foundation, American Enterprise Institute, the Free Congress Foundation, the Cato Institute, Citizens for a Sound Economy, the Hudson Institute and the Hoover Institution.

- *Marketing those ideas and policies to the public:* $16.3 million went to finance alternative media outlets, media watchdog groups and specific reporting on public radio or television that offered conservative angles on public issues.

"Right-wing foundations have developed a truly comprehensive funding strategy, providing grants to a broad range of groups, each promoting right-wing positions to their specific audiences," observes a separate report titled *Buying a Movement*, which was produced in 1996 by the liberal group, People for the American Way. "The grants have created and nurtured an enormous range of organizations all bent on promoting a far-right-wing agenda. Recipients of foundation largesse include the right-wing media; national 'think tanks' and advocacy groups; a budding network of regional and state-based think tanks; conservative university programs; conservative college newspapers; conservative scholars and more. In many of these funding areas, progressive and mainstream foundation giving lags far behind."[29]

There is nothing magical or conspiratorial about these activities. As David Ozonoff of the Boston University School of Medicine has observed, "One can think of an idea almost as one thinks of a living organism. It has to be continually nourished with the resources that permit it to grow and reproduce."[30] Conservative foundations have simply made the nourishment of their ideas a priority, creating a rich environment in which their movement can thrive.

On campus, right-wing foundations work to influence the politics of university campuses, fighting against multicultural education, gender studies and affirmative action. They give millions of dollars to conservative university programs, university endowments, lectures and right-wing student publications, and they help advance the careers of conservative professors by promoting their research in the media. In fact, several conservative think tanks are housed at universities, such as the Hoover Institution on War, Revolution and Peace at Stanford University; the Institute for Humane Studies at George Mason University; the Georgetown Center for Strategic and International Studies; the Bradley Fellows program at the University of Chicago; and the Harvard Center for Risk Analysis. Conservative foundations also support networks of conservative professors such as the National Association of Scholars.[31] The late Allan Bloom, author of *The Closing of the American Mind*, a conservative critique of the "decline" of American academia, headed the University of Chicago's John M. Olin Center for Inquiry into the Theory and Practice of Democracy, which was funded with $3.6 million from the Olin Foundation.[32] Other academic recipients of Olin funding have included conservative thinkers Irving Kristol, Robert Bork, William Bennett and Robert Leiken (a leading supporter of the Nicaraguan Contras in the 1980s). Foundations also fund programs that recruit and train students, ensuring the intellectual future of conservatism by grooming future generations of conservative scholars, activists, journalists and politicians.

Send in the Tanks

The conservative movement's emphasis on funding ideas has made it a major sponsor of "think tanks." Of course, conservatives are not the only players in this game. Labor unions, environmentalists and consumer groups also have their own research organizations, and wealthy individuals with progressive political leanings such as billionaire George Soros have recently begun putting money into liberal foundations and think tanks such as the Center for American Progress, which was launched in October 2003.[33] They have a long way to go, however, before they catch up to the right. The last available annual financial reports showed that the major conservative think tanks—American Enterprise Institute, American Legislative Exchange Council, Cato Institute, Center for Strategic and International Studies, Citizens for a Sound Economy, Family Research Council, Heritage Foundation, Hudson Institute, Hoover Institution and Manhattan Institute for Public Policy Research—had annual budgets totaling $146.5 million. This is more than six times the combined annual budget of $22.6 million for the leading progressive think tanks—the Center on Budget and Policy Priorities, Center for Policy Alternatives, Center for Public Integrity, Economic Policy Institute and Institute for Policy Studies.[34]

Unlike the messy debates that take place on university campuses, foundation-funded think tanks are comparative islands of calm. They do not have their own underground newspapers, free-speech movements or other manifestations of rebellious thought. In contrast with the ideal of academic freedom to which universities aspire (however imperfectly), think tanks are places where people are hired to think the thoughts that their employers tell them to think. This does not mean that the people who work for think tanks are mindless robots who simply follow orders and never disagree with one another. Debates occur, sometimes heated ones, among the "scholars in residence," "distinguished fellows" and other impressively titled individuals who work in the more than 1,000 think tanks that now dot America's intellectual landscape. Within each think tank, debates occur within the boundaries that its sponsors set. At the libertarian Cato Institute, there are no scholars in residence who believe that it would be a good idea to expand the welfare state, and at the Economic Policy Institute, which is funded by labor unions, there are no scholars who believe that the minimum wage should be abolished. This intellectual discipline is maintained by the simple mechanism of market demand. No policy analyst who favors a stronger welfare state would even bother applying to work at the Cato Institute, because they know that no one there would ever consider hiring them.

The term "think tank" originated during World War II as jargon for a secure room where plans and strategies could be discussed, and it reflected a transformation in the way that people in power thought about "thinking." The practice of assembling smart people to advise governments goes back, of course, thousands of years. Aristotle tutored the young Alexander the Great, Niccolò Machiavelli advised the Republic of Florence and Francis Bacon advised the British monarchy. In the latter half of the 19th century, various societies existed for the purpose of theorizing about solutions to social problems such as disease, alcoholism and poverty, but they saw themselves as social reformers and healers rather than as strategic planners. The American Association for the Promotion of Social Science (later abbreviated to the American Social Science Association, or ASSA) began in 1865 as a diverse group of abolitionists in search of a new cause, advocates of public health and sanitation, charity workers and university scholars. "Unlike our era, the distinctions between the professional 'expert' and the knowledgeable 'amateur' had not yet hardened," notes historian James A. Smith. To ASSA's founders, "social science, reform, and notions of Christian charitable obligations were virtually synonymous."[35] A similar spirit lay behind the Russell Sage Foundation, established half a century later with a charter to seek "the permanent improvement of social conditions," with programs that addressed child welfare, tuberculosis and women's working conditions.[36]

It took the First and Second World Wars to transform these committees of thinkers into "social engineers," "efficiency experts" and strategic information warriors. Under the pressure of war, they began to focus on things like helping factories meet their labor needs, monitoring the production of shoe leather and weapons, and studying the motivational psychology of soldiers and civilians. Later, as the Cold War became a "war of ideas," thinking became both a battlefield and a weapon. By the time Ronald Reagan took office in 1981, Smith observes, "the vocabularies of warfare and marketing" had come to "permeate the language of those who work in Washington's think tanks."[37] What warfare and marketing have in common is their use of propaganda to influence the behavior of large groups of people—"target populations," to use the phrase sometimes preferred by both soldiers and marketers when they talk about the public. In the war against communism, a new group of think tanks emerged such as the RAND Corporation that were determined to ensure that capitalist ideas would win and collectivist ideas would lose.

Given the conservative movement's own immersion in the assumptions of the Cold War, it was only natural that they would turn to think tanks as places to formulate and promote their ideas. The Heritage Foundation became one of the first successful conservative think tanks, which former Heritage vice president Burton Yale Pines has described as "the shock troops of the conservative revolution."[38]

Two distinct and often contradictory ideas have driven the conservative movement and are reflected in the think tanks that it sponsors. The first is a libertarian belief in the "free market" and opposition to government interference in business or people's lives. The second is a traditionalist approach to religious and cultural values. Often the traditionalists *demand* government intervention in people's lives. Libertarian philosophy doesn't want the government to regulate corporations, but it also doesn't want the government to tell you whether you can smoke marijuana, buy pornography, or make your own sexual choices. Traditionalists, of course, want the government to control all these aspects of your life, and more. Reconciling these two competing impulses has been a perennial challenge for conservatives, which they achieve by focusing on the area where the two sides agree.

Traditional Values

The Heritage Foundation lies on the traditionalist side of the divide, publishing reports that oppose gay rights, drug use and other perceived deviations from "family values" while also pushing for welfare cuts, tax cuts and keeping the minimum wage as minimum as possible.[39] Established in 1973 by conservative activist

Paul Weyrich with funding from brewery magnate Joseph Coors, Heritage provided the blueprint for many of Ronald Reagan's policies as president, ranging from supply-side economics to Star Wars.[40] It later helped Newt Gingrich draft the Republican Party's "Contract with America." Many of its "scholars in residence" have been former officials from Republican administrations, such as Reagan-era attorney general Edwin Meese and William Bennett, Reagan's education secretary.[41]

The Heritage Foundation also excels at *selling* its ideas. In contrast with older think tanks like the RAND Corporation or the Brookings Institute, which devote themselves to compiling and publishing dense jungles of statistics and technical analysis, Heritage spends only 40 percent of its budget on actual research, devoting the remainder to marketing, fund-raising and public relations. "All this marketing enables the Foundation to successfully attract mass media coverage for its publications and policy proposals," explains writer Sharon Beder. "The Foundation claims that it usually gets 200 or more stories nationwide from each of the position papers it publishes. . . . Its specialty is its 'backgrounders' or 'bulletins' which are short essays (between two and twenty pages) on current issues—'brief enough to read in a limousine ride from National Airport to Capitol Hill.'"[42]

Heritage runs the "Town Hall" website, which links together more than a hundred other websites, conservative think tanks, advocacy groups and like-minded pundits. On its own website, Heritage offers user-friendly, McNugget-sized talking points, predigested for conservatives looking for factoids with which to trounce liberal arguments. Its "taxes" research page, for example, provides articles, backgrounders and WebMemos, with links to multimedia materials and supporting charts and visuals. Another section on the website, called the "Candidate's Briefing Book," provides ready-to-repeat wording that politicians can plug into TV and radio spots, and a downloadable "pocket card" with prepared "talking points" for on-the-go conservatives who need a set of crib notes for the road. Heritage also has a database of "2,200 public policy experts by area of expertise," perfect for speaking at your school, radio show or caucus hearing. And if you're a conservative thinker looking for a place to do your thinking, Heritage also has a job bank that "assists conservatives in finding employment with conservative Congressional offices, faith-based organizations, other public policy organizations, lobbying groups and trade associations."[43]

The Libertarian "Kochtopus"

The other wing of the conservative movement, pro-corporate libertarianism, has been heavily bankrolled by brothers David and Charles Koch. Before their entrance into Republican politics, they were active members of the Libertarian Party, with David Koch even running as the Libertarian candidate for vice president in 1980—a nomination that was cemented by Koch's personal contribution of $1.6 million to the campaign.[81] Dubbed the "Kochtopus" in libertarian circles, they funded a variety of foundations, institutes and centers, including Murray Rothbard's *Libertarian Forum* newsletter, Roy Childs's *Libertarian Review*, Students for a Libertarian Society, the Center for Libertarian Studies, the Institute for Humane Studies, and the Council for a Competitive Economy. The best-known of these groups today is the Cato Institute, co-founded in 1977 by Charles Koch and Edward H. Crane, the Libertarian Party's former national chairman.[45]

The power of Koch money also transformed libertarianism, in ways that members of the party often resented. In the 1970s, the Libertarian Party was an odd mix of anarchists and hippies, nudists, science-fiction fans, and conservative fans of writer Ayn Rand. The Cato Institute was established, according to Crane, as a way of cleaning up libertarian ideas and making them palatable to a mainstream public. "I was always fighting off the crazies," he recalled in a 2002 interview with the *Washington Post*.[46] After opening in San Francisco, the Cato Institute moved to Washington, where it built a lush, six-story headquarters—a signal to the political establishment, explained Cato executive vice president David Boaz, "that we were in Washington to stay and that we had significant resources."[47]

Under Crane's leadership, and with ample infusions of cash from the Koch brothers, Cato pioneered a form of libertarianism that stripped away the hippies and other counterculturalists. It has sometimes dissented from the rest of the conservative movement on issues involving personal liberties and militarism. (For example, Cato heavily criticized the war in Iraq.) Its main focus, however, has been pro-corporate libertarianism, opposing government regulators, taxes and other policies that infringe on the freedom of companies like Koch. The Cato Institute has pushed Social Security privatization since 1980 and has major programs that focus on "Regulatory Studies" and "Risk and Science Studies" that consistently oppose environmental protections. Its staff writes opinion columns and speaks on themes such as "the myth of health effects from exposures to chemicals in the environment"[48] and publishes books such as Ron Bailey's *Eco-Scam: The False Prophets of Ecological Apocalypse* and Thomas Gale Moore's *Climate of Fear: Why We Shouldn't Worry about Global*

Warming. One Cato Institute policy paper characterized the government's "zeal to stamp out pollution" as a "growing threat to civil liberties."[49] Another Cato publication equated environmentalism with "the collectivist desire for social control . . . a kind of religion," and spoke disparagingly of "watermelon environmentalists" who are "green on the outside and red on the inside."[50] This focus has in turn helped attract funding from corporations and corporate trade lobbies that stand to benefit if Cato's policy recommendations are adopted. Its corporate funders have included the American Farm Bureau Federation, American Petroleum Institute, Amoco, ARCO, Association of American Railroads, Association of International Automobile Manufacturers, Coca-Cola, Eli Lilly Endowment, ExxonMobil, Ford Motor Company, Monsanto Company, Pfizer, Philip Morris, Procter and Gamble and Sears Roebuck.

Like other well-heeled think tanks, the Cato Institute has been successful at pushing its ideas into the media. "Today Cato scholars are fixtures on the talk shows and op-ed pages," the *Washington Post* reported in 2001. "Cato-affiliated scholars appeared 1,499 times on radio and television last year, according to the tank's communications department. Also in 2001, Cato scholars wrote 895 opinion pieces for newspapers, including 146 that appeared in the country's 25 largest newspapers."[51]

The Koch brothers also founded Citizens for a Sound Economy (CSE), another Washington-based conservative think tank. CSE describes itself as an organization of "grassroots citizens dedicated to free markets and limited government,"[52] but according to internal documents leaked to the *Washington Post* in January 2000, the bulk of its revenues ($15.5 million in 1998) came not from its 250,000 members but from contributions of $250,000 and up from large corporations. CSE is co-chaired by former Republican Majority Leader Dick Armey and C. Boyden Gray, a Washington attorney who served as counsel to former President George H. W. Bush. The Koch Family Foundations continue to provide some of CSE's funding, but the bulk of its income now comes from corporations including Allied Signal, Archer Daniels Midland, DaimlerChrysler, Emerson Electric Company, Enron, General Electric, Johnson & Johnson, Philip Morris and U.S. West. Other funding comes from the same conservative foundations that finance other conservative think tanks: Castle Rock, Earhart, JM, Olin, Bradley, McKenna and Scaife.[53]

CSE's activities have ranged from a major press and public relations campaign to defeat the Clinton administration's 1993 proposal for an energy tax to filing "friend of the court" briefs in 1999 that sought to declare the Clean Air Act unconstitutional. It produces more than 100 policy papers each year, delivering them to every single congressional office, while also distributing its message via direct mail, advertising, placements of op-ed pieces and outreach to journalists that generates thousands of news articles in print, radio and television. CSE argues that "environmental conservation requires a commonsense approach that limits the scope of government," acid rain is a "so-called threat [that] is largely nonexistent," and global warming is "a verdict in search of evidence."[54] CSE also engages in "grassroots" lobbying, sending out activists to collect signatures on petitions for its various causes. Although tax-exempt nonprofit organizations are supposed to refrain from endorsing specific legislation or candidates, CSE has intervened in elections on occasion, as in 1999 when it worked during the primary election to defeat Joseph Negron, a Republican running for the Florida State Assembly. CSE ran a series of television ads blasting Negron, funded by $460,000 from major corporate donors including rent-a-car companies and Associated Industries of Florida, which represents 10,000 Florida businesses and opposed Negron's position on tort reform. "Our political department orchestrated the whole thing," said Jon L. Shebel, the president of Associated Industries. "We called CSE and said here's the plan, can you do something? They did TV. We did radio, direct mail and all the analytical work."[55]

On other occasions as well, CSE has acted as a conveyor belt for the views of its funders. In 1998, it launched a project to derail a multibillion-dollar plan by the U.S. Army Corps of Engineers to restore the Florida Everglades. In news releases and other publicity materials, CSE claimed that the project would cost every household in Florida $120 and cost the state nearly 3,000 jobs. Shortly after launching the project, CSE received $700,000 in contributions from Florida sugar companies, which stood to lose thousands of acres of land if the federal plan went into effect. As the *Washington Post* reported in January 2000, this was only one of several occasions on which CSE has taken money from specific corporate interests while lobbying on their behalf. It received more than $1 million from Philip Morris while opposing cigarette taxes and another $1 million from the U.S. West phone company while it pushed a deregulation plan that would let U.S. West offer long-distance service. CSE president Paul Beckner dismissed warnings about global warming as "junk science," shortly before receiving $175,000 from ExxonMobil to fund its work on "global climate" issues. Another $380,000 came in from Microsoft while CSE was lobbying in Congress to limit the Justice Department's budget for antitrust enforcement against the software giant.[56]

Heritage, Cato and CSE are only the tip of the think tank ice-berg. Multiply the examples above by several hundred and you begin to get an idea of the scale on which efforts are ongoing to influence the way you and your neighbors—and especially your elected representatives—think about health, taxation, the environment, trade, foreign policy and a host of other issues. And in addition to the national think tanks, conservative funders have built a network of *state* think tanks such as the Wisconsin Policy Research Institute, the Hudson Institute in Indiana, the Heartland Institute in Illinois, the Pacific Research Institute in California and the Manhattan Institute in New York City. Just as the national think tanks push legislation onto the federal agenda, the state groups push local and state governments to adopt policies such as welfare cuts, privatization of public services, parental choice in schools and deregulation of workplace safety.[57] The state and national think tanks reinforce one another, with the national centers serving as sources of leadership and authority while the state organizations develop model programs that can then be replicated nationally.

Many of these state initiatives are coordinated and led by the American Legislative Exchange Council (ALEC), which was established by Paul Weyrich, Jesse Helms, Jack Kemp, Henry Hyde and other New Right leaders in 1973, the same year that Weyrich launched the Heritage Foundation. According to ALEC executive director Sam Brunelli, "ALEC's goal is to ensure that these state legislators are so well informed, so well armed, that they can set the terms of the public policy debate, that they can change the agenda, that they can lead. This is the infrastructure that will reclaim the states for our movement." ALEC had a budget of $5 million in 2002.[58] Its support over the years has come from right-wing foundations such as Bradley, Castle Rock, Koch, Olin and Scaife, along with more than 200 corporations including Amoco, the American Nuclear Energy Council, the American Petroleum Institute, Amway, AT&T, Chevron, the Chlorine Chemistry Council, Coors, Enron, Exxon, Ford, IBM, the Pharmaceutical Research and Manufacturers of America, Philip Morris, R. J. Reynolds, Shell Oil and Texaco.[59]

Enron's Intellectuals

Following the collapse of Enron, the Center for Public Integrity (CPI), a consortium of independent investigative journalists, compiled an extensive report that showed how the energy giant integrated strategic funding of think tanks into the rest of its lobbying activities, which gained favorable treatment from state and national governments on at least 49 occasions between the late 1980s and the company's scandal-ridden bankruptcy in December 2001. "To achieve its legislative goals," the CPI reported, "Enron employed multi-pronged strategies that included doling out campaign contributions to influential politicians, employing a nationwide network of lobbyists and building grassroots support for policy changes by bankrolling think tanks and other organizations that advocated those changes." Think tanks functioned within a network of Enron-funded organizations that advocated for the company's interests, including the Alliance for Lower Electric Rates Today, Americans for Affordable Electricity, Americans for Fair Taxation, the American Legislative Exchange Council, Citizens for a Sound Economy, International Climate Change Partnership and the National Wetlands Coalition. "Before Enron started promoting the nationwide restructuring of the electricity industry," the CPI report stated, "the notion of a 'free market' for electricity was an academic issue discussed by university economists and think tank policy specialists who debated what constituted a natural monopoly. Enron made it into a political issue."[60]

The *Washington Post* also investigated Enron's lobbying machine, which even used a computer program to calculate the exact dollar value to the company of the changes it got politicians to implement. "They called it 'the matrix,'" the *Post* reported, "a computer program that brought a scientific dimension to Enron's effort to seduce politicians and sway bureaucrats. With each proposed change in federal regulations, lobbyists punched details into a computer, allowing Enron economists in Houston to calculate just how much a rule change would cost. If the final figure was too high, executives used it as the cue to stoke their vast influence machine, mobilizing lobbyists and dialing up politicians who had accepted some of Enron's millions in campaign contributions."[61] (In the end, of course, the program failed to account for the company's own cooked books, which kept the economists from noticing that Enron was hemorrhaging money even as they thought they were counting every penny.)

In addition to using election campaign contributions to cultivate support, the *Post* reported, "Enron 'collected visible people' by gathering up pundits, journalists and politicians and placing them on lucrative retainers. For a couple [of] days spent chatting about current events with executives at Enron's Houston headquarters, advisers could walk away with five-figure payments."[62] From 1989 to 2001, Enron gave 74 percent of its election contributions to Republicans,[63] and most of the pundits on the payroll were conservatives as well, such as *Weekly Standard* editor

William Kristol, commentator Larry Kudrow of the *National Review*, Bush economic adviser Lawrence B. Lindsey, *Wall Street Journal* columnist and former Reagan speechwriter Peggy Noonan, and Republican National Committee chairman Mark Racicot. (Princeton economist Paul Krugman was one of the few liberal thinkers hired to serve on Enron's advisory panel, from which he resigned when he later became a columnist for the *New York Times*.)[64]

These disclosures prompted a bit of soul-searching from Robert W. Hahn, director of the heavily corporate-funded American Enterprise Institute–Brookings Joint Center for Regulatory Studies. Hahn penned an essay for the *Policy Review*, a publication of the conservative Hoover Institution, in which he frankly admitted that Enron was only the tip of the iceberg with respect to conflicts of interest affecting thinkers and the thoughts they think. "I am aware of many people who write opinion pieces on a particular subject for direct compensation. Some disclose that information while many others do not," Hahn wrote. "No one seems to care, except editors at major newspapers. They are less likely to publish op-eds that come with some kind of disclosure statement because they do not want to be viewed as supporting free advertisements for a particular point of view. This creates an incentive not to disclose. . . . The basic problem is that we are all walking conflicts of interest because most of us have to work for a living. And in exchange for money, most of us make compromises. . . . Should I note on the bottom of my op-eds that a small part of my compensation at AEI and Brookings is linked to the number of op-eds I publish in newspapers? This, indeed, has an effect on the number of op-eds I write, if not their bias." Hahn went on, however, to conclude that full public disclosure of these financial conflicts of interest "would actually do more harm than good by reducing the pool of experts and encouraging people to circumvent the system. . . . Indeed, if disclosure requirements are enforced more rigorously, I would expect more think tanks to emerge that serve as fronts for all sorts of preferred interest group policies."[65]

The financial unraveling of media mogul Conrad Black provided yet another example of rich people who collect conservative thinkers the way other people collect stamps or autographs. Until his resignation, Black, a British lord, was CEO of Hollinger International, a media conglomerate whose holdings included more than 100 newspapers around the world such as the *Chicago Sun-Times*, the *Daily Telegraph* and *Spectator* newspapers in London and the *Jerusalem Post*. Black himself sat on the board of directors of two think tanks—the Hudson Institute and the Nixon Center. His resignation from Hollinger in December 2003 occurred after the company fell into financial crisis, prompting minority shareholders to form an investigative committee, which found more than $32 million in payments that "were not authorized or approved by either the audit committee or the full board of directors of Hollinger."[66] By January, the investigation had uncovered more than $200 million in dubious transactions, prompting the company to file a lawsuit against Black, alleging that he had "diverted and usurped corporate assets and opportunities from the Company through systematic breaches of fiduciary duties owed to the Company and its non-controlling public shareholders." The "systematic breaches" included "excessive, unreasonable and unjustifiable fees" paid from Hollinger to another company owned by Black, as well as other irregularities and "sham transactions."[67] They also involved other tangled financial dealings reflecting what the *New York Times* described as a "seemingly porous boundary among Lord Black's social, political and business lives."[68]

Prior to his fall from grace, Black had built a reputation for himself as a deep thinker in his own right, publishing a thick biography of Franklin D. Roosevelt, its dust jacket decorated with laudatory blurbs from conservative intellectuals including Henry Kissinger, columnist George F. Will, and *National Review* founder William F. Buckley, Jr. "What the blurbs did not mention was that each man was praising the work of a sometime boss," the *Times* reported. "During the 1990's, Lord Black had appointed all three to an informal international board of advisers of Hollinger International, the newspaper company he controlled. For showing up once a year with Lord Black to debate the world's problems, each was typically paid about $25,000 annually."[69] In addition to Buckley, Kissinger and Will, Black's advisory board included luminaries such as former British Prime Minister Margaret Thatcher, former U.S. National Security Advisor Zbigniew Brzezinski, and Richard Perle, the former assistant secretary of defense to Ronald Reagan.

Most of these illuminati had received payments of more than $100,000 over the years but hadn't felt compelled to disclose the payments when they publicly praised or disseminated Black's political views. During the buildup to war with Iraq, for example, George Will had written a column praising a hawkish speech that Black gave in London. After the *New York Times* called to ask if he should have disclosed his financial relationship with Black at the time, Will snapped, "My business is my business. Got it?"[70]

Buckley was a bit more polite but equally evasive. When Black's financial scandal began making the news in November

2003, Buckley had written a defense of the embattled mogul, calling him "extraordinarily learned, profoundly instructed, modest in demeanor, eloquent in speech and in kindnesses." Responding to editorial criticism of Black in the *New York Observer*, Buckley blasted the editorial as "febrile with hate" and added, "Since your mind inclines in that direction, hear this: he has never donated a nickel to any of my enterprises."[71]

Technically, that might have been true, since the money Buckley received over the years was payment for services, not a "donation." But it was a lot more than a nickel. When queried by the *New York Times*, Buckley estimated that Black had paid him at least $200,000.[72]

CHAPTER TWO

The Echo Chamber

It was May 20, 1993, and George Stephanopoulos, President Clinton's senior adviser, was having a bad hair day. His afternoon press briefing had begun normally enough, with talk about Clinton's economic plan, Social Security and an effort at fiscal compromise with the Republican-led Senate Finance Committee. Then came the real meat.

"There were stories in the paper today," a reporter began, "that the president was delayed on the runway in Los Angeles while he had Monsieur Cristophe come in—"

"Another haircut story," Stephanopoulos replied. He'd already read about it.[1]

Three days previously, Clinton had arranged for Cristophe, a top Beverly Hills hairdresser who normally charges $200 for his services, to cut his hair aboard Air Force One as the plane sat on a tarmac at Los Angeles International Airport. Now the newspapers and TV were reporting that Clinton's haircut had shut down the airport for nearly an hour, delaying travelers. In the *New York Times*, columnist Thomas Friedman called it "the most expensive haircut in history."[2] An editorial in the *Journal of Commerce*, a magazine for the business community, fumed that "Clinton continues to argue for more infrastructure including airport facilities. Better he should get his hair cut someplace else so we can use the infrastructure we've got."[3] Newspaper headlines referred to the incident as "Hairgate" or "Scissorgate"—a premonition of the "Travelgate," "Troopergate," "Whitewatergate" and "Monicagate" scandals that would soon dog the Clintons.[4]

"Is the White House at all concerned that this makes the president look a little foolish and self-indulgent?" someone asked at the press conference.

"No," Stephanopoulos said. "I mean, the president has to get his hair cut. Everybody has to get their hair cut. . . . I think he does have the right to choose who he wants to cut his hair."[5]

The reporters weren't about to let the matter drop there. One asked if Cristophe charged Clinton his normal rate or offered a discount. Stephanopoulos said he didn't know. Another wanted to know what kind of security arrangements were necessary so that Cristophe could board the plane. Another asked if Cristophe always cut the president's hair or if he used other barbers as well. Stephanopoulos didn't know the answer to those questions either. All told, he fielded 27 questions about Clinton's haircut. In a separate news conference that same day, White House press secretary Dee Dee Myers fielded another 20.[6] And the story didn't die there. It continued to circulate for weeks, becoming the butt of jokes by late-night standup comedians.

Speaking on CNN's *Crossfire*, conservative commentator Pat Buchanan explained that the haircut was a "symbol" that "exemplifies the suggestion that this guy is not Bubba at all. He's a yuppie, and he gets a $200 haircut from a Hollywood star."[7]

Libertarian pundit Virginia Postrel commented that Clinton's Air Force One haircut "was unbelievably stupid of him. It was unbelievably inconsiderate of him, not because the haircut cost $200. If he'd had, you know, the $10 Ross Perot special, it would have been equally stupid and inconsiderate to hold up, you know, all the traffic at this huge international airport."

Detroit News columnist Tony Snow, a former speechwriter to the Reagan and first Bush administrations, opined that Clinton had shown "contempt" for other people: "When you keep people waiting on a runway for an hour and you keep planes circling around, the President is acting imperial rather than simply saying, 'I need to get a haircut.'"[8]

Republican congressman Dan Burton complained that Clinton "spent thousands of your tax dollars waiting to get a haircut for 200 bucks from Hillary's hairdresser. He ought to be more concerned about trimming the deficit than his own hair."[9]

The story of Clinton's Hollywood haircut in fact has lived on more than a decade since its inception. A Google search in January 2004 found 28,000 hits for the keyword combination of "Clinton" and "Cristophe." And the story found new resonance in December 2002 when Internet columnist Matt Drudge reported that Democratic presidential hopeful John Kerry had also gotten a cut from Cristophe.[10] As Bill Whalen noted in the *National Review*, Drudge's exclusive on Kerry's haircut was quickly picked up by the mainstream press. In case any readers had forgotten, Whalen reminded them that Kerry's barber was "yes, the same

Cristophe who tied up LAX in knots back in 1993 by attending to Bill Clinton's coif."[11]

All of this might seem like a lot of attention to pay to a politician's haircut—especially since most of the commonly believed "facts" about Clinton's haircut are actually false. Clinton did indeed get a haircut from Cristophe aboard Air Force One, but it didn't "tie up Los Angeles Airport in knots." According to Federal Aviation Administration records obtained through the Freedom of Information Act, Clinton's haircut caused no significant delays of regularly scheduled passenger flights—no circling planes, no traffic jams on the runways. The only flight that suffered any inconvenience at all was a single unscheduled air taxi flight that got delayed for a mere two minutes—a holdup that might seem unusual in Switzerland but is fairly ordinary in the United States.[12] To this day, no one other than the Clintons knows what price Cristophe actually charged for his services aboard Air Force One. All we know for sure is that it didn't cost taxpayers a dime, since Clinton paid for it out of his own pocket. And to answer one of the questions that Stephanopoulos couldn't on the day of the news conference, Cristophe was not Clinton's regular stylist. His usual barber charged $20, not $200.[13] As for John Kerry, his haircut in December 2002 cost $75—more than most people would pay, but only half the $150 cited in Drudge's original "exclusive."[14]

The news reports on Clinton's haircut followed a pattern that has now become familiar—a trivial event that becomes elevated, through exaggeration and distortion, into a "scandal" in which both conservative and mainstream pundits become drawn into extended discussion of factoids that are imagined to have some symbolic bearing on the character and judgment of the politician under scrutiny. This phenomenon is not limited to Clinton, and it has happened to politicians of both parties. Jimmy Carter had his "killer rabbit," and the elder George Bush faced similarly tendentious scrutiny when he was caught expressing amazement at the capabilities of a supermarket price scanner, which became a symbol for Bush's detachment from the commonplace world of regular Americans. The *New York Times* dryly observed that "some grocery stores began using electronic scanners as early as 1976," while the *Boston Globe* commented that his unfamiliarity with scanners was "just one of the many aspects of everyday life from which a president (or vice president) is shielded in the private life of public office." (In reality, Bush's "amazement" was probably nothing more than an attempt at polite small talk when the scanner was demonstrated for him during a campaign stop.)[15]

What seems new, however, is the conservative movement's success at developing its own echo chamber that deliberately creates and amplifies these sorts of stories with disturbing regularity and increasing virulence. The Clinton years were marked by an unending cycle of pseudo-scandals that focused enormous public scrutiny on topics with no bearing on public policy and scant evidence of actual presidential wrongdoing—Scissorgate, Travelgate, the alleged "murder" of Vince Foster and a series of so-called "bimbo eruptions" that trivialized and personalized American politics as never before. For eight years, the serious business of government became a *Seinfeld*-like sitcom, in which "nothing happened" but everyone talked about it. This occurred in large part because the conservative movement successfully used a three-part strategy to dominate the news cycle:

1. It has used the complaint of "liberal bias" to pressure the mainstream media into giving more sympathetic coverage to conservative politicians and causes.
2. It built its own, ideologically driven media network as an alternative to the mainstream.
3. It has developed an effective system of promoting conservatives *within* the mainstream media—helping them find jobs and advancing their careers and exposure.

These resources do not always enable the conservative movement to dictate the direction of American journalism, but more often than not they give conservatives a disproportionate capacity to do so.

Networks of Their Own

Over the years, both the left and right wings of American politics have lamented the state of the mainstream media, and both established their own alternatives, such as *National Review* on the right or *The Nation* on the left. In the 1960s, leftist activists also established a number of other media outlets that have survived, including "alternative weeklies" such as the *Village Voice, Los Angeles Weekly, San Francisco Bay Guardian* and the *Texas Observer*. From the perspective of the 1970s or even the 1980s, it might have appeared that the left was beating the right at the media game. Over time, however, the conservative movement has been able to leverage its superior financing with clever marketing techniques to build a media juggernaut.

Early on, the conservative movement seemed to grasp that the term "media" is plural rather than singular. To begin with, there are different *types* of media. The forms that come most readily to mind are the mass media: radio, television and print. However, telephones, letters and the human voice are also media through which people communicate. During the civil rights movement in the American South, beauty parlors and beauty shops became places where activists gathered to communicate and organize, as did local and national churches. Churches are in fact superb communicators. It was the Catholic Church that popularized the term "propaganda," establishing the Sacred Congregation of Propaganda in 1622 to oversee its missionary work in non-Christian countries. (Then, as now, propaganda was tied with warfare. The Sacred Congregation was created shortly after the start of the Thirty Years' War, which pitted Protestants against Catholics.)

During the Cold War, Christian evangelism became closely tied with conservative politics, as religion became one of the ways that the United States proclaimed its moral superiority over the atheistic Soviet Union. The ultra-conservative John Birch Society took its name from John Morrison Birch, a Baptist missionary and U.S. Air Force intelligence officer who was killed by Chinese Communists in 1945. Ben Armstrong, the first executive secretary of National Religious Broadcasters (a conservative nemesis of the National Council of Churches), began his career designing anti-Communist religious broadcasts that targeted the Soviet Union and Eastern Europe.[16] Campus Crusade for Christ founder Bill Bright consciously modeled his evangelical movement to mimic and defeat his concept of how Communists organize, setting up "revolutionary cells." Bright called himself "the head of a large international movement...

involved with thousands of others in a 'conspiracy to overthrow the world.' Each year we train tens of thousands of high school and college students from more than half of the major countries of the world in the art of revolution, and daily these 'revolutionists' are at work around the globe, spreading our philosophy and strengthening and broadening our influence."[17]

The evangelist rise was also assisted by a couple of little-noted changes in the regulations for television issued in 1960 by the Federal Communications Commission (FCC). TV stations were required to set aside a certain amount of time each week for "public interest programming," much of which went to religious programming. Initially, this was interpreted to mean that the stations had to give away this time for free. The 1960 rule, however, declared that the stations could fulfill their public interest obligation by *selling* the airtime to religious programmers who paid for it, just like other commercially sponsored programs. The FCC also gave religious broadcasters an advantage over secular programs: whereas the secular programs were limited in the number of minutes they could devote to commercials each hour, the FCC stated that these rules "do not apply to paid-time religious program time." TV stations quickly realized that they could maximize their profits by offering airtime to paying religious broadcasters, which in turn favored a specific *type* of religious broadcaster. As Sara Diamond observes in her book, *Spiritual Warfare*, "paid-time *religious* programs were allowed to become, essentially, program-length fund-raisers. The ability to buy air time became the main criterion for spreading a particular brand of Christianity. The mainline denominations, with their staid Sunday morning inspirationals and public affairs talk shows, simply could not or would not compete with the more zealous fundamentalist broadcasters

who seemed not the least bit squeamish about passing the proverbial collection plate on the air."[18] Programs like *The Lutheran
Hour* faded from the scene and were replaced by televangelists
like Jerry Falwell, Jim and Tammy Faye Bakker, Pat Robertson
and Jimmy Swaggart, who brought the carnival-like showmanship
of revivalist tent shows to television religion. By the 1980s, the TV
preachers were raking in hundreds of millions of dollars each year
in contributions.

Poison Pens

Conservatives also pioneered another form of alternative media —
direct mail, which was pioneered by "funding father" Richard
Viguerie in the 1960s. Viguerie began his career as the executive
secretary for Young Americans for Freedom, an organization affiliated initially with both the John Birch Society and William F.
Buckley.[19] His initiation into direct-mail fund-raising came in
1965 when he learned that the names of all electoral campaign
donors who had contributed more than $50 were registered with
the clerk of the U.S. House of Representatives. He hand-copied a
list of 12,000 donors to Goldwater, which became his first direct-
mail list.[20] Viguerie went on to become a leading figure in the
New Right, raising contributions for the National Conservative
Political Action Committee, Paul M. Weyrich's Committee for
the Survival of a Free Congress, Howard Phillips's Conservative
Caucus and the Congressional Club of North Carolina Senator
Jesse Helms. In the 1980s, he raised money to support prayer in
public schools, Ollie North and the Nicaraguan Contras, and to
oppose gay rights, abortion rights and publicly funded "weird art."

His clients have also included Judicial Watch, an organization that spent the 1990s attempting to insinuate that Clinton was responsible for the murder of individuals including Vincent Foster and former U.S. Commerce Secretary Ron Brown.

Initially, the New Right was seen as a force separate and apart from the Republican Party. In 1976, Viguerie even managed direct-mail fund-raising for the presidential primary campaign of right-wing Democrat George C. Wallace—a fiery segregationist who had previously run in 1968 on a third-party ticket—when Wallace campaigned against Jimmy Carter for the Democratic Party nomination. Although Carter won the nomination and went on to win the presidency, the Wallace campaign put together one of the most successful direct mail operations ever in terms of dollars and contributors, raising $6.9 million from more than 70,000 contributors—three and a half times the number on Carter's donor list.[21] Actually, though, the dollars were less significant than the messages in the New Right's direct mail appeals, which tended to cost nearly as much money as they raised. In 1976, New Right political action committees raised $10.7 million in contributions, but actually gave less than $1 million to conservative candidates, with the rest of the money eaten up by postage, printing, administrative costs and consultant fees. "How can these groups raise all this money, and distribute only such a small amount to candidates—and still have debts at the end of the year?" complained Wyatt Stewart III, director of finance and administration of the National Republican Congressional Committee.[22]

Viguerie himself readily admitted that raising money was not the main goal of direct mail or the standard by which it should be judged. "The U.S. mail is the principle method of communication for conservatives," he declared. "We sell our magazines, our books, and our candidates through the mail. We fight our legislative battles through the mail. We alert our supporters to upcoming battles through the mail. We find new recruits for the conservative movement through the mail. . . . Without direct mail, we might have no *National Review,* no *Human Events,* no *Conservative Digest,* no conservative PACs, no effective organizations in Right to Work, Right to Life, pro-gun, anti-busing, national defense, pro-family, no large national conservative organizations and youth training. You can think of direct mail as our TV, radio, daily newspaper and weekly magazine. Some people persist in thinking of direct mail as only fund raising. But it's really mostly advertising."[23]

There is, however, a difference between Viguerie's operations and conventional "TV, radio, newspapers and magazines." Traditional media were expected to maintain a firewall of separation between opinions and news as well as between editorial content and advertising. Those distinctions do not exist in direct mail, which is relentlessly partisan and opinionated—the more so the better, from a fund-raiser's perspective. Direct mail appeals have only a few seconds to capture the attention of a reader before they get dumped in the trash, so copywriters are constantly looking for gimmicks to grab and hold attention—from words like "Urgent!" on the envelope to emotional, hot-button language. As conservative direct marketers learned to craft these appeals in the 1970s and the '80s, they developed the "mad as hell" rhetoric of the angry underdog that later became the natural vocabulary of conservative talk radio and cable television.

By the 1980s, conservatives dominated the direct mail terrain. In 1982, the Republican National Committee had an active donor list of more than 1.6 million members, nearly ten times the 180,000 names on the Democrat list. Viguerie's database controlled an even larger list—4.5 million names, categorized according to issues, such as gun control and taxes. Viguerie explained his success by saying, "The Democrats went to sleep in the '60s. They didn't develop the new technologies. Conservatives felt by necessity they had to bypass the media monopolies. This is a skill that is learned not in a month or a year. It takes years and years to operate at the national level. Of the 50 major political direct-mail consultants, about 40 are conservative-Republican. It takes eight or nine years to become a heavyweight."[24]

In Oliver North's unsuccessful campaign for the U.S. Senate in 1994, he hired six different direct mail vendors, including Viguerie, to mail out more than 13 million letters. Asking donors "to help me battle the liberal army . . . no matter what the liberals do or how viciously they attack me,"[25] the North campaign spent $11 million on direct mail, which raised $16 million out of the campaign's $20.3 million in total contributions.[26]

Scarlet Letters

Sometimes the overheated rhetoric of direct mail and its tendency to target senior citizens have raised ethical eyebrows. In 1994, Viguerie's company, American Target Advertising, came under investigation from U.S. postal inspectors for giving the 60-Plus Association, a conservative senior-citizens group, just $93,000 of $1.3 million raised during a campaign drive to "save Medicare" (by cutting benefits to seniors).[27] In 1998, the *San Francisco Examiner* described some of the direct mailers' fund-raising practices. It told the story of Faye Shelby, an 86-year-old woman who lives in a retirement home in Oakland, California. During just a four-month period, Shelby received 700 mailings, some marked "Urgent!" "Personal" or "Jury Duty Notice." The letters frequently contained vitriol directed at Bill or Hillary Clinton, alongside warnings that "Social Security is going bankrupt" or, "The liberal monster is primed to rip your Social Security to shreds." According to the *Examiner,* the letters distressed Shelby so much "that she often sat up nights, fretting over which crisis most deserved her help. Fearful that her benefits might expire, she regularly responded with small donations."[28]

"Seniors are a top target of these folks," said a spokesman for the American Association of Retired Persons. "There are seniors who receive volumes of mail that say if you don't give me $25, $50 or $100, the sky is going to fall down. . . . Their common strategy is to use very open-ended and misleading language. . . . What you end up with is frightened and scared older Americans who are giving away their money to organizations that aren't going to provide them with important services or information."[29]

The *Examiner* interviewed Amy Moritz Ridenour of the National Center for Public Policy Research (NCPPR), a conservative public policy group promoting "Social Security reform." During the four months that the *Examiner* spent tallying Faye Shelby's mail, the NCPPR alone had sent her 160 separate fund-raising pitches. Ridenour defended the practice, on grounds that it was effective. "It's just that you're competing with a lot of other organizations. People seem to respond better to emotion than they do with letters that have lots and lots of facts," Moritz said. "You have to give something that is light enough that people will be willing to read it upon receipt. . . . If they don't read it right at that moment, all the studies show they never will."[30] In fact, NCPPR does almost nothing *but* mail out fund-raising appeals. In 2001, it spent more than $5 million of its $5.8 million budget on fund-raising, of which $457,802 went to fund-raising consultant fees and the remainder went to postage, printing and other direct mail expenses. Another $409,579 went to salaries and benefits—more than half of which went to Amy Ridenour and her husband, David—which left barely $400,000 for office rent, travel, printing and other activities mostly related to media outreach.[31]

Bruce Eberle, another conservative direct-marketing guru who got his start raising money for Ronald Reagan in the mid-1970s, has also repeatedly attracted charges of emotionally exploitative fund-raising, the most notorious of which was a campaign in the 1980s that used phony prisoner-of-war sightings to solicit money for former Air Force colonel Jack Bailey's Operation Rescue. Bailey claimed to be on the verge of saving American prisoners of war still being held in Vietnam. One solicitation took the form of a "handwritten letter" signed by Bailey, who claimed to be writing from aboard his rescue ship, the *Akuna III*. "Please excuse the handwriting. But I'm writing at a makeshift desk on the deck of the Akuna III," the letter read. "The China sea is tossing and rolling." In reality, the letter had been written by Eberle, not Bailey, and the *Akuna III*, which was not even seaworthy, had been docked for more than two years.[32] Eberle's direct mail appeals enabled Bailey's group to raise nearly $2.3 million between 1985 and 1990, of which 88 percent was actually spent on "fund-raising expenses" instead of rescue missions (and of course, no rescue mission ever actually succeeded in rescuing anyone). When these facts surfaced during a Senate committee hearing, the revelations prompted outrage from Vietnam veterans on the committee, including John Kerry, who termed the operation "fraudulent," "disingenuous" and "grotesque."[33]

Republican Senator John McCain offered similar sentiments. "In my opinion, they are criminals and some of the most craven, most cynical and most despicable human beings to ever run a scam," McCain said. "They have preyed on the anguish of families, and helped to turn an issue which should unite all Americans into an issue that often divides us."[34]

Eberle shrugged off these charges, claiming to have "one of the highest reputations for integrity in the business."[35] Apparently his clients agree. In addition to Operation Rescue, he has raised money for Young Americans for Freedom;[36] Stacey Koon, one of the Los Angeles police officers convicted in the 1991 beating of Rodney King;[37] Pat Buchanan's 1992 campaign for the Republican presidential nomination;[38] Public Advocate, a conservative response to Common Cause;[39] Jesse Helms's Congressional Club;[40] Oliver North;[41] Grover Norquist's Americans for Tax Reform;[42] Paula Jones, the former Arkansas state worker whose lawsuit accused Bill Clinton of sexual harassment;[43] the Linda Tripp Legal Defense Fund;[44] the anti-environmental Mountain States Legal Foundation[45] and the Southeastern Legal Foundation;[46] conservative Missouri Senator John Ashcroft (now U.S. attorney general);[47] and Radio America, an all-conservative nationwide network of radio stations.[48]

Radio Days

Direct mailers have integrated their campaigns with other forms of media, notably talk radio, which took off in the 1980s with the demise of AM music and the repeal of the Fairness Doctrine that required stations to grant equal airtime to opposing views. The number of talk radio stations in the United States jumped from 200 in 1986 to more than 1,000 eight years later, mostly featuring conservative hosts and heavily Republican audiences. "Republicans have it down to a science," the *Detroit Free Press* reported in 1994. "At the House Republican Study Committee, for example, they have a list of 300 talk radio programs. During big legislative battles—when they need folks to pressure Congress—they pump out GOP opinion, by fax, all over the country." By contrast, the Democratic National Committee had a fax list of just 100 stations considered friendly enough to be worth contacting.[49] Outside the party's formal structure, its network of think tanks and GOP consultants extended the advantage. Craig Shirley, a conservative political consultant who represents the NRA and the American Conservative Union, had his own fax list of 735 talk stations.[50] Tax reports filed by Amy Ridenour's NCPPR in 1995 showed that its regular activities included sending out tip sheets to 1,200 radio talk-show hosts twice a week offering a right-wing perspective on issues in Washington.[51]

Conservatives have also used the Internet effectively as part of an integrated communications strategy, which, like direct mail, blurs the boundaries between news, commentary, advertising and partisan advocacy. Bruce Eberle's Omega List Company, which manages and rents mailing lists of potential donors, now sells similar services for Internet fund-raising, boasting that it is "a pioneer in the endorsement e-mail field." In 2000, the Omega List website featured a presentation by conservative talk radio personality Blanquita Cullum, who explained how "endorsement e-mail" works. "You do what you do best!" Cullum said. "Get on the air and talk to your listeners! Drive them to your website by conducting a daily survey or a contest on the topic of your choosing."[52]

Eberle's "polling wizard" software then captures the names of respondents so that they can be hit up for money. "What happens next is a cakewalk," Cullum says. "Omega will call you with an opportunity to send an endorsement e-mail to your list . . . and receive a royalty for lending your name to a cause, organization or product you believe in. . . . Omega gives you their specialized software absolutely FREE and presents you with an opportunity to earn an extra $25,000 or more annually."[53]

Viguerie also adapted his direct-mail operations to the Internet in the 1990s, launching websites such as ConservativeHQ.com and the now defunct BeCounted.com, which said its mission was "to empower Joe or Jane Sixpack again" by giving "Americans the power to state their views and opinions, and . . . decision-makers the means to hear what they have to say." On the surface, BeCounted.com looked like an online opinion poll, but its real purpose was fund-raising. Visitors to BeCounted.com were asked to submit their opinions on a hot issue of the day. The surveys were actually meaningless, since there was no attempt to ensure that the result reflected any kind of representative sampling of the public, and there was no mechanism for conveying the results to political decision-makers. Their real purpose was to collect the names and other contact information of survey participants, which the site justified as a way to "prevent someone from 'cheating' in one of our online petitions or polls by voting more often than the rules allow."

People who signed up would then start receiving a stream of e-mail pitches, including commercial offers such as "incredible deals on wireless products and services"[54] or "a win-win offer from Rogaine."[55] Most, however, combined right-wing activism with opportunities to part with your money, inviting recipients to "sign a thank you card to Jesse Helms";[56] "help the Boy Scouts against political correctness" (by donating to scout troops that continue to discriminate against gays);[57] "celebrate Earth Day by countering radical environmentalist propaganda";[58] or buy books, videos and audio tapes about topics ranging from the Chinese Communist threat to Fox News commentator Bill O'Reilly's latest musings.

Subsidized Media

Conservative foundations have also financed media-watch organizations that work to pressure media organizations into airing conservative viewpoints or that attack programs for perceived "liberal bias," including Reed Irvine's Accuracy in Media; David Horowitz's Committee for Media Integrity (COMINT); the Center for Media and Public Affairs; and L. Brent Bozell III's Media Research Center. In addition, they have financed their own media outlets, ranging from highbrow to tabloid. Some examples include:

- The Bradley, Olin and Scaife foundations have poured more than $6.1 million into *The New Criterion*, a monthly cultural review founded to counter the allegedly pernicious effects of 1960s leftist radicalism on art criticism.[59] It has been characterized as an "organ for respectable neoconservative opinion" that challenges "the leftists on the battleground of ideas" by Herbert London, a John M. Olin Professor of Humanities at New York

University and president of the Hudson Institute, a leading conservative think tank.[60]

• Another $7.9 million has gone into Irving Kristol's National Affairs, Inc., which publishes *The National Interest* and *The Public Interest.*[61] Kristol's publications have editorial boards that include Henry Kissinger, Midge Decter, Charles Krauthammer, Richard Perle and Daniel Pipes. They enjoy endorsements from other conservative luminaries such as William Bennett and David Brooks. *The National Interest* published Francis Fukuyama's influential essay "The End of History," and Fukuyama has returned the favor by writing a promotional blurb for *The Public Interest,* touting its "large impact" on "the intellectual history of the late twentieth century America. . . . No other magazine has had a comparable effect."[62]

• More than $6 million has gone to *The American Spectator,* which played a key role in attacking Anita Hill after she testified before Congress that she had been sexually harassed by U.S. Supreme Court nominee Clarence Thomas.[63] *The Spectator* also originated many of the most salacious stories about President Clinton that dominated public attention throughout his eight years in office, including Whitewater, Troopergate and the Monica Lewinsky scandal.

Not all conservative media projects have been successful. Even Richard Viguerie suffered financial losses in the 1980s and was rescued from near-bankruptcy when the Rev. Sun Myung Moon's Unification Church hired him for several lucrative fund-raising projects on behalf of the Moon-controlled American Freedom Coalition.[64] The first conservative attempt to create a secular cable news network, National Empowerment Television (NET), also floundered financially and eventually went under.

Launched in December 1993 as a project of Paul Weyrich's Free Congress Foundation, NET was unabashedly partisan. The *Columbia Journalism Review* profiled it in 1994, noting that "One-third of the programs on NET are produced by 'associate broadcasters' — organizations handpicked by Weyrich to share NET's airtime. Among the dozen associate broadcasters on NET are Accuracy in Media, the National Rifle Association, and the American Life League, an anti-abortion group. Though these programs can look like 'Discovery Channel' documentaries, they are in fact unrestrained, unfiltered, political infomercials."[65] NET programs included "The Progress Report," hosted by then House Minority Whip Newt Gingrich; "Direct Line," featuring Weyrich himself; "Borderline," a forum for discussion of conservative views on immigration policy; the "Cato Forum," sponsored by the Cato Institute; "Science Under Siege," co-produced by the industry-funded Competitive Enterprise Institute; the NRA's "On Target"; and "Straight Talk," produced in conjunction with the anti-gay Family Research Council.

NET was also regarded as an ally by the tobacco industry, which gave $200,000 to the network in 1994 and drafted plans for working with NET to develop programs defending secondhand cigarette smoke from regulations and opposing cigarette excise taxes proposed as part of Clinton's health plan. "Since NET is a TV network, we could fund these activities via product advertisements from the food and beer business," stated an industry memo, which also suggested that the company "could increase the impact of NET's coverage by assisting the network in getting additional cable companies to carry their broadcasts."[66] However, the network suffered from low ratings and bled money.[67] In its first year alone, its budget was $5.6 million, with advertising and on-air fund-raising expected to bring in only $627,500.[68] Despite generous grants from foundations such as Scaife and Bradley, the network's failing finances led to its reorganization in 1997, with another $20 million in seed money, as a for-profit TV channel called America's Voice. However, Weyrich's strident political tone brought him into conflict with Robert Sutton, a broadcast executive who had been hired to run the reorganized network. Sutton persuaded the network's board to force out Weyrich in a hostile takeover, but the station continued to lose money. In 2000, America's Voice was purchased by E-Cine, a Dallas-based multimedia company, which briefly returned Weyrich to the airwaves before succumbing to bankruptcy later that year.[69]

Talk Radio on TV

By 2000, however, another conservative cable channel had begun to flower—Fox News, a branch of billionaire Rupert Murdoch's media empire. Launched in 1996, Fox had the advantage of Murdoch's deep pockets and his already substantial media holdings. Beginning in his home country of Australia, Murdoch has built a network of 175 newspapers around the world, and has extended his reach into other media including the Fox broadcast networks, Fox Sports, FX, 20th Century-Fox studios, dozens of local U.S. television stations, the HarperCollins publishing house and the Sky and Star satellite systems in England and Asia. Although Murdoch is an ideological conservative, he is first and foremost a practical businessman. The notable exceptions to his priority on profit-seeking have been the *Weekly Standard*, edited by Bill Kristol (the former chief of staff to Vice President Dan Quayle) and the *New York Post*, a conservative tabloid newspaper. Both publications lose money ($40 million a year for the *Post*), but they help cement Murdoch's standing with Republican policymakers, and he is able to use the *Post* to cross-promote his Fox television holdings.[70]

"When Ted Turner launched the Cable News Network in 1980, CNN took the idea of all-news radio and transferred it to television," observes *New Yorker* media columnist Ken Auletta. "The Fox News idea was to make another sort of transition: to bring the heated, sometimes confrontational atmosphere of talk radio into the television studio."[71] Its conservative tone is precisely what attracts many of its viewers. Whereas the efforts of conventional television news programs to appear objective come across as bland and evasive, Fox is gleefully opinionated, which appeals to many people as refreshingly candid. Matt Gross, a former Fox News editor, says network employees were instructed: "Seek out stories that cater to angry, middle-aged white men who listen to talk radio and yell at their televisions. . . . The facts of a story just didn't matter at all. The idea was to get those viewers out of their seats, screaming at the TV, the politicians, the liberals—whoever—simply by running a provocative story."[72]

To lead Fox News, Murdoch hired Roger Ailes, a television producer and former media consultant to the tobacco industry as well as to Republican presidential candidates including Richard Nixon, Ronald Reagan and George Herbert Walker Bush. Before becoming a political consultant, Ailes produced *The Mike Douglas Show*, a popular TV talk and variety program of the 1960s and seventies. Over the years, Ailes has moved back and forth between the entertainment industry and politics, often mingling the two. In 1991, he produced Rush Limbaugh's short-lived television show before becoming president of NBC's cable channel CNBC and another NBC cable show called *America's Talking* (the forerunner of today's MSNBC). Ailes brought to Fox a combination of right-wing politics and the ratings-building skills of a seasoned media showman. Also, he had the backing of Murdoch's deep pockets. Fox News arrived on the scene at a time when media analysts were predicting that the market for new cable stations was nearing saturation and the price that cable operators were willing to pay for new programming was dropping. Murdoch boldly declared that rather than *charge* for Fox News, he would actually *pay* cable operators $10 per subscriber to carry it.[73] During its first two years on the air, Fox lost $150 million—a price that Murdoch was willing to pay while it built its audience.[74]

Like talk radio, part of the secret to Fox's success has been the fact that "talk is cheap." It has a smaller reporting staff than its competitors but compensates with better bluster, hiring on-air talent such as Matt Drudge, Sean Hannity, Oliver North, Bill O'Reilly and Geraldo Rivera. Even by cable standards, Fox spends less on actual news-gathering than any of the other networks. In 1999, it spent $4 million on a promotional campaign calling itself "the most powerful name in news" at a time when its news staff was only one-third the size of the staffs at either NBC or CNN.[75] Even by the time of the Iraq War, Fox News had just 1,250 full-time and freelance employees and 17 news bureaus, only six of them overseas, with operating costs of about $250 million. By contrast, CNN had 4,000 employees and 42 bureaus, 31 of them overseas, at a cost of about $800 million. In the Middle

East, Fox had only 15 correspondents, compared to at least 100 apiece for ABC, CBS, NBC and BBC.[76] As U.S. tanks rolled on Baghdad, Fox was forced to purchase video footage of Baghdad from Al-Jazeera, the Arab network. "We don't have the resources overseas that CNN and other networks have," admitted Fox correspondent Rick Leventhal, who was with the First Marine Light Armor Reconnaissance unit. "We're going in with less money and equipment and people, and trying to do the same job. You might call it smoke and mirrors, but it's working." By the end of the war, Fox had the lead in the cable ratings.[77]

"The Clinton scandals helped Fox to find its political base, but the attacks of September 11th had a more profound effect: Fox, far more than any other television enterprise, went to war," observed the *New Yorker*'s Ken Auletta in May 2003. "And in doing so it defined itself. To be sure, news coverage in wartime tends to be less reflective, more emotional; in the aftermath of the deadliest attack on American soil, this was particularly so. But Ailes and Fox News went further. Geraldo Rivera, whom Ailes had recruited from CNBC to be a war correspondent, armed himself with a pistol and proclaimed that he would be honored to kill Osama bin Laden. Fox anchors and reporters spoke not of 'United States troops' but of 'our troops.' "[78]

Fox claims to be "fair and balanced," but by "balanced" what it really means is that its conservative tone offsets the alleged liberal bias of other networks. Charlie Reina, who worked for six years as a Fox News producer, explained in October 2003 how the political line is maintained at the network. "Editorially, the FNC newsroom is under the constant control and vigilance of management. The pressure ranges from subtle to direct. First, it's a news network run by one of the most high-profile political operatives of re-

cent times. . . . Roger [Ailes] is such a high-profile and partisan
political operative that everyone in the newsroom knows what his
political feelings are and acts accordingly. I'd never worked in
a newsroom like that," Reina said in an interview with the *Los
Angeles Times*. "Never. At ABC, for example, I never knew what
management or my bosses' political views were, much less felt
pressure from them to make things come out a certain way."[79]

Writing on the online forum of the Poynter Institute for journalists, Reina stated, "The roots of Fox News Channel's day-to-day
on-air bias are actual and direct. They come in the form of an executive memo" written by John Moody, the network's vice president for news, and "distributed electronically each morning,
addressing what stories will be covered and, often, suggesting how
they should be covered. To the newsroom personnel responsible
for the channel's daytime programming, The Memo is the bible.
If, on any given day, you notice that the Fox anchors seem to be
trying to drive a particular point home, you can bet The Memo is
behind it," Reina explained. "The Memo was born with the Bush
administration, early in 2001, and, intentionally or not, has en-
sured that the administration's point of view consistently comes
across on FNC. This year, of course, the war in Iraq became a
constant subject of The Memo. But along with the obvious — information on who is where and what they'll be covering — there
have been subtle hints as to the tone of the anchors' copy," he
wrote. On the day that war commenced in Iraq, for example,
Moody's memo told Fox employees that there was "something
utterly incomprehensible about [United Nations Secretary Gen-
eral] Kofi Annan's remarks in which he allows that his thoughts
are 'with the Iraqi people.'" On another occasion, "The Memo
warned us that anti-war protesters would be 'whining' about U.S.

bombs killing Iraqi civilians, and suggested they could tell that to the families of American soldiers dying there. Editing copy that morning, I was not surprised when an eager young producer killed a correspondent's report on the day's fighting—simply because it included a brief shot of children in an Iraqi hospital."[80]

The Bias of "Bias"

The notion that there is a "liberal bias" in the news media has been a component of conservative ideology in the United States for decades. This notion was at the center of William Rusher's 1988 book, *The Coming Battle for the Media*. Rusher was a former Wall Street attorney and publisher of William F. Buckley, Jr.'s *National Review*, which was one of the first conservative efforts to counter this alleged liberal bias by creating a conservative alternative. In *The Coming Battle for the Media*, Rusher claimed that "the principal media in the United States, responding to liberal intellectual trends once dominant but now much less so, have allied themselves with those political forces promoting liberal policies (meaning primarily the Democratic party), and have placed news coverage at the service of those policies."[81] Like most complaints about bias, however, Rusher devoted the bulk of his book to detailing examples of allegedly one-sided reporting, while struggling to provide a coherent explanation of *how* the media had become biased. In a chapter titled "Who Is Behind the Media's Bias?" he searched for culprits, only to conclude that "journalists are at least as sensitive as the rest of us to the world around them—the intellectual milieu, the popular sociological concepts, the significant political trends. In a society as wholly dominated (intellectually speaking) by liberalism as America was between 1945 and, say, 1975, it was . . . simply to be expected that professional journalists would, in the great majority of cases, share that pervasive coloration."[82] Journalists had a liberal bias, in other words, because *all of society* had a liberal bias.

As Rusher's comment illustrates, the concept of bias is itself a highly subjective term. On other occasions, conservatives have looked for evidence of bias by arguing that the news media's values are *different* from the values of the rest of society, by counting the number of reporters who vote Democrat versus Republican, or by studying the frequency with which the words "conservative" or "liberal" appear alongside politicians' names. What all of these methodologies assume is that there is some "natural" and "unbiased" ratio for these things. In their more candid moments, however, conservatives are willing to acknowledge the basic contradiction in their complaint. In May 2003, JournalismJobs.com, an employment advertising service affiliated with the *Columbia Journalism Review*, interviewed Matt Labash, the senior editor of Murdoch's *Weekly Standard*. The interviewer asked, "Why have conservative media outlets like the *Weekly Standard* and Fox News Channel become more popular in the past few years?"

"Because they feed the rage," Labash replied. "We bring the pain to the liberal media. I say that mockingly, but it's true somewhat. We come with a strong point of view and people like point-of-view journalism. While all these hand-wringing Freedom Forum types talk about objectivity, the conservative media likes to rap the liberal media on the knuckles for not being objective. We've created this cottage industry in which it pays to be un-objective. It pays to be subjective as much as possible. It's a great way to have your cake and eat it too. Criticize other people for not being objective. Be as subjective as you want. It's a great little racket. I'm glad we found it actually."[83]

"The conservative press is self-consciously conservative and self-consciously part of the team," says Grover Norquist. "The liberal press is much larger, but at the same time it sees itself as the establishment press. So it's conflicted. Sometimes it thinks it needs to be critical of both sides, to be nonpartisan."[84]

In the battle over bias, one side sees itself as a boxer, while the other side sees itself as a referee. Guess which one is going to get beat up. And in reality, the supposedly liberal mainstream isn't as liberal as the conservatives like to pretend. In addition to building their own, aggressively partisan media outlets, conservatives have systematically worked to insert their people and ideas *into* the mainstream media. "Think about it," writes *Nation* columnist Eric Alterman. "Who among the liberals can be counted upon to be as ideological, as relentless and as nakedly partisan as George Will, Robert Novak, Pat Buchanan, Bay Buchanan, William Bennett, William Kristol, Fred Barnes, John McLaughlin, Charles Krauthammer, Paul Gigot, Oliver North, Kate O'Beirne, Tony Blankley, Ann Coulter, Sean Hannity, Tony Snow, Laura Ingraham, Jonah Goldberg, William F. Buckley, Jr., Bill O'Reilly, Alan Keyes, Tucker Carlson, Brit Hume, the self-described 'wild men' of the *Wall Street Journal* editorial page, etc., etc.? In fact, it's hard to come up with a single journalist/pundit appearing on television who is even remotely as far to the left of the mainstream spectrum as most of these conservatives are to the right."[85]

As with many aspects of conservative success, their growing influence in the mainstream media is no accident. Liberals do not have an organized system for recruiting, nurturing and promoting the careers of left-leaning journalists, but conservatives do. It begins on college campuses, where the Collegiate Network, which began as a project of the Institute for Educational Affairs, serves as a networking resource and spends more than $300,000 per year funding 80 conservative student newspapers.[86] From 1995 to 2002, the Collegiate Network received more than $4 million from conservative funders.[87] Its alumni have gone on to work for both right-wing and mainstream media, including CNN, the *Washington Post*, *Wall Street Journal*, *Time*, *Newsweek*, Fox News, *National Review*, the *Weekly Standard*, *Detroit News*, *New York Post*, *Commentary*, the *Charlotte Observer* and the *Atlantic Monthly*.[88]

Another group, the National Journalism Center (NJC), helps bridge the gap from college to actual careers. Founded in 1977, it has been described by current director Ken Grubbs, Jr., as "a juggernaut for creating journalists."[89] The NJC offers scholarships to young reporter-wannabes so that they can attend its six-to-twelve-week training sessions, where they receive instruction in the technical skills of reporting, combined with "economic fellowships" that provide ideological orientation about topics such as Social Security, federal land policies, environmental regulation and taxation. For career advice, they attend seminars featuring speakers from the world of conservative politics and journalism such as columnist Robert Novak, *Washington Times* political correspondent Donald Lambro, or *Wall Street Journal* editorial columnist John Fund (himself an NJC alumnus). The NJC also helps the reporters-in-training build their résumés by arranging internship opportunities at both conservative and mainstream media, and it operates a job bank to help place graduates of its programs in permanent positions.

"Over 1,400 students have now graduated from the NJC's 12-week training sessions, held three times a year, and we estimate some 900 of these have gone on to media and media-related positions," declares the NJC website. "Among the media outlets where NJCers have worked are the *New York Times, Washington Post, USA Today* and *Wall Street Journal*; ABC, CBS, NBC, Fox, PBS, NPR, CNN, MSNBC, CNBC and C-SPAN; *Time, Newsweek, New Yorker, Harper's, Esquire, National Geographic, Reader's Digest, Wired, George, Details, Stuff* and *Forbes*; AP, UPI, Dow Jones Newswire, Bloomberg News Service, Copley News Service, Knight Ridder News Service and hundreds more."[90]

Some of the journalists trained in this fashion are individuals whose names you will never see, because they now work behind the scenes as producers, research assistants, public relations consultants or as editors and reporters for local and state media rather than national publications. Others have gone on to prominence, such as *National Review* editor Rich Lowry, *New York Post* and Fox News contributor John Podhoretz and CNN correspondent Jonathan Karl, all of whom worked on Collegiate Network publications in their student days. Ultra-right pundit Ann Coulter passed through both the Collegiate Network *and* the National Journalism Center on her path to fame, starting as editor of the CN-backed *Cornell Review*.

The story of Dinesh D'Souza epitomizes how conservative foundations have created a career track for aspiring conservatives. D'Souza, a native of India, began as the editor of the *Dartmouth Review*, a Collegiate Network publication that was notorious both for its attacks on alleged liberal bias at the university and for its sneering bigotry. Under D'Souza's editorship, the *Review* published an offensive parody titled "Dis Sho Ain't No Jive Bro," which mocked the way African-American students supposedly speak. ("Dese boys be sayin' that we be comin' here to Dartmut an' not takin' the classics. You know, Homa, Shakesphere; but I hea' dey all be co'd in da ground, six feet unda, and whatchu be askin' us to learn from dem?") It also outed a number of gay students by obtaining and publishing stolen correspondence, including personal letters, prompting one of the outed students to consider suicide and embarrassing another when his family learned of his sexual orientation.[91] After Dartmouth, D'Souza became the editor of *Prospect*, a magazine funded by conservative Princeton alumni. Under D'Souza's tenure, *Prospect* attacked women's studies and published an exposé on the sex life of a female undergraduate student without her permission.[92] He wrote a complimentary biography of Moral Majority leader Jerry Falwell, followed by a stint as senior domestic policy analyst in the Reagan administration before becoming a John M. Olin Scholar at the American Enterprise Institute, a gig that paid more than $100,000 per year. At AEI, a grant from the Olin Foundation helped pay for the writing of *Illiberal Education: The Politics of Race and Sex on Campus*, which attacked affirmative action on campus. *Illiberal Education* was heavily promoted by conservative publications such as the *National Review* and became a bestseller.

D'Souza went on to write *The End of Racism*, a book that managed to offend even conservatives with its declaration that black culture is pathologically inferior to white culture and that "the criminal and irresponsible black underclass represents a revival of barbarism in the midst of Western civilization."[93] D'Souza's history of southern segregation characterized it as merely misguided paternalism, "based on the code of the Christian and the gentleman" and designed to *protect* blacks: "Segregation was intended to assure that blacks, like the handicapped, would be insulated from the radical racists and—in the paternalist view—permitted to perform to the capacity of their arrested development."[94] The book's declarations were so extreme that two prominent African-American conservatives, Robert Woodson, Sr., and Glenn Loury, renounced their affiliation with the American Enterprise Institute to protest AEI's sponsorship of the book. According to Loury, AEI marketed *The End of Racism* extensively in business circles, and "Republican staffers on Capitol Hill are said to have eagerly anticipated how the book might move the affirmative action debate in the 'right direction.'"[95] None of this, of course, has meant any kind of setback in D'Souza's career as a public intellectual. In 2004, he had a fellowship at the Hoover Institution, and his website boasted that "Mr. D'Souza has been featured on numerous TV programs, including *Nightline, Crossfire, The Today Show, The O'Reilly Factor, Hannity & Colmes, Good Morning America,* and *Moneyline.* . . . He speaks at top universities and business and civic groups across the country. Among his recent engagements are World Presidents Organization meetings, *Forbes* CEO Conference, National Association of Credit Management, Emory University, and Bucknell University."[96]

The nastiness of the attacks that D'Souza oversaw beginning with his *Dartmouth Review* days was no accident, and this sort of thing continues today. Stanley Ridgley's *Start the Presses,* a 2000 guidebook for starting conservative campus newspapers, advises "causing a stir" to "attract more donations, staff, and subscriptions." Controversy, Ridgley explains, "must become grist for your paper's mill."[97] Provocative rhetoric helps influence students while they are young and naturally inclined toward rebellion. It also places university faculty and administrators on the defensive, forcing them to choose between tolerating behavior that creates a hostile environment for other students or taking action that invites accusations of censorship. The *Cornell Review*, Ann Coulter's old stomping grounds, followed this strategy in 1997 when it reprised the tone of "Dis Sho Ain't No Jive Bro" with its own mocking parody of black speech. ("Da white man be evil an he tryin' to keep da brotherman down. We's got Sharpton and Farrakhan so who da white man now, white boy?")[98]

Similarly, the *Hawk's Right Eye*, a monthly newsletter for college Republicans at Roger Williams University in Rhode Island, devoted the front page of its September 2003 issue to an attack on Judy Shepard, whose son Matthew was beaten to death in Wyoming for being gay. After Shepard gave a talk on campus about the murder of her son, *Hawk's Right Eye* editor Jason Mattera accused her of "preying on students' emotions and naivety" [sic] so that she could become "a mascot for the homosexual agenda." The same issue published a lurid description of the homosexual rape of a young boy and threw in a joke about "pedophiles nationwide" who "condemned the FDA's food pyramid as 'bigoted' and 'hateful' because 'anus' and 'penis' were not listed as separate food groups."[99] As a student publication, *Hawk's Right Eye* receives funding from the university to pay for its printing costs. Its attack on Shepard prompted the university administration to take the bait, denouncing the publication and freezing its funding. Conservative groups nationwide responded on cue, accusing the university of censorship. Young America's Foundation decried "harassment by university officials" and their "heavy-handed approach to silencing ideas that oppose the leftist orthodoxy so prevalent on college campuses."[100] David Horowitz's *Front Page* magazine took up the cry, as did another Horowitz group, Students for Academic Freedom.[101] The local *Providence Journal* noted that the controversy "has launched Jason Mattera, the 20-year-old editor of the monthly newsletter, into the national spotlight. While in Washington, D.C., yesterday, Mattera spoke at a news conference on the Student Bill of Rights, which would require colleges to balance their so-called liberal bias in faculty hiring and promotions."[102] Mattera was in Washington for his summer internship at the *National Review,* which was in turn arranged through his fellowship at the National Journalism Center.[103]

The Real David Brock
and the Surreal Anita Hill

David Brock, who was one of the luminaries of right-wing journalism before experiencing a change of heart in the late 1990s, has described the ease with which he was able to climb aboard the conservative career escalator in his 2002 mea culpa, *Blinded by the Right: The Conscience of an Ex-Conservative.* "Most of us," he writes (by which he means cohorts such as Ann Coulter, Dinesh D'Souza, Laura Ingraham and John Podhoretz), "were involved in alternative campus publications—in the '80s, 'alternative' meant conservative—funded by a right-wing outfit in Washington called the Institute for Educational Affairs. The foundation was chartered in 1978 by former Nixon and Ford treasury secretary William Simon and Irving Kristol, the ex-Trotskyite intellectual known as the godfather of conservatism, in a bid to recruit and program cadres of young people and send them forth into ideological battle. While it appeared to us as if the left was an all-powerful force, the truth is that in terms of movement building, the left didn't have the money, the discipline, or the single-mindedness of the right."[104]

After a tumultuous year as a conservative editor of Berkeley's student newspaper, the *Daily Cal*, Brock was "approached about editing the *Berkeley Review*, an even more crude version of its sister publication at Dartmouth." Brock had qualms about the "racist, homophobic" stance of the *Berkeley Review*, so he declined the offer but was helped instead to "found another outlet, a dignified, neoconservative weekly magazine we called the *Berkeley Journal*." While still in college, Brock also began writing for the Heritage Foundation's *Policy Review* and the editorial page of the *Wall Street Journal*, and fresh out of college he was able to step into a job at Rev. Sun Myung Moon's *Washington Times*, followed by a stint at the Heritage Foundation and from there to the *American Spectator*, itself a recipient of more than $6 million in grants from Bradley, Olin and other conservative foundations.[105]

Brock's big break, though, came in 1991 when Anita Hill, a professor of law at the University of Oklahoma, testified before Congress that she had been sexually harassed by U.S. Supreme Court nominee Clarence Thomas. The Bradley Foundation contributed $11,850 specifically to finance Brock's research as he wrote an attack on Hill, which appeared first as an "investigative report" in the *American Spectator*.[106] Brock's article, which declared that Hill was "a little bit nutty and a little bit slutty," was then expanded into a book titled *The Real Anita Hill*, which portrayed her testimony before Congress as part of an orchestrated left-wing conspiracy to derail Thomas. The book extensively quoted Hill's detractors, many of them anonymous, who described her as "untrustworthy," "bitter," "militantly anti-male," "subject to wild mood swings," "a full-fledged campus radical" and "the world's kinkiest law professor."[107]

In *Blinded by the Right*, Brock admits that his attacks on Hill were "a witches' brew of fact, allegation, hearsay, speculation, opinion, and invective. . . . I didn't know what good reporting is. Like a kid playing with a loaded gun, I didn't appreciate the difference between a substantiated charge and an unsubstantiated one." In fact, Brock stated, "Every source I relied on either thought Thomas walked on water or had a virulent animus toward Hill. . . . I had no access to Hill's supporters, and therefore no understanding of their motivations, no responses to any of my charges, and no knowledge of whatever incriminating evidence they might have gathered against Thomas that was not introduced in the hearing. . . . The conspiracy theory I invented about the Thomas-Hill case could not possibly have been true, because I had absolutely no access to any of the supposed liberal conspirators. . . . All of my impressions of the characters I was writing about were filtered through their conservative antagonists, all of whom I believed without question."[108]

Although *New York Times* columnist Anthony Lewis dismissed *The Real Anita Hill* as "sleaze with footnotes," the actual book review in the *Times* was flattering, and it spent eight weeks on the *Times* bestseller list. In fact, the critique from Lewis and a few other liberals actually generated controversy that helped boost sales of the book. A raft of conservatives rose to Brock's defense, including William F. Buckley, Cal Thomas, Mona Charen, and the editorial pages of the *New York Post* and the *Washington Times*. "In my world of conservative Washington, I was a hero overnight," Brock recalled. "I was suddenly a star and a stud. My friend Ann Coulter, a conservative lawyer and future TV pundit and author, told me that when I walked into a room full of conservatives, it was like Mick Jagger had arrived."[109]

Some Girls

With the election of Bill Clinton, Brock switched from defending Thomas against allegations of sexual misconduct to investigating Clinton for similar offenses. The campaign against Clinton, he states, was instigated by Peter Smith, a conservative financier and top contributor to GOPAC, Newt Gingrich's political action committee. Brock says he received $5,000 initially from Smith to investigate allegations that Clinton had fathered a child with an African-American prostitute named Bobbie Ann Williams in Arkansas. "I was programmed to spring to action like a trained seal," Brock recalls in his book. "Peter offered me $5,000 for my trouble, not through the *Spectator* but paid directly to me by check; getting by on my Anita Hill book advance, I was a whore for the cash. Although accepting a payment like this was most unusual and unethical for a journalist, in my mind it was no different from taking money from politically interested parties like the Olin and Bradley foundations."[110]

The Bobbie Ann Williams story originated during the 1992 election, when it appeared on the cover of *The Globe*, the supermarket tabloid. Reporters from mainstream publications looked into the Clinton's "love child" allegations but declined to print them because there was no confirmation beyond the word of a drug-abusing prostitute who was paid by *The Globe* for her story. Even Brock was unable to find enough evidence to support a hatchet job, as was Daniel Wattenberg, another journalist at the *American Spectator*, who was given a videotape of Williams telling her story. "My notes of the tape describe her as 'addled' and her speech as 'slurred,' but that's unfair to crack addicts," Wattenberg recalled later. "The noddy, scratchy, mumbly woman on that tape looked like a junkie to me. No reporter of sound mind would have gambled his journalistic reputation on an unauthenticated tape of this woman."[111]

Although the Clinton "love child" story didn't pan out, a year later Smith introduced Brock to Arkansas Republican activist Cliff Jackson, who put him in touch with four Arkansas state troopers claiming to have personally observed Clinton's sexual shenanigans while he was governor. Brock was unable to verify any of the troopers' allegations, and the details that he was able to check independently turned out to be false.[112] After conversations with several Republican friends, however, Brock went ahead with the "Troopergate" story, which ran in the *Spectator*'s January 1994 issue.[113] "I threw in every last titillating morsel and dirty quote the troopers served up. I even published what the troopers conceded was their idle conjecture, such as the claim that Hillary Clinton had been having an affair with her former law partner Vince Foster," he says. "The right-wing construct of 'Bill' and 'Hillary' now had 'facts' to back it up. My article depicted 'Bill' as a sexually voracious sociopathic cipher, while 'Hillary' appeared as a foulmouthed, castrating, power-mad harpy, joined together in a sham power marriage. The piece left such an indelible image in the minds of the media and the public as it led network newscasts and became a staple of Jay Leno monologues and *Saturday Night Live* skits that it would be possible in the future to say and write and broadcast any crazy thing about the first couple and get away with it. The Clintons were moral monsters."[114]

Although Brock's article dwelt on the role played by Clinton loyalists in trying to prevent embarrassing "bimbo eruptions" from reaching the media, he omitted any mention of the role that Cliff Jackson and Peter Smith had played in *creating* the bimbo eruptions by feeding him his story and even paying him to write it. He also didn't mention that the troopers who dished dirt on the Clintons each received a check of $6,700 from Smith, and that Jackson helped fan the flames by promising them a million-dollar book deal.[115]

Brock's article in turn helped pave the way for Paula Jones and her lawsuit accusing Clinton of sexual harassment, as part of a multimillion-dollar campaign financed by Richard Mellon Scaife. Called the "Arkansas Project," the campaign was coordinated closely from the outset with *The American Spectator*, which received checks of $50,000 per month to keep the project running, generating a steady stream of scandalous allegations about the Clinton administration. According to Brock and *Spectator* editor R. Emmett Tyrrell, Jr., the initial discussions that led to the Arkansas Project took place on a Chesapeake Bay boat trip in mid-1993, involving four men — Tyrrell, Scaife aide Richard Larry, Washington lawyer Stephen Boynton, and longtime *Spectator* board member David Henderson, a retired public relations executive.[116] "Several sources at *The Spectator*, all of whom asked for anonymity, said they thought Tyrrell had agreed to undertake the investigation to please Larry and Scaife, the magazine's most generous supporter since 1970," the *Washington Post* reported in 1999.

Brock, in *Blinded by the Right*, concurs. "The anti-Clinton scandal machine became quite a profitable business for right-wing publishers, pundits, and radio talk show hosts, and we at the *Spectator* were pioneers," he recalled. "In the three years that the $2.5 million Arkansas Project ran, Henderson paid himself $477,000 and Boynton made $577,000. Of course, my own greed motivated me to play along with these Keystone Kops, who knew nothing about journalism. Yet I took down their preposterous accusations that the Clintons were involved in everything from sex orgies to drug-running to murder as if they were legitimate, and did what I could to check them out. This was part of my job at *The Spectator,* and I was paid handsomely for it. All of us at *The Spectator* were in it together at some level or another, scamming Scaife."[117]

The Spectator's allegations, echoed by other conservative publications and pundits, regularly made their way into the mainstream press. Allegations of wrongdoing prompted calls from Republican congressmen for investigations, which led to the appointment of White House Special Prosecutor Kenneth Starr—a member of the Federalist Society for Law and Public Policy Studies, a network of law students, attorneys and judges devoted to the spread of conservative legal principles. The society is a recipient of more than $9.6 million in funding from conservative foundations including Scaife, Bradley and Olin.[118]

Of course, there was a basis for part of the right wing's case against Bill Clinton—specifically, the charge that he was a philanderer and lied about it. Even in this regard, however, the known facts about Clinton's sex life are actually fairly tame by comparison with the known facts about other presidents, including Grover Cleveland (who reportedly fathered a son out of wedlock 11 years before becoming president), Warren Harding (whose affair with Nan Britton produced a daughter), Franklin D. Roosevelt (who had an affair with his wife's secretary) and of course, John F. Kennedy.[119] Most of the other lurid allegations against the Clintons have never been substantiated, notwithstanding eight years of concerted effort from the right. This of course did not stop the right-wing echo chamber from continuing to spread the stories.

In 1998, even the long-discredited story about Clinton's alleged "love child" resurfaced while the Monica Lewinsky scandal was in full swing. Conservative outlets including NewsMax.com, Rupert Murdoch's *Times* of London, the *Drudge Report*, Fox News and the *Washington Times* all carried stories claiming that the Williams family was trying to establish Clinton's paternity of Bobbie Ann's teenage son, Danny. Photographs of the boy were published, accompanied by breathless commentary about his resemblance to a young Bill Clinton. Matt Drudge ran a "world exclusive" headlined, "White House Hit with New DNA Terror; Teen Tested for Clinton Paternity," while the alleged "scandal" reverberated on right-wing talk radio. On January 3, 1999, the front page of Murdoch's *New York Post* carried a photo of Clinton with a screaming headline, "CLINTON PATERNITY BOMBSHELL: DNA test will determine if prez is father of teen." The story bled over to the *New York Daily News* and even the BBC. *Tonight Show* host Jay Leno devoted a week of monologues to the paternity allegations, joking, "Only President Clinton could distract people from a sex scandal with another sex scandal." The *Washington Times* reported that the media were "abuzz with rumors" about the paternity allegations and that *The Star* (another supermarket tabloid) had paid Bobbie Ann Williams a sum "in the low six figures" for her cooperation, which included turning over DNA samples for comparison with Clinton's DNA profile published in the Ken Starr report.[120] The LexisNexis news database recorded 98 stories just in the month of January 1999 about Clinton and his alleged love child, in publications including the *New York Daily News*, the *Guardian* of London and the online journal *Slate*.

On January 9, the DNA test came back negative, confirming that Clinton was not the father. "There was no match. Not even close," said a source at *The Star*.[121] The *New York Post*, which had considered the story important enough to fill its entire first page only a few days previously, buried the news that Clinton had been exonerated in a brief, seven-sentence notice on an inside page.[122]

Stossel's Big Break

The career of John Stossel on ABC's *20/20* offers another example of the way the echo chamber works to place conservative ideas into the mainstream media, while hiding the interests of the people who promote those ideas. Stossel's programs regularly rely on interviews and information provided by conservative think tanks, which in turn help advance and defend Stossel's career. Writer David Mastio (himself a conservative pundit who writes for publications such as *National Review*) detailed some of those relationships in a February 2000 report for Salon.com. Mastio noted that Stossel has a business arrangement with the Palmer R. Chitester Fund, a conservative, tax-exempt nonprofit organization that is partly financed by the Bradley and Olin foundations. Through the Chitester Fund, Stossel's ABC specials are also used as classroom educational materials. The Chitester Fund hires conservative economics instructors at George Mason University, which is itself a magnet for more than $36 million in funding from Olin, Koch, Bradley, Scaife and other conservative foundations. The economics instructors write study guides to go with several of Stossel's TV shows, and the Chitester Fund sells them to schools through a program that it calls "Stossel in the Classroom." The Heartland Institute, a conservative think tank in Illinois also funded by Bradley, Scaife and the others, advertises "Stossel in the Classroom" in its publication, the *School Reform News*.[123]

Stossel's programs themselves have a decidedly corporate-friendly slant, which is emphasized further by the study guides. One of the programs is titled "Greed," which begins with the famous Michael Douglas line from the movie *Wall Street* in which Douglas declares that "greed is good." Stossel sets out to demonstrate that Douglas was right. According to the promotional materials for "Greed," Stossel "discovers that in order to get money from people, you generally have to provide value for them in return, thus everybody wins. He also examines how the profit motive has spurred civilization's accomplishments. So why then is greed so vilified?"[124] Another program, "Freeloaders," questions "how some people in America get something for nothing" and features an interview with Walter Williams, the John M. Olin Distinguished Professor of Economics of George Mason University.[125] (Williams has also served on the board of directors of the Chitester Fund and supervised the economics instructors who wrote the study guides for Stossel's series.) Yet another "Stossel in the Classroom" show is called "Are We Scaring Ourselves to Death?" and dismisses health risks from pesticide and other chemical exposures. The study guide goes further, attacking the government for changing dietary recommendations to emphasize fruits and vegetables over meat and dairy products. As Mastio observes, "Many, if not most, of the 35 to 40 footnotes accompanying each guide cite predictably conservative sources like the Heritage Foundation, the Cato Institute, the Hoover Institution, the Young America's Foundation and the *Wall Street Journal* op-ed pages."[126]

Mastio notes other connections between Chitester, Stossel and ABC News: Stossel has contributed some of his lecture fees to

Chitester. An ABC vice president helped edit one of the study guides. Chitester used to own Stossel.org and several other Internet domain names based on John Stossel's name. ABC News also gets a percentage of the proceeds from sales of "Stossel in the Classroom."[127]

Stossel's reporting style is aggressively assertive and opinionated, but often sloppy and misleading. In "Greed," for example, he dismisses a protest rally on Wall Street highlighting the widening wage gap between American workers and bosses and the fact that compensation of CEOs has risen by 500 percent over the past 15 years. "Still, this doesn't mean the workers were hurt," Stossel responds. "Factory wages were up, too—up 70 percent." While technically accurate, his statistics failed to adjust for inflation. When inflation is taken into account, real wages for workers rose by only 3 percent, while bosses' real incomes went up by more than 360 percent.[128]

"ABC News policy says employees are allowed to speak to groups they cover or could potentially cover, but they can't accept money for it," noted writer Ted Rose in *Brill's Content* magazine. "Yet Stossel does. He says charging people is his way of thinning out invitations. In addition to conservative political organizations such as [the American Legislative Exchange Council] and the Federalist Society, Stossel has spoken to The Michigan Petroleum Association and to Chase Manhattan Bank." During a two-year period, he earned $263,000 in speaking fees, most of which he said he gives away to charities—such as the Palmer R. Chitester Fund.[129]

Stossel has been caught simply fabricating facts to fit his ideological agenda. On February 4, 2000, he broadcast a scathing attack on organic foods. Titled "The Food You Eat—Organic Foods

May Not Be as Healthy as You Think," Stossel's *20/20* segment suggested that organic farmers' failure to use pesticides actually make their food *less* safe. "We searched the records and found there have been no tests done that actually compare bacteria counts in organic vs. normal food," Stossel told *20/20* viewers. "So we did our own laboratory testing." The results, he claimed, showed that neither conventional nor organic produce had pesticide residues, but that organic produce was more likely to contain dangerous E. coli bacteria. "By a small margin, more of the organic produce was contaminated than the conventional stuff," Stossel said. "But the real bad news for you organics buyers is that the average concentration of E. coli in the spring mix [a bag of organic lettuce] was much higher. And what about pesticides? Our tests surprisingly found no pesticide residue on the conventional samples or the organic." In reality, the pesticide tests that Stossel claimed were conducted were never done at all. Tests *had* been done for bacterial contamination, but according to the scientists hired to perform them, the tests were incapable of proving the food safety problems that Stossel attributed to the results.[130]

Based on this nonexistent research, Stossel then cornered Katherine DiMatteo of the Organic Trade Association (OTA), which represents sellers of organic foods. After telling her that the organic foods had tested higher for E. coli, he held up a bag of organic lettuce. "You've seen our research," he said. "Does this bother you? . . . So maybe we shouldn't buy this?" The cameras captured DiMatteo's defensive response. After the interview was over, the OTA reviewed ABC's research claims and discovered the deception, but during the three months between the interview and the program's broadcast, neither Stossel nor ABC responded to its repeated complaints and demands that the information should be corrected. The Environmental Working Group (EWG), a Washington-based environmental organization, also waded into the fray.[131] Nevertheless, the program was broadcast on four separate dates without any corrections.

In a July 2000 letter to the network, EWG president Kenneth Cook complained about the network's "remarkable breach of journalistic ethics and conduct. . . . ABC News has reported these nonexistent laboratory results, invoking the scientific authority such findings normally convey, in a false and reckless manner. . . . We consider it implausible, if not impossible, that Mr. Stossel and his producer, David Fitzpatrick, were unaware that they were falsifying the pesticide test results reported on *20/20*. Indeed, we raised the issue directly with them in a letter, phone messages and e-mail within days of the original February 4 broadcast—and four months before the story re-aired July 7 and July 11."[132] The network did not issue a retraction until August, after EWG circulated a 16-page report exhaustively documenting the fraud. After the story was picked up and reported in the *New York Times*, the network responded with a one-paragraph statement admitting the error, and Stossel made a half-hearted apology on the air, but there were no further consequences for his journalist career. In fact, the conservative echo chamber sprang into action in Stossel's defense. Industry-funded think tanks including the Cato, Hudson and Competitive Enterprise institutes all sent out op-ed pieces, defending Stossel and disparaging his critics as censors. CEI went further and launched a "Save John Stossel" website (subsequently renamed SupportJohnStossel.org), praising "his unique ability to debunk conventional wisdom and expose special interests, politicians, and politically correct causes."[133]

Stossel struck again the following year with another attack on environmentalists. On March 27, 2001, a pesticide-industry advocacy group called Responsible Industry for a Sound Environment (RISE) sent around an e-mail to its members, urging them to assist CEI's Michael Sanera, who heads a CEI project aimed at eliminating environmental education in schools. "Mr. Sanera has been contacted by ABC News," the e-mail explained. "A producer for John Stossel is working on a program on environmental education. He needs examples of kids who have been 'scared green' by schools teaching doomsday environmentalism. . . . Let's try to help Mr. Stossel. He treats industry fairly in his programs."[134]

When an organization circulates a message to multiple parties, sometimes copies get forwarded to other people as well, and a copy of the RISE message wound up in the hands of John Borowski, an environmental science teacher who lives in Oregon. A few days later, he was surprised to receive a phone call himself from Ted Balaker and Debbie Colloton, who identified themselves as television producers with ABC News. Without mentioning Stossel's name, they said that they had read a piece Borowski wrote supporting environmental education and that they wanted to interview him for a piece they were doing about environmental issues. After he hung up the phone, Borowski did a bit of sleuthing. Using an assumed name, he pretended to be a parent upset at "environmental scaremongering in the classroom" and contacted Angela Bendorf Jamison, a public relations consultant to RISE. Jamison directed him to Sanera, whom she confirmed was "working with Stossel's people on this."[135] Borowski ended up not doing the interview.

John Quigley, the executive director of Earth Day in Los Angeles, was not so lucky. He was contacted by Colloton for permission to film a field trip at which some 2,000 kids learned about clean-energy solutions. Through Quigley, Colloton also arranged for several elementary schoolkids to be interviewed in an ABC studio as they talked about the environment. When Stossel showed up to conduct the interview, Quigley says, "He started asking leading questions, and it was very clear what he wanted to get. He would say, 'Wow, it's really scary, isn't it?' And the kids weren't scared at all and so they just looked at him. He asked that question repeatedly. . . . These were bright kids, and they were responding well. He was clearly trying to elicit certain responses on tape. When he didn't get the verbal response he wanted, he had the crew shoot from behind and had the students raise their hands while he asked, 'Is the air getting dirtier or cleaner?' It was clear that he wasn't interested in honest dialogue but was trying to elicit certain responses for a script he had already written."[136]

After the children's parents complained that their kids had been manipulated, Stossel appeared on Bill O'Reilly's program on Fox News to say that the parents had been "brainwashed" by "the totalitarian left. They want to silence people who criticize them."[137]

In May 2003, Stossel was promoted to co-anchor of *20/20*. "These are conservative times," an ABC source told *TV Guide*. "The network wants somebody to match the times."[138] But shouldn't a record of fair and accurate reporting be more important than bending to the current political wind?

Reinventing Al Gore

During the 2000 presidential campaign, the campaign to ridicule Al Gore was organized through the congressional office of Texas

Republican Dick Armey, the House majority leader. "We would just kind of compile stuff and send it out to talk radio and to members," said Armey spokeswoman Michele A. Davis. Grover Norquist's Americans for Tax Reform also helped out, starting a website to track and publicize Gore's "misstatements."[139]

The same pattern appeared repeatedly during the 2000 campaign. Instead of discussing budgets, health plans and other topics that actually pertain to governance of the country, reporters fell prey to a game of trivial untruths that came to define the public's perception of candidate Al Gore. Through a series of contrived controversies, Gore was portrayed as someone who had a habit of embellishing and stretching the truth. He was reported to have claimed that he "invented the Internet." He was pilloried for saying that he and his wife, Tipper, were the models for the lead characters in Erich Segal's novel, *Love Story*, and he was ridiculed for saying he had grown up doing chores on his family's farm. Let's look briefly at each of these supposed exaggerations or lies by candidate Gore:

The Internet. Contrary to what almost everyone today believes, Gore never said he "invented" it. During a March 9, 1999, interview with CNN, what Gore actually said was, "During my service in the United States Congress, I took the initiative in creating the Internet."[140] As is clear from this sentence and the context that surrounded it, Gore was not saying that he invented the Internet in a technical or engineering sense. He was saying that he did the political work and articulated a public vision that made the Internet possible. It is not unusual for politicians to publicly tout their achievements, and Gore's boast was accurate, according to Vinton Cerf and Robert Kahn, the two computer engineers who actually designed the basic architecture and the core protocols that make the Internet work. (Cerf is the person most often called the "father of the Internet.")[141] After Gore's comment began to attract public ridicule, Cerf and Kahn wrote a public declaration describing Gore's comment as "a straightforward statement on his role." Moreover, they stated, "Al Gore was the first political leader to recognize the importance of the Internet and to promote and support its development. . . . No other elected official, to our knowledge, has made a greater contribution over a longer period of time. . . . The fact of the matter is that Gore was talking about and promoting the Internet long before most people were listening."[142]

The statement by Cerf and Kahn, however, was barely noticed against the huge background noise of the Republican echo chamber, which quickly transformed the meaning of Gore's statement. Senator Trent Lott mockingly claimed to have taken "the initiative in creating the paper clip." A news release by House majority leader Dick Armey declared, "If the Vice President created the Internet then I created the Interstate highway system." Within a week after Gore made his original comment, the phrase "took the initiative in creating" was truncated to "created," and "created" was then glossed as "invented," with Dan Quayle quipping, "If Gore invented the Internet, I invented spell-check."[143] From there it was off to the races, with newspaper editorials, TV pundits and TV standup comedians all mocking Gore's statement. For the month of March 1999 alone, the LexisNexis database lists 146 news stories stating that Gore claimed he invented the Internet, with headlines such as "Gore's Gaffe," "Pure Invention," "There's No Reconciling Al Gore's Rhetoric with Reality" and "Actually, Gore Hasn't Even Invented a Way to Fib Convincingly."[144]

Love Story. Like the Internet hoax, this one takes a bit of explaining. As a student at Harvard, Al Gore was friendly with novel-

ist Erich Segal, who went on to write *Love Story* and drew on
Gore (and on Gore's roommate, actor Tommy Lee Jones) in creating the character of Oliver, the uptight preppy who was later
played by Ryan O'Neal in the movie adaptation of the book. During Segal's promotional tour following the publication of *Love
Story*, he mentioned this to a reporter for the *Tennessean*, a newspaper in Gore's home state. When the reporter wrote up the story,
he stretched things a bit and said that Tipper Gore had also been
the role model for Jennifer, Oliver's spunky girlfriend, who was
played in the movie by Ali McGraw. Years later, while Gore was
flying back from Texas to Washington on Air Force Two in December 1997, he spent a couple of hours on the plane chatting
about movies with two reporters and mentioned his acquaintance
with Segal and the story that had appeared in the *Tennessean*.
Contacted later for comment, Segal acknowledged that Gore had
been a model for Oliver but made it clear that Jennifer was not
based on Tipper. The only error in this case was the part about
Tipper being the inspiration for Jennifer, and that error originated
with the *Tennessean*.[145] Nevertheless, it became a major example
of Gore's pathological tendency to fib. "How does Al Gore explain
all of these sort of wacky things about I invented the Internet, I was
the inspiration for *Love Story*?" asked Tony Snow on Fox News,
prompting Brit Hume to respond that Gore needs to "stop doing
this stuff."[146] The *Washington Times* rehashed the tale, describing
it as "an assertion Mr. Segal emphatically denied."[147] As with the
Gore-invented-the-Internet hoax, the *Love Story* hoax had no sig-
nificance at all in terms of understanding whether Gore would
pursue better policies or perform better than Bush in the office
of president. Bob Somerby, another college classmate of Gore,
called the media feeding frenzy over *Love Story* "a misreported,

silly tale that would have been trivial even had it been true,"[148] adding that he was "embarrassed to think that such silly disputes can be a part of our national discourse."[149]

Gore's chores. In a March 16, 1999, interview with the *Des Moines Register,* Gore described the summers he spent as a teenager on his family farm, where his father "taught me how to clean out hog waste with a shovel and a hose. He taught me how to clear land with a double-bladed ax. He taught me how to plow a steep hillside with a team of mules. He taught me how to take up hay all day long in the hot sun and then, after a dinner break, go over and help the neighbors take up hay before the rain came and spoiled it on the ground."[150] Two days later, Rupert Murdoch's *New York Post* declared that Gore's description of his experiences on the farm was "a load of bull" and further evidence of "a tendency to fake his past to burnish his image."[151] On Fox News, Fred Barnes scoffed, "This is the guy who grew up in a luxury hotel in downtown Washington, D.C." Brit Hume marveled, "Gore is now claiming that—that he grew up shoveling hog poop!"[152] In the *Washington Times,* Donald Lambro said the incident displayed "the deeply dishonest side of Al Gore," and Cal Thomas explained that Gore was actually the pampered son of a U.S. senator & and "attended elite private schools in Washington, where he has delivered a lot more rhetorical hog waste than he ever shoveled in Tennessee."[153] In the *Washington Post,* conservative columnist Michael Kelly wrote a parody titled "Farmer Al," which depicted Gore trying to do farm chores at his luxury Washington hotel and swinging his double-bladed ax to clear away "some of that Louis XV furniture."[154] In *USA Today,* Michael Medved said Gore's story of the chores showed he had a "delusional view of himself."

Everyone had a good laugh at the vice president's latest stupid lie—even though, once again, it happened to actually be the truth. Gore spent his summers growing up on the family farm in Tennessee, where his father—even though he was a U.S. senator—believed that hard manual labor would instill character. Even Bob Zelnick, who wrote a hostile biography of Gore for the conservative Regnery publishing house, noted that young Gore's regimen of farm chores often stretched from sunup to sundown.[155] According to another biography of Gore by Bill Turque, "For parts of virtually every summer through high school, Gore worked with the farmhands and was often assigned an extra project by his father. . . . Even the local kids, who might have enjoyed watching a city slicker sweat some, were appalled at how hard Gore was worked. 'It was horrendous,' said one woman who knew him well as a teenager."[156]

It may feel like a waste of time even bothering to set the record straight about these sorts of stories. After all, who really cares how much of Al Gore ended up in Erich Segal's novel, or what kind of chores he did when he was a teenager? The only thing that makes these stories serious is the role they played in shaping the public's opinion of Gore's character. "Everyone knows that Al Gore's biggest problem is a tendency to lie," declared conservative columnist Mona Charen, citing *Love Story* and the Internet among her list of examples.[157] According to the *Washington Times*, Gore's "increasingly bizarre utterings" were evidence of "a nervous or mental disorder."[158] But anyone who cares to examine the record closely can see that in fact Charen and her fellow conservative politicians and pundits were the ones who were lying, even as they claimed to make honesty the litmus test for judging Gore's character and fitness to become president. In ensuing years, none of the reporters and pundits who smirkingly commented on Gore's "pattern of making things up" has bothered to set the record straight about their own misstatements.[159]

The real damage that this sort of propaganda does is to democracy itself. Robert Parry is one of the few journalists who actually bothered to investigate and debunk the media's portrayal of Gore-as-liar. "How can voters have any hope of expressing an informed judgment when the media intervenes to transform one of the principal candidates—an individual who, by all accounts, is a well-qualified public official and a decent family man—into a national laughingstock?" Parry asked in the *Washington Monthly*. "What hope does a candidate have when the media can misrepresent his words so thoroughly that they become an argument for his mental instability?"[160]

CHAPTER THREE

The One-Party State

In a democracy, Alexander Hamilton believed: "The differences of opinion, and the jarrings of parties . . . often promote deliberation and circumspection; and serve to check the excesses of the majority."[1] Although these jarrings and clashings sometimes seem messy, contentious and wasteful, in fact they are one of the great strengths of democracy in both peacetime and wartime.

If, however, a single viewpoint or party is able to drown out or suppress the views of others, a different dynamic sets in. One-party dominated states and hierarchical, command-driven social systems are notorious for their tendency to make disastrous decisions, in the areas of both domestic and foreign policy. China's cultural revolution and the Soviet Union's failed economic development plans are among the most extreme but not the only cases in point. In the field of foreign affairs, Napoleon and Hitler both disdained dissenting advice and found doom attacking Russia. Saddam Hussein met a similar fate when, after fighting a debilitating war with Iran, he invaded Kuwait and triggered the wrath of other nations.[2] As we detailed in our previous book *Weapons of Mass Deception*, the Bush administration seems to have made the same mistake when it believed its own propaganda promoting war with Iraq.[3]

The U.S. military has a term for this type of information system: "incestuous amplification," which *Jane's Defense Weekly* defines as "a condition in warfare where one only listens to those who are already in lock-step agreement, reinforcing set beliefs and creating a situation ripe for miscalculation."[4] Psychologists have a similar term: "group polarization," which describes the tendency for like-minded people, talking only with one another, to end up believing a more extreme version of what they thought before they started to talk.[5]

The Republican Party's philosophy and political organizing strategies have been remarkably successful at helping the party achieve and consolidate power in the late 20th and early 21st centuries. Simultaneously, however, they have created conditions that make incestuous amplification and group polarization more likely in disparate areas of America's political arena, from government agencies to business lobbies and even within traditionally independent bodies such as the government's scientific advisory boards.

The Revolving Door

Shortly after President Bush took office, one of his most trusted campaign advisers, Ed Gillespie, took a brief break from heading up his own lobbying and PR firm, Quinn Gillespie & Associates.

Gillespie, whose clients have included Microsoft, Enron and Verizon, as well as the steel and logging industries, went to work for a few days as acting director of public affairs for the U.S. Commerce Department, where he assisted Secretary Donald Evans with the agency's reorganization under the new Bush administration. Among his other activities, Gillespie arranged for the department to hire as its press secretary one of his own employees at Quinn Gillespie, Jim Dyke. Gillespie finished his work at the Commerce Department on February 15, 2001, and the following day he was back at work in his own office.

"Federal law requires departing government officials to wait one year to lobby agencies that employed them," observed *Wall Street Journal* reporter Jim VandeHei. "But that doesn't apply to Mr. Gillespie; his brief, 15-day tenure made him a temporary worker exempt from the cooling-off period. As a result, Mr. Gillespie is free to contact Mr. Evans on behalf of clients."[6]

Gillespie was not alone. More than 150 Republican lobbyists worked on Bush's transition team. Diane Steed of the Coalition for Vehicle Choice, which was created by the Motor Vehicle Manufacturers of America to fight against higher fuel-efficiency standards, advised the Department of Transportation. Jack Abramoff, a Republican lobbyist for Indian gambling, advised the Interior Department. Many of Bush's permanent employees have also come from an inner circle of party-affiliated industry lobbyists. For the number-three spot at the Department of Labor, for example, Bush tapped Eugene Scalia, the son of Supreme Court Justice Antonin Scalia and a labor lawyer who has specialized in representing management in labor disputes related to worker safety, especially the dangers of repetitive-stress injuries.[7] With regard to environmental-policy jobs, virtually all of Bush's appointees have consisted of attorneys and lobbyists for the very industries they were appointed to oversee. Timber industry lobbyist Mark Rey became assistant secretary for agriculture with responsibility for national forests. Steven Griles, a leading lobbyist for the oil, gas and coal industries, became deputy secretary at the Department of the Interior. A lobbyist for drilling in the Arctic National Wildlife Refuge went to work as the Interior's envoy to Alaska. At the U.S. Justice Department, Wyoming attorney Tom Sansonetti—a Republican activist who has lobbied on behalf of coal-mining operations—was appointed to head the enforcement of environmental and natural resource laws.[8]

The revolving door between private lobbyists and government officials existed, of course, long before George W. Bush became president—but Bush has taken it to new levels. When Bill Clinton assumed the presidency, people who assisted with his presidential transition were barred from lobbying agencies they helped for six months. The Bush administration, by contrast, saw no problem with having someone like Gillespie work for the White House one day and literally go to work as a lobbyist on the following one. "Helping out this administration is good for the country," Gillespie told the *Wall Street Journal*. "Anything we can do to help President Bush initially or from here on out we are happy to do."[9]

Send My Regards to K Street

Much of the real power and influence-peddling in Washington, D.C., begins on K Street, a nondescript corridor of office buildings located a few blocks north of the White House. K Street is where the big lobbying firms and corporate trade associations have their headquarters. It is sometimes referred to as the fourth branch of government. Many of the top K Street lobbyists are, in fact, former government officials—senators, congressmen and their staffs who, after retiring from office (or after losing their last election) go to work as hired advocates for companies and industries. Their ability to influence government policy comes in part from the personal relationships they have with their former colleagues, and from the campaign contributions that corporations can channel to politicians who do their bidding. Lobbyists, as columnist Michael Kinsley has observed, are "a group of people who charge a lot of money to give disproportionate influence in our democracy to people with even more money."[10]

Historically, however, the power of corporate lobbyists has been somewhat mitigated by the two-party system. Since the party in power could vary from one election to the next, K Street had to hire top names from both major parties as a way of ensuring access. Ideological differences between the parties therefore limited the ability of corporations to control the policy agenda. In addition to corporations, the Democratic Party needed to appeal to constituencies including the labor movement, minorities, environmentalists and other liberals who have historically turned out as voters and activists in support of the party's candidates. As Nicholas Confessore observed in the July/August 2003 issue of the *Washington Monthly*, the relationship between Democrats and lobbyists contained an "inherent tension": "For the most part, K Street groups supported Democrats because they had to and Republicans because they wanted to. The Democrats needed corporate money to stay competitive, but were limited by the pull of their liberal, labor-oriented base. Although the party became generally more pro-business during the 1980s, it had few natural constituencies on K Street."[11] After Republicans achieved control over all sectors of the federal government in the early 21st century, however, corporate lobbyists were happy to jettison bipartisanship and throw their weight solidly behind the Republican machine, which targeted control of K Street by pressuring the major lobbying firms to hire only Republicans.

Party strategist Grover Norquist is one of the leading masterminds of this strategy. Working with Tom DeLay, the House majority leader, he launched the K Street Project in 1995 to compile a database of lobbyists. The database lists lobbyists' names, where they work, which party they belong to, where they have worked politically and how much money they have contributed to the candidates and causes of both parties. The purpose of the list is to decide who "deserves" access to the White House, Congress and federal agencies. Contributions to the wrong party can "buy you enemies," explained Congressman Thomas M. Davis III of Virginia, chairman of the National Republican Congressional Committee.[12] According to Marshall Wittmann, a former Christian Coalition staffer who now works for Senator John McCain, the pressure on lobbyists has made DeLay "the 'Dirty Harry of Capitol Hill, the bad cop. Every K Street lobbyist is shaking in their boots because K Street lives on access, and DeLay can shut off their oxygen."[13]

Pennsylvania Senator Rick Santorum is another key player in the K Street Project. In the months following the 2000 elections that gave Republicans the White House, Santorum began convening a private meeting each Tuesday morning of Republican lobbyists, attended sometimes by representatives from the White House and other senators. Democrats and journalists were not invited. "The chief purpose of these gatherings is to discuss jobs—specifically, the top one or two positions at the biggest and most important industry trade associations and corporate offices," Confessore reported. "Every week, the lobbyists present pass around a list of the jobs available and discuss whom to support. Santorum's responsibility is to make sure each one is filled by a loyal Republican—a senator's chief of staff, for instance, or a top White House aide, or another lobbyist whose reliability has been demonstrated. After Santorum settles on a candidate, the lobbyists present make sure it is known whom the Republican leadership favors."[14]

Republican dominance on K Street has further enhanced the party's fund-raising advantage over Democrats. "An analysis of political donations by industry groups shows that over the past decade, 19 major sectors have shifted from a roughly 50–50 split between the two main parties—or in some cases, a slightly pro-Democratic tilt—to a solid alignment with the Republican Party, which now enjoys advantages exceeding 5 to 1 in some of these sectors," the *Washington Post* reported in November 2002.[15] Key industries that have shifted Republican include accounting, aerospace, alcoholic beverages, commercial banking, defense, health care and pharmaceuticals. "Just like the Democrats get a 90–10 split from the trial lawyers and labor, we will have 90–10 in the staffing on K Street and 90–10 business giving," Grover Norquist gloated in November 2002.[16] But trial lawyers and labor give only a fraction of the amount that corporations donate to election campaigns. In 2002, contributions from businesses accounted for 73 percent of all election giving, compared to only 7 percent for labor. (Most of the remainder came from "ideological" or "other" donors, such as environmental groups, the National Rifle Association, clergy or nonprofit organizations.)[17]

In place of the "inherent tension" that existed between Democratic politicians and K Street lobbyists, their ideological closeness with Republicans has made the party and its corporate supporters virtually indistinguishable. "Tom DeLay, Grover Norquist, and others have set up a K Street patronage operation that effectively obliterates the distinction between conservatives and corporatists," conservative columnist David Brooks observed in June 2002. "And remember, when they brag about the growing merger between conservatives and the business community, they are talking about something akin to a merger between Sam's Video Shack and Blockbuster. The culture of the corporate community is bound to dominate the culture of conservatism, not the other way around."[18]

Another indicator of the growing closeness of the corporate-conservative relationship is that corporations and their trade lobbies have gone beyond merely trying to influence politicians in Washington and have become propaganda machines that work to sell the Bush administration's policies to the general public. "Beginning in the 1990s, Washington's corporate offices and trade associations began to resemble miniature campaign committees, replete with pollsters and message consultants," Confessore writes. "To supplement PAC [Political Action Committee] giving, which is limited by federal election laws, corporations vastly increased their advocacy budgets, with trade organizations spending millions of dollars in soft money on issue ad campaigns in congressional districts. And thanks to the growing number of associations whose executives are beholden to DeLay or Santorum, these campaigns are increasingly put in the service of GOP candidates and causes."[19] During the Iraq War, for example, radio conglomerate Clear Channel Communications had its stations sponsor pro-war rallies nationwide and even banned the Dixie Chicks from their playlist after one band member criticized Bush. Companies such as General Motors, Verizon and Morgan Stanley have lobbied their stockholders and customers to promote Bush administration tax cuts, and the pharmaceutical industry both helped write and promote Bush's Medicare plan.[20]

Double Standard

While Bill Clinton occupied the White House, the nonprofit Center for Public Integrity stirred a major public scandal when it obtained a list of White House guests and found that Democratic Party donors and fund-raisers, who raised hundreds of thousands of dollars, were among the guests who spent nights in the historic Lincoln bedroom. The CPI's 1996 report, titled "Fat Cat Hotel," sparked a Republican-led Senate investigation and became the topic of thousands of news reports and critical editorials, with headlines such as "Clinton's Cash Hunt,"[21] "Lincoln Bedroom Becomes Another Soiled Symbol,"[22] "Dozing for Dollars"[23] and "Anatomy of a Scandal."[24] By contrast, there was almost no reporting—let alone outrage or Senate investigation—when the CPI reported, seven months after Bush took office, that the "fat cat hotel" was "still open for business." According to a list released by the White House, many of the new administration's guests had been major political donors, including at least six "Bush Pioneers"—people who raised more than $100,000 for his presidential campaign.[25] In a Republican-dominated political climate, no one raised an eyebrow about this sort of thing, because the investigating body—the U.S. Senate—was controlled by the same political party that ran the hotel.

Haley Barbour, who was elected governor of Mississippi in 2003, exemplifies the synergistic relationship between lobbying and fund-raising. Barbour is the former chairman of the Republican National Committee and also owns his own lobby shop, Barbour, Griffith & Rogers, which represents 50 major clients, including representatives of the tobacco, automobile, pharmaceutical, health-care and transportation industries. Shortly after Bush took office, the company was named by *Fortune* magazine as the number one lobbying firm in Washington.[26] It is also all-male and all-Republican. "Even receptionists and secretaries have to be Republican to be hired," noted the *New York Times* in a July 2001 profile.[27] Barbour is also the man in charge of raising money for Republican Senate campaigns. For some of them, including Mississippi Senator Trent Lott, he has raised millions of dollars, much of it coming in the form of large contributions from Barbour's own clients. Not surprisingly, money translates into influence. According to Charles Lewis, executive director of the nonprofit Center for Public Integrity, Barbour gave his corporate clients "a pipeline into Republican members of the Senate," and Barbour himself pretty much agrees. "People in the Senate have already made up their mind about me," he says. "I can't improve on my standing with these guys. I've worked closely with them over the years. They've been nice to me, and doors open to me, and they are willing to listen to my opinion on issues that they are dealing with on behalf of my clients. If you called anyone in town, they would tell you I cannot improve my standing with these senators."[28]

Barbour's company is also closely tied to another firm, New Bridge Strategies, which was set up in June 2003 to help companies get the sweetest contracts for rebuilding Iraq. The president of New Bridge is Joe Allbaugh, a longtime close adviser of President Bush and a member of the so-called "iron triangle" of advisers—himself, Karen Hughes and Karl Rove—who have formed Bush's inner circle since he first ran for governor in 1994. The other top officers at New Bridge Strategies are Ed Rogers and Lanny Griffith—Barbour's partners at Barbour, Griffith & Rogers, where Allbaugh's wife Diane also happens to work as an attorney. You might think these guys waste a lot of time shuttling back and forth between their jobs at BG&R and their jobs at New Bridge. Fortunately, that's not much of a problem, because they all share office space on the same floor of the same building, a couple of blocks from the White House.[29]

And Barbour isn't the only well-connected Republican with one foot in government and the other in the Iraq contracting business. Douglas Feith is the U.S. undersecretary of Defense and was one of the most influential advocates within the Bush administration for war with Iraq. Feith is currently in charge of reconstruction at the Pentagon, while his former law partner, Marc Zell, is "assisting regional construction and logistics firms to collaborate with contractors from the United States and other coalition countries" through their former law firm—previously called Feith & Zell, now rechristened Zell, Goldberg & Co.[30]

With this kind of Republican clout, it isn't terribly surprising that the actual contracts for rebuilding Iraq have also gone to companies that give big donations to the Republicans. Weeks before the first bombs dropped in Iraq, the Bush administration began its plans for rebuilding the country. The plans were developed in secret, according to ABC News, with only a handful of companies allowed to bid on contracts for the reconstruction of Iraqi schools, airports, roads, bridges, hospitals and power plants.

The companies allowed to bid were all generous political donors, mostly to Republicans: Bechtel, Fluor, Parsons, the Washington Group and Halliburton—Vice President Dick Cheney's old firm.[31] In October 2003, the Center for Public Integrity tallied the contracts that had been awarded by then to projects in Iraq and found that the recipient companies "donated more money to the presidential campaigns of George W. Bush—a little over $500,000— than to any other politician over the last dozen years." The biggest winner by far was KBR, a subsidiary of Halliburton. KBR got $2.3 billion in Iraq contracts, followed by Bechtel ($1 billion) and International American Products ($527 million).[32]

The pattern is this: companies like Halliburton give money to support Republican politicians, who in turn use their clout to ensure that the companies get fat contracts, who in turn give a portion of their profits to keep Republicans in power. Around and around the circle goes, and everybody gets a piece—except, of course, for the rest of the American people, who pay the bill for all this fun with their tax dollars and the mounting federal deficit.

The relationship between corporations, lobbyists, industry-funded think tanks and the Republican Party has become so intertwined that simply listing all the overlapping relationships can boggle the mind. During the buildup to war in Iraq, some of the relationships between corporate and government supporters of the war were summarized in *Energy Compass*, an expensive newsletter ($2,195 per year) that offers insider intelligence on the oil industry to corporate executives. As *Energy Compass* reporter Jill Junnola observed, "The overlap among members of foundations, think tanks and increasingly, the Bush team, borders on the incestuous."[33] Her 2002 summary is worth quoting at some length. If you have a hard time keeping track of all the names and organizations listed below, don't worry. The point here is not to memorize every detail or connect every dot, but simply to get a sense of how things work:

The Smith Richardson Foundation, funded by Vicks VapoRub money, gave $1.16 million to AEI [the American Enterprise Institute] in 2000, of which $125,000 went toward a study on US foreign entanglement led by none other than the State Department's John Bolton. AEI fellows include Richard Perle, head of the quasi-government Defense Policy Board, Irving Kristol, the grand-daddy of neocons, and Michael Ledeen, a fellow Reagan appointee and the first executive director of the Jewish Institute for National Security Affairs (JINSA). Ledeen has been leading the call for putting Iran next on the US's hit list. Former AEI fellow Michael Rubin, who was also affiliated with the Washington Institute for Near East Policy, joined the Pentagon this month to help shape a post-Saddam Iraq policy. AEI's board includes Lee Raymond, chairman and CEO of ExxonMobil, and William Stavropoulos, chairman of Dow Chemical Co.

The current president of the Lynde and Harry Bradley Foundation, Michael Grebe, also sits on the board of overseers of the Hoover Institute at Stanford University, where National Security Adviser Condoleezza Rice was formerly provost. Of the $101 million-plus that had been raised in a funding drive by August 2000, nearly 70% came from its well-heeled Board of Overseers, which boasts among its members Defense Secretary Donald Rumsfeld and Richard Mellon Scaife, an heir to the Mellon family's industrial, oil and banking fortune.

During the Reagan and Bush Senior administrations, Richard Scaife sat on the US Advisory Commission for Public

Diplomacy, which oversees the US Information Agency—which cynics have long regarded as the acceptable face of the CIA. He helped found the Heritage Foundation in 1973, and now heads three of four Scaife family foundations. . . . Former Heritage visiting fellow Alvin Felzenberg is now working with Rumsfeld at the Department of Defense.[34]

The danger in all of these interlocking relationships is that it breeds the "incestuous amplification" of one-sided thinking, leading to serious errors of judgment by policymakers. This helps explain how the Bush administration managed to convince itself that Iraq truly did possess awesome weapons of mass destruction, that it was closely tied to Al Qaeda, and that the people of Iraq would greet a U.S. invasion of their country as liberation. Much of the administration's intelligence information about Iraq actually came from the Iraqi National Congress (INC), an organization created and funded by the U.S. government at the behest of the first Bush administration for the purpose of creating conditions for Saddam Hussein's overthrow. Not surprisingly, the information from the INC and its head, Ahmed Chalabi, tended to reinforce the already existing assumptions of policymakers in the second Bush administration, even when that information contradicted other reports coming from the U.S. Central Intelligence Agency. The INC's "intelligence isn't reliable at all," said Vincent Cannistraro, a former senior CIA official and counterterrorism expert. "Much of it is propaganda. Much of it is telling the Defense Department what they want to hear. And much of it is used to support Chalabi's own presidential ambitions. They make no distinction between intelligence and propaganda, using alleged informants and defectors who say what Chalabi wants them to say, [creating] cooked information that goes right into presidential and vice-presidential speeches."[35]

Lysenkoism Lite

"Incestuous amplification" can also distort other types of information, such as science. One-party rule had absurd and horrific consequences for science in Hitler's Germany, where Nazi scientists denounced Einstein's relativity theory as a Jewish corruption of Isaac Newton's "organic" laws of nature. Science also suffered under the Soviet Union's one-party system in the mid-20th century, when the Communist Party began to insist that scientific ideas must conform to Marxist ideology. This policy had especially disastrous consequences for Soviet agriculture, which fell under the sway of Trofim Lysenko, a party-backed biologist who insisted that genetics was a "reactionary," "bourgeois" and even "fascist" form of "idealism" that deviated from Marxist philosophy. Geneticists were accused of "useless scholasticism," charged with sabotage, terrorism and Trotskyism, and fired from their jobs. Biologists were publicly denounced as "enemies of the people," arrested, tortured, placed on trial, sent to prison, and executed. By the time Lysenkoism peaked around the end of World War II, the best Soviet scientists had been silenced and scattered, while the Soviets attempted to grow crops on the basis of Lysenko's increasingly bizarre ideas, such as the theory that wheat seeds can be "trained" to produce rye. Eventually, of course, Lysenko's ideas were discredited. When science and politics meet, nature is the ultimate referee. By the time Lysenkoism fell from favor, however, the Soviet Union had lost a generation of its best scientists, and it had missed the agricultural revolution in productivity that other countries enjoyed thanks to genetic innovations such as hybrid corn.[36]

Under Republican rule, of course, scientists are not being arrested or shot, but the Bush administration has begun a disturbing process of subordinating science to politics, with potentially dangerous consequences. To inform its decisions on issues including sex education, environmental health, global warming, workplace safety and AIDS, the Bush administration has used a variety of political litmus tests to create scientific panels stacked heavily with members who have scant scientific credentials but strong industry ties and right-wing agendas. It has altered official government websites, removing scientific information that contradicts the political views of industry groups and the conservative movement. In some cases, scientists have been ordered to remain silent by their politically appointed higher-ups.[37] Here are a few examples:

● In accordance with the Christian right's opposition to sex education and its determination to promote abstinence, information has been pulled from the CDC's website showing that condom use is effective at preventing AIDS.

● The website of the National Cancer Institute was altered to suggest that abortion increases a woman's risk of breast cancer—a claim that is overwhelmingly contradicted by actual research.[38]

● In 2001, Bush signed an executive order banning all federal funding for stem-cell research using new human embryonic cell lines. Scientists and advocates for the disabled believe that embryonic stem-cell research is vital to finding new cures for debilitating diseases, such as paralysis, Lou Gehrig's Disease,

Parkinson's Disease and Alzheimer's Disease. Some religious groups, however, equate it with abortion because it involves the extraction of stem cells from a fertilized egg. "We've had a severe violation of the separation of church and state in the handling of what to do about this emerging technology," responded disabled actor Christopher Reeve, a strong advocate for stem-cell research. "Imagine if developing a polio vaccine had been a controversial issue," Reeve said. "There are religious groups—the Jehovah's Witnesses, I believe—who think it's a sin to have a blood transfusion. What if the president for some reason decided to listen to them? . . . Where would we be with blood transfusions?"[39] Bush's position also disturbed Nancy Reagan, who normally avoids criticizing other Republicans out of a sense of party loyalty but issued a rare dissent on the stem-cell issue. "A lot of time is being wasted," she said. "A lot of people who could be helped are not being helped."[40]

- The U.S. Department of Agriculture (USDA) has told top scientists at its Agricultural Research Service that they need to ask for permission before they can publish research related to "sensitive issues," including "agricultural practices with negative health and environmental consequences, e.g., global climate change; contamination of water by hazardous materials (nutrients, pesticides, and pathogens); animal feeding operations or crop production practices that negatively impact soil, water, or air quality."[41]

- In response to a request from the National Pork Producers Council, the USDA has forbidden microbiologist James Zahn from publishing or speaking publicly about his study finding antibiotic-resistant bacteria in the air near factory farms with large-scale hog confinement operations.[42]

- In September 2002, the *Washington Post* reported that the Bush administration had begun "a broad restructuring of the scientific advisory committees that guide federal policy in areas such as patients' rights and public health, eliminating some committees that were coming to conclusions at odds with the president's views and in other cases replacing members with handpicked choices. In the past few weeks, the Department of Health and Human Services (HHS) has retired two expert committees before their work was complete. One had recommended that the Food and Drug Administration expand its regulation of the increasingly lucrative genetic testing industry, which has so far been free of such oversight. The other committee, which was rethinking federal protections for human research subjects, had drawn the ire of administration supporters on the religious right, according to government sources."[43]

- HHS Director Tommy Thompson has also transformed the CDC's Advisory Committee on Childhood Lead Poisoning and Prevention, rejecting the nominations of renowned scientists with extensive experience in studying the health effects of lead on children. Drs. Michael Weitzman, Bruce Lanphear and Susan Kitzman have been dropped from the panel or had their nominations rejected. The new appointees have included Dr. William Banner, a paid expert witness for the lead industry; Dr. Joyce Tsuji, a staff scientist for a company whose corporate clients have included several large lead firms; and Dr. Kimberly Thompson, who is affiliated with the heavily industry-funded Harvard Center for Risk Assessment—three of whose funders have Superfund sites with lead contamination.[44] Banner's appointment especially is hard to defend on scientific grounds. Whereas Weitzman, Lanphear and Kitzman have all authored numerous peer-reviewed scientific papers on lead poisoning, Banner's only published research in the field deals with experimental treatment of rats. In courtroom testimony for his corporate clients, Banner has claimed that a lead level of 70 micrograms per deciliter is safe for a child's brain—seven times the level currently considered safe by the CDC and every other scientific organization or expert outside the lead industry itself.[45]

- In August 2002, HHS replaced virtually every member of the advisory committee for CDC's National Center for Environmental Health, which provides advice on a range of public issues from pollution to bioterrorism. The 15 new members appointed to the 18-member committee included individuals with close ties to regulated industries, including Lois Swirsky Gold, a risk-assessment specialist who has minimized reports linking environmental pollutants with cancer, and Dennis Paustenbach, a toxicologist whose firm does paid risk assessments for industry. Paustenbach's résumé also includes serving as an expert witness for California utility Pacific Gas and Electric in a trial involving allegations that the company had poisoned drinking water with a deadly form of chromium—the theme of the movie *Erin Brockovich*.[46] The transformation of HHS prompted a protest from ten leading scientists. "Scientific advisory committees do not exist to tell the secretary what he wants to hear but to help the secretary, and the nation, address complex issues," they warned in an editorial for *Science* magazine. "Every administration advances its agenda by making political appointments of scientists and managers to direct its agencies. But disbanding and stacking these public committees out of fear that they may offer advice that conflicts with administration policies devalues the entire federal advisory committee structure and the work of dedicated scientists who are willing to participate in these efforts."[47]

- The Bush administration's process for screening scientists was glaringly political in the case of Dr. William Miller, a professor of psychology and psychiatry. Miller was initially asked to join the National Advisory Council on Drug Abuse, which provides expert advice to the National Institutes of Health. Before he could be appointed, however, he received a disturbing phone call from an aide in Thompson's office. The caller wanted to know if Miller was sympathetic to faith-based initiatives, whether he supported abortion rights, whether he supported the death penalty for drug dealers and whether he had voted for President Bush—none of which had any relevance to his qualifications to serve on a panel that deals with drug abuse. "I need to vet you to determine whether you might have any views that would be an embarrassment to the president," the aide explained. When Miller said that he had not voted for Bush, the aide asked, "Why didn't you support the president?" Miller was not appointed to the panel.[48]

Storming Warming

The issue of global warming has occasioned some of the most intense political battles involving science in recent years. Measures to address global warming would gore the interests of the automobile, oil, coal and manufacturing industries. The Bush administration has confronted it by behaving like the proverbial ostrich with its head in the sand. Among scientists who work in the field of climate research, there is strong agreement that action is necessary now to counteract the effect that human industrial emissions of carbon dioxide and other greenhouse gases are having on the global climate, but Bush has acted as though the problem doesn't exist.

The best indicator of scientific opinion worldwide is the Intergovernmental Panel on Climate Change (IPCC), which was established in 1988 by the World Meteorological Organization and the United Nations Environmental Program to provide scientific, technical and economic assessments of the current state of knowledge about various aspects of climate change. Some 2,000 scientists, experts and government officials from more than 170 countries have prepared and signed off on the IPCC's conclusions. "Globally, it is very likely that the 1990s was the warmest decade and 1998 the warmest year in the instrumental record, since 1981," it declared in its 2001 report. Moreover, "CO_2 concentration has not been exceeded during the past 420,000 years and likely not during the past 20 million years. The current rate of increase is unprecedented during at least the past 20,000 years. . . . [M]ost of the observed warming over the last 50 years is likely to have been due to the increase in greenhouse gas concentrations," and "Emissions of CO_2 due to fossil fuel burning are virtually certain to be the dominant influence on the trends in atmospheric CO_2 concentration during the 21st century."

These conclusions have been supported and amplified in reports by other leading scientific bodies, such as the American Geophysical Union,[49] the American Meteorological Society[50] and the National Academy of Sciences (the most prestigious general scientific body in the United States.[51] Recognizing the threat that global warming poses to the environment and human beings, more than 120 countries—with the notable exception of the United States—have ratified the Kyoto Protocol, a commitment to reduce greenhouse emissions that was negotiated in Kyoto, Japan, in 1997.

During his 2000 campaign for president, Bush declared that global warming was "an issue that we need to take very seriously."[52] His first appointee as head of the Environmental Protection Agency, former New Jersey governor Christine Todd Whitman, also made the right noises initially, declaring that Bush "has also been very clear that the science is good on global warming. It does exist. There is a real problem that we as a world face from global warming."[53] In March 2001, she told an environmental summit of the eight major industrialized nations in Italy that global warming was "at the top of his agenda."[54]

Within the administration, however, Whitman's position was nothing if not controversial. "When I said it over there, what happened was, everybody back here interpreted that as meaning we were going to support the Kyoto Protocol. And that set people nuts," Whitman would recall two years later.[55] Bush began backpedaling furiously. After the release of the IPCC's 2001 report, ExxonMobil lobbied the Bush administration to demand the ouster of Dr. Robert Watson, the U.S. scientist who had chaired the panel since 1996.[56] The U.S. State Department obligingly opposed Watson's re-election, offering no scientific rationale for its position, and Watson was ousted the following year.[57] Princeton University atmospheric scientist Michael Oppenheimer called the administration's action "scandalous," an "invasion of narrow political considerations into a scientific process."[58]

In May 2002, the Environmental Protection Agency issued a report, titled *U.S. Climate Action Report 2002*, in compliance with its reporting obligations under a global-warming treaty that the elder George Bush signed at the United Nations Earth Summit in 1992.[59] The report confirmed that global warming was a real problem and that urgent action was needed to keep it from getting worse. In its assessment of likely impacts in the United States, the EPA report said global warming was likely to disrupt snow-fed water supplies, cause increased flash floods in Appalachia, create more stifling heat waves and the permanent disappearance of Rocky Mountain meadows and coastal marshes and displace forests with grasslands in the Southeast. Its publication sent the administration into full denial mode, traces of which are evident in e-mail correspondence that was discovered later between Myron Ebell of the Exxon-funded Competitive Enterprise Institute and Phil Cooney of the White House Council for Environmental Quality. "Thanks for calling and asking for our help," wrote Ebell, CEI's global-warming policy director. "It's nice to know we're needed once in a while," Ebell continued. "I want to help you cool things down. . . . We made the decision this morning to do as much as we could to deflect criticism by blaming EPA for free-lancing. It seems to me that the folks at EPA are the obvious fall guys, and we would only hope that the fall guy (or gal) should be as high up as possible. Perhaps tomorrow we will call for Whitman to be fired. I know that this doesn't sound like much help, but it seems to me that our only leverage to push you in the right direction is to drive a wedge between the president and those in the Administration who think that they are serving the president's best interests by pushing this rubbish. . . . So I'm willing and ready to help, but it won't be possible to do much without some sort of backtracking from the Administration."[60]

Christine Todd Whitman managed to keep her job for the time being by distancing herself from the report that had been written under her leadership, declaring that she hadn't even known about its existence until news organizations reported on it.[61] Bush himself dismissed it as "the report put out by the bureaucracy."[62]

In July 2003, the *Washington Post* reported that it had obtained leaked confidential documents detailing White House efforts to suppress climate-change research in an environmental survey of the U.S. that was published that June. A four-page memo from the EPA revealed that Bush's staff had made "major edits" to the climate-change section of the report and were telling the EPA that "no further changes may be made." In addition to deleting sections on the ecological effects of global warming and its impact on human health, White House officials had sprinkled numerous qualifying words such as "potentially" and "may" throughout the document. As a result, the EPA memo complained, "Uncertainty is inserted where there is essentially none." The changed version, according to scientists at the EPA, "no longer accurately represents scientific consensus on climate change." Unable to persuade the White House to accept a scientifically credible version, the EPA decided to remove the entire global-warming section from the report.[63]

Whitman was left in an awkward situation. On the one hand, she admitted, there was "scientific consensus within the agency. I mean we were ready to say stuff. And we were ready to say it in pretty strong language. Other departments and agencies weren't." As a result, EPA's judgment was overruled by the White House Council on Environmental Quality (CEQ), which Whitman describes as "the gatekeeper for all of the agencies that have anything to do with the environment."[64] Unlike the EPA, however, there are no scientists at the CEQ. It is run by James Connaughton, a former lobbyist for power and electric utilities, which have long opposed action to address global warming.

Eric Schaeffer, the EPA's director of enforcement, resigned from the agency in 2002 to protest White House interference in EPA assessments. "I'm used to compromise," Schaeffer said. "I've worked in government most of my life. Under the Bush administration I saw something else. This was not a matter of trying to find a reasonable balance, but of taking whatever the industry gave us and feeling like we had to eat it. We had to accept it no matter how wrong it was."[65]

Similar concerns have been expressed by Jeremy Symons, whose frustrations with White House interference led to his own resignation as EPA climate policy adviser in April 2001. According to Symons, scientists at the agency are afraid to conduct research for fear of angering the White House. "They do good research," he said. "But they feel that they have a boss who does not want them to do it. And if they do it right, then they will get hit or their work will be buried."[66]

In May 2003, Whitman herself resigned, telling reporters she was "interested in taking some time off."[67] As the *Washington Post* noted, however, her departure capped "months of speculation" that she was on her way out. "Bruising fights within the administration over key issues had left her drained and eager to depart

Washington," the *Post* reported, adding, "Secretary of State Colin L. Powell once described Whitman as the administration's 'wind dummy'—a military term for an object shoved from an airplane to determine how the wind is blowing over a landing zone. Repeatedly, she found herself losing policy battles with the White House and other agencies."[68]

Denying Dust

Prior to assuming his post at the White House Council on Environmental Quality, James Connaughton defended corporate clients including leading defendants in cases involving asbestos, a major liability concern for corporations because of its proven link to a number of life-threatening respiratory diseases including lung cancer. It is not terribly surprising, therefore, that CEQ played an important role in covering up information about asbestos and other toxins in the air in New York City following the terrorist attacks on September 11, 2001. Asbestos was used as an insulating material during construction of the first 40 stories of the first World Trade tower, and it joined the concrete, glass and other materials that were pulverized into a huge cloud of dust when the towers collapsed.[69] Literally before the dust had cleared, however, New York City Mayor Rudolph Giuliani joined the White House and the EPA in assuring people that the city's air was safe. The day after the attacks, the chief of staff for EPA Deputy Administrator Linda Fisher sent an e-mail to senior agency officials, saying that "all statements to the media should be cleared" first by the National Security Council, Bush's main forum for discussing national-security matters.[70] Fisher, a Bush appointee, had worked previously as a chief lobbyist and political fund-raising coordinator for the Monsanto Company, a defendant in asbestos liability cases involving millions of dollars.[71]

The original draft of the EPA's statement on air quality, written two days after the 9/11 attack, contained a clear warning: "Even at low levels, EPA considers asbestos hazardous in this situation." Before releasing it to the public, however, the White House reworded it to say almost the exact opposite: "Short term, low level exposure to asbestos of the type that might have been produced by the collapse of the World Trade Center buildings is unlikely to cause significant health effects."[72]

The changes were made, according to a report issued two years later by the EPA's inspector general, at the behest of Connaughton's Council on Environmental Quality. "As a result of the White House CEQ's influence," the report noted, "guidance for cleaning indoor spaces and information about the potential health effects from WTC debris were not included in the EPA's issued press releases. In addition, based on CEQ's influence, reassuring information was added to at least one press release and cautionary information was deleted from EPA's draft version of that press release. . . . Every change that was suggested by the CEQ contact was made." According to the EPA chief of staff, in fact, "no press release could be issued for a three- to four-week period after September 11 without approval from the CEQ contact."[73]

On September 16, the EPA and OSHA issued another news release stating that "the majority of air and dust samples monitored at the crash site and in lower Manhattan do not indicate levels of concern for asbestos."[74] In another statement two days later, Whitman said she was "glad to reassure the people of New York and Washington, D.C., that their air is safe to breathe and their water is safe to drink."[75] Within a space of ten days after the attacks, the EPA had issued five statements, all of them reassuring the public that the air around the World Trade towers was safe to breathe. Rescue workers at the site trusted those assurances as they dug frantically in hope of finding survivors, often without face masks or other respiratory protection. In fact, those reassurances were as toxic as the air the rescue workers inhaled. It wasn't until June of the following year that the EPA determined that air quality had returned to pre-9/11 levels, by which time respiratory ailments and other problems began to surface in hundreds of New Yorkers.

Corporate-funded think tanks went even further, declaring not only that the air was safe but that asbestos *safety regulations* had contributed to the death toll from the terrorist attack. "Asbestos fibers in the air and rubble following the collapse of the World Trade Center are adding to fears in the aftermath of Tuesday's terrorist attack," wrote Steven Milloy, a columnist for Fox News and an "adjunct scholar" at the Cato Institute. "The true story in the asbestos story, though, is the lives that might have been saved but for 1970s-era hysteria about asbestos." In his column, which was published on the Fox News website just three days after the 9/11 attacks, Milloy went on to speculate that asbestos insulation might have delayed the steel framework of the building from melting "by up to four hours."[76] The only individuals Milloy quoted to support his theory, however, were scientists who had previously worked as paid expert witnesses for the asbestos industry during product liability lawsuits filed by cancer victims. None of these experts had actually done research comparing asbestos to other heat-resistant insulating materials in an event like the 9/11 attack, and there is no scientific evidence whatsoever to support the claim that asbestos would have delayed the collapse of the towers by even five seconds, let alone four hours. "If you look at what *Marks' Standard Handbook for Mechanical Engineers* and the *Fire Protection Handbook* have to say about structural steel insulation, it becomes clear that there is nothing magical about asbestos in this application," says Jim Dukelow, a senior research engineer for the U.S. Department of Energy. "It was used because it was less expensive than the other spray-on materials and cheaper to apply than the non-spray-on alternatives. Other materials, specifically mineral wools, have equivalent or better insulation properties."[77]

The official reassurances failed to satisfy Alyssa Katz, who edits *City Limits*, a nonprofit magazine about New York City affairs. On September 11, she watched as a giant plume of smoke settled over her home in Brooklyn. "The whole neighborhood was raining paper and dust," she recalled.[78] As the months passed, New Yorkers began experiencing health problems. "Many people who live or work in lower Manhattan are convinced that they have not been told the truth," she reported. "They say that they're sick— throats sore, lungs hacking. Cleanup workers, local residents, and, most of all, firefighters at ground zero attest to intense respiratory illnesses unlike anything they recall experiencing before."[79]

On October 26, 2001, *New York Daily News* columnist Juan Gonzalez wrote a front-page story contradicting the official government line, detailing EPA test findings of notable quantities of toxic substances including dioxins, PCBs, benzene, lead and chromium in addition to asbestos.[80] The day Gonzalez's column appeared, EPA officials held a joint press conference with New York Mayor Rudy Giuliani to dismiss the story, calling it irresponsible, and Gonzalez came under increased scrutiny from his own paper, and several different editors were assigned to review his subsequent columns on the topic. "From that day on, the whole attitude toward the story changed," he says. "I did several more columns, but every one of them was highly scrutinized."[81]

Within the EPA as well, dissent was marginalized. Prior to the 9/11 attacks, the EPA had an ombudsman, Robert Martin, who was assigned to independently assess and comment on EPA decisions. Martin and his chief investigator, Hugh Kaufman, criticized the agency's handling of air-quality information following the terrorist attacks. On April 16, 2002, Kaufman spoke to *The NewsHour with Jim Lehrer*. The terrorist attack's "first set of victims," he said, "are the people who were killed when the attack happened. The second set of victims are the people who are exposed to the chemicals: to lead, to mercury, to cadmium, dioxin, benzene, asbestos, all these chemicals that have spread throughout lower Manhattan and have landed in their apartments, in their schools, in the office buildings—and these Americans who are also suffering from the attack have been abandoned by the government. And that's not right. It's our job at EPA not to count the dead bodies ten or twenty years down the line, not to operate on people to get rid of cancer. It's our job to prevent cancer. And we fell down on the job."[82]

A few days later, while Martin was out of town on EPA business, the agency announced a plan to place the ombudsman's office under the direct control of its inspector general, a move that would effectively end its autonomy (the whole purpose of an ombudsman in the first place). New rules were imposed, forbidding the ombudsman from mediating disputes between the public and the agency, or from talking with lawmakers or reporters without permission.[83] Martin returned to his office to find that the locks of his office were changed, and his files and computer had been taken. He and Kaufman resigned in protest. "They have portrayed this transfer as granting more independence for the ombudsman function when, in fact, it destroys it completely," Martin said. "I cannot operate with that falsehood."[84]

A year after the attacks, the *New England Journal of Medicine* published a study by David Prezant, the deputy chief medical officer for the New York City Fire Department. It showed that 332 city firefighters had developed "World Trade Center cough" and that roughly half of them remained on medical leave or light duty.[85] "Although no firefighters have retired from respiratory problems, nearly 500 firefighters may have to retire by year's end because of their failing health," the *Washington Post* reported.[86]

"We asked many times, is it safe here?" says Jack Ginty of the Uniformed Fire Officers Association, many of whose members died in the towers' collapse, while others went on to dig frantically in the rubble, searching for survivors. "We were told by city officials, federal officials, 'oh, yeah, we've tested the air, the air is fine,'" Ginty recalled in August 2003. "Now, finally the truth comes out that they have been lying to us all the way along. Had we known, we could have operated in a different fashion."[87]

CHAPTER FOUR

Pumping Irony

We deal in illusions, man. None of it is true. But you people sit there day after day, night after night, all ages, colors, creeds. We're all you know. You're beginning to believe the illusions we're spinning here. You're beginning to think that the tube is reality and that your own lives are unreal. You do whatever the tube tells you. You dress like the tube. You eat like the tube. You even think like the tube. In God's name, you people are the real thing, we are the illusion.

—Howard Beale, in the movie *Network*

For Jay Leno, it was a big night, scoring the highest Nielsen rating that *The Tonight Show* had seen for a Wednesday in more than four years. The big guest was movie muscleman Arnold Schwarzenegger, who was coming on the show to announce whether he would run in California's recall election against Governor Gray Davis. The buzz had been in the air for weeks. A month and a half earlier, when Schwarzenegger visited the show to promote his latest film, *Terminator 3: Rise of the Machines*, Leno had playfully introduced him as "the next governor from the great state of California."[1] And although Arnold's advisers had been hinting lately that the star was planning to forgo his shot at electoral office, Arnold had a surprise in store.

Bounding onstage, Schwarzenegger began with a warm-up joke, quipping that his decision was the most difficult in his career since his 1978 dilemma whether to get a bikini wax. Then he got serious. "The politicians are fiddling, fumbling and failing," Schwarzenegger said. "The man that is failing the people more than anyone is Gray Davis. He is failing them terribly, and this is why he needs to be recalled, and this is why I am going to run for governor." The announcement prompted whoops and cheers from Leno's studio audience, and Schwarzenegger rewarded them with some of the lines he had made famous in his movies. "Say 'Hasta la vista' to Gray Davis," he said, promising to "pump up Sacramento."[2]

He also paraphrased a line from another movie — Paddy Chayefsky's 1976 film, *Network*. The people of California, Schwarzenegger said, were "mad as hell, and we're not going to take it anymore."[3]

The movie *Network* is a satire about television sensationalism run amok. In the movie, Peter Finch plays Howard Beale, a deranged newscaster who has rejuvenated his network's ratings by promising to kill himself live in front of the cameras. Instead of committing suicide, though, Beale urges his viewers to join him in chanting that they are "mad as hell," and a cult-like movement forms around his diatribes against "the system." Ironically, Beale's anger eventually becomes a predictable television ritual, his ratings drop again, and the network itself arranges to have him killed. The movie's message was that even when the public gets "mad as hell," nothing changes in the end. It was a grim and cynical cinematic statement—almost as cynical as Schwarzenegger's seemingly nonironic use of Beale's line.

By all accounts, Arnold Schwarzenegger is a shrewd man, and his remarks on *The Tonight Show* were carefully crafted. He made a point, for example, of getting out in front of the main criticisms that his campaign would encounter. "I know that they're going to throw everything at me—I am a womanizer, no experience, a terrible guy," Schwarzenegger said. "We all know that Gray Davis can run a dirty campaign better than anyone, but we also know he doesn't know how to run a state."[4]

Months previously, Schwarzenegger's approach had been spelled out by Republican pollster Frank Luntz, who conducted focus-group research for the party's "Rescue California" campaign to recall Davis. In a memo to "Rescue California," Luntz outlined 17 ways to "kill Davis softly." It was important, he advised, to "trash the governor," but, "Issues are less important than attributes and character traits in your recall effort." Accordingly, Schwarzenegger carefully avoided mentioning the budget or raising any policy questions during his Leno appearance, sticking to Luntz-tested lines such as, "Do your job for the people and do it well, otherwise you are '*Hasta la vista*, baby!'"[5]

There is an art to "going negative" in political campaigns. Gray Davis was indeed an unpopular governor facing a voter backlash in a bleak economic year, and his centrist policies had alienated Democrats as much as Republicans. He had won re-election against Bill Simon less than a year before the recall drive began, but the race was marked by ugly mudslinging on both sides that left voters disgusted and gave his opponents plenty of material to use against him. Campaign consultants often advise that the best way to go negative is to find a lighthearted way to do it, preferably with a bit of humor. As Democratic campaign operative Deno Seder explains, humor "induces the flow of endorphins and other brain hormones, creating a sense of well-being or euphoria. . . . Such 'statements' can cripple the opposition, yet they leave the viewer with a pleasant feeling, not the bitter aftertaste that often accompanies sober attack ads. Instead of earning the resentment of the targeted audience for presenting a 'downer,' leaving them laughing creates a feeling of goodwill toward the sponsor, while actually accentuating the sting of the attack on the opponent. We all know that when Jay Leno or David Letterman starts making jokes about a candidate, the effect can be devastating."[6]

Schwarzenegger, however, was *on* Jay Leno, and he had the audience laughing *with* him. Calling Davis "fiddling, fumbling and failing" was itself a negative attack, but in the jovial context of the Leno show, it didn't feel negative. And by being the person to bring up the allegations of his inexperience and womanizing, Schwarzenegger was inoculating voters against his most obvious weaknesses as a candidate. Two years previously, *Premiere* magazine had published a report that described him as a womanizer and recounted numerous instances in which he had allegedly groped or otherwise harassed women without their consent.[7] Schwarzenegger had originally considered running for governor in the regular 2002 election, but had declined after Davis strategist Gary South launched a pre-emptive strike by blast-faxing copies of the *Premiere* piece around to reporters.[8]

The Running Man

Schwarzenegger's declaration on *The Tonight Show* may have appeared off-the-cuff and spontaneous, but months of planning and preparation had gone into both the recall petition that made his election possible and the campaign itself. Conventional wisdom suggests that Republican presidential candidates write off left-leaning California's 54 electoral votes, but such a substantial prize is hard to ignore. An associate of top Bush strategist Karl Rove calls the state "Karl's Ahab."[9] Aside from the ambition of winning California in the presidential race, the party stood to benefit in other ways by electing Schwarzenegger, such as an increase in Republican voter registration with the potential to influence future elections. It also forces Democratic presidential candidates to spend more time and money in the state in 2004. "We can distract the opposition long enough to make them vulnerable elsewhere on the national political landscape," said California Republican strategist Dan Schnur. Longtime Republican strategist Kenneth L. Khachigian, who worked with recall backer and bankroller Congressman Darrell Issa, characterized the recall as "fundamentally a conservative Republican mainstream movement. That's where all the momentum and energy behind the recall comes from."[10] Several other California GOP leaders, including former state legislator Howard Kaloogian, political consultant Sal Russo, and strategist David Gilliard, worked hard on the recall drive. Schwarzenegger's proclaimed liberal views on social issues such as abortion and gay rights were accepted by party activists as pragmatic necessities in California's cultural environment. As conservative strategist Matt Cunningham explained, "When a man is lost in the desert and dying of thirst, he's not going to insist on Perrier."[11]

One of several Republican Party figures cheering Schwarzenegger in *The Tonight Show* studio was political consultant George Gorton.[12] A year previously, Gorton had directed Schwarzenegger's campaign for Proposition 49—a noncontroversial measure providing grants for after-school programs—which many political insiders saw as a planned precursor to a future run for governor. Two weeks before the announcement on Leno, in fact, the *Political Pulse*, a newsletter of California politics, published a report by Anthony York noting that Schwarzenegger had recently raised nearly half a million dollars in new money for his already-concluded Prop. 49 campaign. "Is money in the Prop. 49 kitty going to be used for the upcoming governor's race?" York asked, adding, "At the very least, the fund-raising does prime the pump."[13]

Two months prior to his appearance on *The Tonight Show*, Schwarzenegger supporters conducted focus groups in San Francisco and the San Fernando Valley to determine participants' views of the actor and of Davis. The results guided a media strategy that more closely paralleled PR blitzes around Schwarzenegger's major movies than most political campaigns. Capitalizing on the uniquely short time frame of the recall election, it was a remarkably controlled and image-focused campaign. Voters in California—the most populous and one of the most diverse states in the country—had only two months to decide whether they wanted to recall Governor Davis and, if so, which of the more than 130 registered candidates should replace him.

Schwarzenegger required all of the aides and consultants to his campaign to sign a five-page confidentiality agreement. The agreement, which itself was supposed to be confidential (but leaked anyway to the *Los Angeles Times*), stated that Schwarzenegger "is a public figure and substantial effort and expense have been dedicated to limit the constant efforts of the press, other media and the public to learn of personal and business affairs" in which he was involved. Campaign aides agreed not to "take any photographs, movies, videos, or make any sketches, depictions or other likenesses of Arnold Schwarzenegger or Arnold Schwarzenegger's family, friends, associates or employees, all of which constitute confidential information." They also agreed not to divulge "financial, business, medical, legal, personal and contractual matters" and "any letter, memorandum, contract, photograph, film or other document or writing pertaining in any way" to Schwarzenegger "or any Related Parties."[14] Nondisclosure agreements of this type are common in Hollywood but unusual for political candidates.

Newspapers and more serious television news shows were, for the most part, ignored by the Schwarzenegger camp, which waited until 30 days into his campaign before agreeing to his first interview with California newspapers. Instead, carefully crafted yet vague messages were relayed to the public via entertainment-focused venues such as *Access Hollywood, The Oprah Winfrey Show, The Howard Stern Show* and *Larry King Live*. According to Sean Walsh, the campaign's co-director of communications, "We ran away from the established media. We went to the real mass media. We make no apologies for doing lots of radio or TV. It gave us five, seven, eight minutes of unfiltered opportunities to get out our message every day."[15]

The campaign finale was an elaborate bus tour through the state, with journalists in tow. Each bus was named after a different

Schwarzenegger film—"The Running Man" for Schwarzenegger himself and his immediate retinue, "Total Recall" for VIP tagalongs, and four buses for reporters, dubbed "Predator 1–4" by the campaign staff. Writing in the conservative *Weekly Standard*, Matt Labash called the caravan "the No Talk Express—in which he invites hundreds of access-starved journos along for the ride, then essentially tells them to buzz off. . . . Since it is fairly clear early on that access to Arnold will be next to nil, journalists interview other journalists from foreign countries."[16]

The campaign was dominated by slogans parroting his movie taglines: "I'll be back,"[17] or "Gray Davis has terminated opportunities! Now it is time that we terminate him!"[18] The campaign even had its own special effect: a giant wrecking ball, used at a campaign stop to crush a car as a way of dramatizing Schwarzenegger's opposition to the state's auto tax.[19]

As Schwarzenegger had anticipated on Leno, one of the areas that did come under scrutiny was his long-standing reputation as a womanizer. Reports of his rough handling of women were prominent in Wendy Leigh's 1990 book, *Arnold: An Unauthorized Biography*. According to Leigh, the actor's publicity team had responded to the book with lawsuits, threats and efforts to sabotage the book's publicity campaign.[20] The 2001 report in *Premiere* magazine also left questions hanging about the candidate's character. The truncated time frame of the recall campaign, however, left little time for further investigations. The *Los Angeles Times* conducted its own investigation and compiled a list of 15 women with stories of sexual harassment. The *Times* was able to find corroboration of each woman's story, either from independent witnesses or from friends or relatives who said the women had told them of the incidents long before Schwarzenegger's run for governor. The

Times report, however, did not appear until the last week of the campaign and was quickly dismissed by the Schwarzenegger camp as a smear orchestrated by Davis.[21] In its own bit of last-minute smearing, the Schwarzenegger campaign circulated an e-mail attacking the character of Rhonda Miller, a stuntwoman who said she had been manhandled on the set of *Terminator 2*. The e-mail pointed reporters to the website of a Los Angeles Superior Court, which showed that Rhonda Miller had an extensive rap sheet for theft, forgery, drugs and prostitution. After the election, it turned out that the felon in question was a different Rhonda Miller.[22]

If anything, the reports of Schwarzenegger's sexual misconduct may have helped rather than hindered the campaign. More than 1,000 *Times* readers cancelled their subscriptions, accusing the paper of last-minute partisan attacks—a charge that editor John S. Carroll vigorously disputes, calling the stories "solid as Gibraltar" and noting that publishing them earlier would have been impossible given the amount of research needed to confirm them. "It was a daunting feat to get all this accomplished during the 62 days of Schwarzenegger's campaign, a year less time than we'd have to cover a normal gubernatorial race," Carroll wrote. The *Times*, he said, understood that publishing it late in the campaign was likely to "touch off an outcry against the newspaper. We had no illusion that it would be warmly received." But the only other options were either to "never publish it," which "could be justified only if the story were untrue or insignificant," or to "hold it and publish after the election," which would "prompt anger among citizens who expect the newspaper to treat them like adults and give them all the information it has before they cast their votes."[23]

Like the campaign itself, Schwarzenegger's victory celebration resembled a Hollywood gala as much as anything political. The crowd surrounding him at the Century Plaza Hotel in Los Angeles could have been the receiving line at an NBC promotion. Prominent faces at the celebration included his wife, *Dateline NBC* correspondent Maria Shriver; actor Rob Lowe of NBC's *Lyon's Den*; and Pat O'Brien of NBC's *Access Hollywood*. The man who announced his victory and introduced him to the crowd of cheering supporters was Jay Leno. And the following night, Schwarzenegger made another appearance on *The Tonight Show*, this time as governor-elect. During his unbilled but clearly pre-planned appearance, Leno's band played "Happy Days Are Here Again" while the studio audience chanted, "Arnold! Arnold!"[24]

NBC representative Rebecca Marks attempted to play down the impression that the network had thrown its support behind the man now called California's "governator." Leno's election-night introduction, Marks said, "was something he agreed to do with Arnold as a friend. He was not in any way endorsing him politically. It was a personal appearance."[25]

Marty Kaplan, associate dean of the University of Southern California's Annenberg School for Communication, disagreed. "What Leno's presence did is give legitimacy to the notion that it wasn't a partisan event, it wasn't a political event, it was somehow an American cultural event," Kaplan said. "It was like welcoming home an astronaut from a safe voyage. In so doing, it played into a campaign strategy that this was a campaign for all, beyond politics. Which is not true; he's a Republican candidate. . . . It gives the impression of taking it out of the political realm into an extraterrestrial domain where politics don't matter, where we're all friends. It puts people who value dispute and debate [into the position] where we're all seen as earthly and petty, as if we should get with the program."[26]

Dancing Elephants

Conservatives frequently decry the "liberal bias" of the mass media. The grain of truth in their complaint is that people who work in the entertainment and news industries—television, movies, popular music, books, magazines and newspapers—tend to lean Democratic. People from these industries give about two-thirds of their campaign contributions to Democrats, and one-third to Republicans.[27] People who work in the media are different in this regard from many other leading corporate sectors such as oil, livestock, trucking, chemicals, tobacco, railroads and the automobile and restaurant industries, all of which give more than 70 percent of their contributions to Republicans.[28] There is no shortage of liberal performers in Hollywood—Ed Asner, Martin Sheen, Tim Robbins, Susan Sarandon, Rob Reiner and Barbra Streisand, to name just a few. While vocal in their views, however, Democratic-leaning actors have rarely sought political office and have almost never held it, preferring to advance their views through activism, lobbying and the arts. By contrast, acting has been a stepping-stone to political careers for numerous Republicans. In addition to Arnold Schwarzenegger, examples include:

- George Murphy, an actor, dancer and former president of the Screen Actors Guild who served as a U.S. senator from California from 1965 to 1971.

- Ronald Reagan, the former governor of California and two-term president of the United States.
- Clint Eastwood, who served two years as mayor of Carmel, California in the 1980s.
- Fred Grandy, who played the character of Gopher on the TV sitcom *The Love Boat* before serving as a congressman from the state of Iowa from 1986 to 1995.
- Sonny Bono, who followed his split from Cher by becoming the mayor of Palm Springs, California, followed by his election to the U.S. House of Representatives in 1994.
- Fred Thompson, who was elected to the U.S. Senate from Tennessee in 1994 following an acting career that included roles in films such as *In the Line of Fire* and *The Hunt for Red October* (and, more recently, the district attorney role on NBC's *Law and Order*).

Following Schwarzenegger's declaration of his candidacy, *Backstage*, a professional magazine for actors, published a story on actors who had run successfully for political office, but the only example it cited from the Democratic side was Sheila Kuhn, a California state senator who many years previously had been a child actor on *The Many Loves of Dobie Gillis* (from which she was fired when CBS discovered that she was a lesbian).[29] We were able to find only one other example—Ben Jones, who played the character of Cooter on the *Dukes of Hazzard* and then served two terms as a Democratic U.S. congressman from Georgia before losing in 1992.

There are several reasons for this disparity. One is that the Republican Party has actively recruited and supported candidates from the entertainment world. Another is that Republicans often run as "antigovernment" or "nonpolitician" candidates, so that an actor's lack of political experience can actually be an advantage for his campaign. And although Bill Clinton was clearly a master of showmanship, for the most part Republicans have shown greater mastery of the rules of postmodern politics, in which style is as important as substance and issues are less important than personality. Republican candidates understand these unwritten rules because they and their campaign consultants, some of whom actually started in the entertainment industry, played a big part in inventing them.

It is no accident that several of the names on the list above came from California. The first political-campaign firm in the United States, Campaigns Inc., was also established in California in the 1930s by the husband-and-wife team of Clem Whitaker and Leone Baxter. Whitaker and Baxter drew on the culture of nearby Hollywood as they developed techniques for "selling" candidates through the mass media. Incumbent California Governor Frank Merriam hired Whitaker and Baxter to defeat a 1934 election challenge by muckraking journalist and social reformer Upton Sinclair. Whitaker and Baxter developed a smear campaign to defeat Sinclair, arranging to have false stories printed in newspapers about Sinclair seducing young girls. To combat Sinclair's Depression-era populism, they worked with Hollywood studios, which controlled movie theaters throughout the state, to place phony newsreels in cinemas featuring fictional "Sinclair supporters" in rags advocating a Soviet-style takeover.

After their victory, Whitaker and Baxter explained the cynical philosophy behind their success: "The average American doesn't want to be educated, he doesn't want to improve his mind, he doesn't even want to work consciously at being a good citizen. But every American likes to be entertained. He likes the movies, he likes mysteries; he likes fireworks and parades. So, if you can't put on a fight, put on a show."[30] In Whitaker's words, they transformed elections from "a hit or miss business, directed by broken-down politicians" into "a mature, well-managed business founded on sound public relations principles, and using every technique of modern advertising."[31]

Whitaker and Baxter were in turn succeeded by another Californian, Murray Chotiner, who took Richard Nixon under his wing in 1945 and groomed him in the techniques of political campaigning. Nixon's career spanned the rise of television as a new medium that transformed both entertainment and politics. "It was Nixon's television performance in his Checkers speech that saved his place as Dwight Eisenhower's running mate in 1952," notes historian David Greenberg, the author of *Nixon's Shadow: The History of an Image*. "In a historic piece of image-craft, Nixon talked earnestly about his onerous childhood and his struggles upon returning from the Navy—and adorned his speech with folksy touches about his wife's cloth coat and his daughters' cocker spaniel. So effective was his self-portrait that telegrams flooded in to the studio praising his sincerity, forcing Eisenhower to retain him. Only a handful of liberal critics dissented, warning that Nixon was using insidious new techniques to misrepresent himself—and endanger democracy. But Nixon innovated further."[32] Following his defeat in the 1960s election against John F. Kennedy, Nixon set out to reinvent himself, hiring professional image manipulators including William Safire, then a New York public relations executive; advertising executives H. R. Haldeman and Harry Treleaven; and television producer Roger Ailes (whose more recent role as the head of Fox News is described in Chapter

Two, "The Echo Chamber"). Long before Bill Clinton played the saxophone on *The Arsenio Hall Show* or Arnold Schwarzenegger traded quips with Jay Leno, Nixon paved the way by appearing on the comedy show *Laugh-In* to say "Sock it to me" as part of his 1968 campaign strategy for overcoming his humorless image.[33]

Before Roger Ailes met Nixon, he was an executive producer of *The Mike Douglas Show,* a popular TV talk and variety program. They met in 1967, while Nixon was waiting to appear as a guest on the show. "It's a shame a man has to use gimmicks like this to get elected," Nixon said.

"Television is not a gimmick," Ailes replied, and Nixon hired him.[34]

The problem for the Nixon campaign, Ailes said, is that "a lot of people think Nixon is dull. Think he's a bore, a pain in the ass. They think he's the kind of kid who always carried a book bag. . . . Now you put him on television, you've got a problem right away. He's a funny-looking guy. He looks like somebody put him in a closet overnight and he jumps out in the morning with his suit all bunched up and starts running around saying, 'I want to be President.' I mean this is how he strikes some people."[35]

To change this image, the campaign paid to produce a series of television shows, in which Nixon fielded questions from panels of citizens. Although the shows were broadcast live, both the audiences and the panels were prescreened by the campaign, chosen carefully to have the right demographics—just enough blacks, for example, but not *too* many. Panel members were chosen so they would ask just enough tough questions to make the shows feel spontaneous, and since the audience was all Republican, applause was guaranteed. "The audience is part of the show," Ailes said during a discussion with Harry Treleaven about whether to allow reporters to watch the tapings. "And that's the whole point. Our television show. And the press has no business on the set. And goddammit, Harry, the problem is that this is an electronic election. The first there's ever been. TV has the power now. Some of the guys get arrogant and rub the reporters' faces in it and then the reporters get pissed and go out of their way to rap anything they consider staged for TV. And you know damn well that's what they'd do if they saw this from the studio. You let them in there with the regular audience and they see the warmup. They see Jack Rourke [the show's warm-up man] out there telling the audience to applaud and to mob Nixon at the end, and that's all they'd write about it."[36]

In 1968, Nixon's success in reinventing himself as the "New Nixon" helped him win the White House. When journalist Joe McGinniss detailed this strategy the next year in *The Selling of the President*, shamefaced reporters vowed to get wise to such manipulation, but the Nixon campaign was just the beginning.[37] Although his impeachment in the Watergate scandal meant a temporary setback, the Republicans roared back into the White House in 1980 with Ronald Reagan, the first actor ever to become president. Reagan also relied on the talents of Ailes, who served as a consultant to his 1984 re-election campaign. Ailes oversaw production of the now legendary "Morning in America" campaign television ads, designed by Madison Avenue executive Philip Dusenberry and featuring swelling violin music and emotional, issue-free imagery of weddings, flag-raising, home-buying and peaceful, scenic vistas.

Ailes used a similar strategy in 1988, when he worked with Lee Atwater to mastermind George H. W. Bush's come-from-behind victory over Michael Dukakis.[38] The Bush/Quayle '88 campaign combined morning-in-America imagery with ads that ridiculed Dukakis through deceptive visual imagery. One TV spot took Dukakis to task for pollution in Boston Harbor, displaying a sign that said, "Danger / Radiation Hazard / No Swimming." The sign actually had nothing to do with pollution or Dukakis. It was posted to warn Navy personnel not to swim in waters that had once harbored nuclear submarines under repair.[39] The most egregious ads, however, used visual imagery to exploit racial feelings. One featured a threatening photograph of William Horton—a black inmate who had escaped from a prison-furlough program and raped a woman—to suggest that Dukakis was unusually soft on crime. (Actually, Massachusetts was one of 45 states with prison-furlough programs at the time of Horton's crime.)[40] A second prison-furlough ad depicted a "revolving door" through which a line of white men entered prison, while blacks and Hispanics exited. "That phrase 'revolving-door prison policy' implies, of course, that Massachusetts criminals could, thanks to Governor Dukakis, slip out of jail as easily as commuters streaming from a subway station," observes Mark Crispin Miller. "But the image makes an even more inflammatory statement. . . . The 'revolving door' effects an eerie racial metamorphosis, implying that the Dukakis prison system was not only porous, but a satanic source of negritude—a dark 'liberal' mill that took white men and made them colored."[41]

True Lies

By its nature, television is expensive to produce and broadcast (although that may be changing, thanks to the Internet and other technological advances). It therefore lends itself to control by the people who can afford to pay for the considerable costs of production. It is also a highly emotional medium. Unlike print, which requires that the audience make a conscious effort, television is often absorbed unconsciously, as pure images and background in our information environment.

Reporter Leslie Stahl tells a story in her memoir, *Reporting Live*, of an experience she had in 1984 when she broadcast a piece for the CBS *Evening News* about the gap between rhetoric and reality under the Reagan administration. She juxtaposed images of staged photo opportunities in which Reagan picnicked with ordinary folks or surrounded himself with black children, farmers and happy flag-waving supporters. These images, she pointed out, often conflicted with the nature of Reagan's actual policies. "Mr. Reagan tries to counter the memory of an unpopular issue with a carefully chosen backdrop that actually contradicts the president's policy," she said in her *Evening News* piece. "Look at the handicapped Olympics, or the opening ceremony of an old-age home. No hint that he tried to cut the budgets for the disabled or for federally subsidized housing for the elderly."[42]

Stahl's piece was so hard-hitting in its criticism of Reagan, she recalled, that she "worried that my sources at the White House would be angry enough to freeze me out."[43] Much to her shock, however, she received a phone call immediately after the broadcast from White House aide Richard Darman. He was calling from the office of Treasury Secretary Jim Baker, who had just watched the piece along with White House press secretary Mike Deaver and Baker's assistant, Margaret Tutwiler. Rather than complaining, they were calling to *thank* her. "Way to go, kiddo," Darman said. "What a great story! We loved it."

"Excuse me?" Stahl replied, thinking he must be joking.

"No, no, we really loved it," Darman insisted. "Five minutes of free media. We owe you big-time."

"Why are you so happy?" Stahl said. "Didn't you hear what I said?"

"Nobody heard what you said," Darman replied.

"Come again?"

"You guys in Televisionland haven't figured it out, have you? When the pictures are powerful and emotional, they override if not completely drown out the sound. Leslie, I mean it, nobody heard you."

Stahl was so taken aback that she played a videotape of her segment before a live audience of a hundred people and asked them what they had just seen. Sure enough, Darman was right. "Most of the audience thought it was either an ad for the Reagan campaign or a very positive news story," Stahl recalls. "Only a handful heard what I said. The pictures were so evocative—we're talking about pictures with Reagan in the shining center—that all the viewers were absorbed. Unlike reading or listening to the radio, with the television we 'learn' with two of our senses together, and apparently the eye is dominant. When we watch television, we get an emotional reaction. The information doesn't always go directly to the thinking part of our brains but to the gut. It's all about impressions, and the White House understood that."[44]

The George W. Bush administration also understands this lesson. At the Republican National Convention that nominated Bush in 2000, only 4 percent of the actual delegates were black, compared to 20 percent at the Democratic Convention, but the talent onstage looked quite different: not just Colin Powell, but comedian Chris Rock, the Temptations, a gospel choir, rhythm-and-blues and salsa singers, and Representative J. C. Watts (the only black Republican in Congress). "It's all visuals," Karl Rove told campaign finance chief Don Evans. "You campaign as if America was watching TV with the sound turned down."[45]

In our previous book, *Weapons of Mass Deception*, we described the extraordinary level of detail that went into preparing Bush's May 1, 2003, landing in a fighter jet aboard an aircraft carrier to celebrate what he called the end of "major combat operations in Iraq."[46] Orchestrating the event cost about $1 million in taxpayer dollars.[47] In reality, the aircraft carrier was so close to shore that it had to be repositioned in the water to keep TV cameras from picking up the San Diego shoreline.[48] In order to get the light just right and keep the ship from arriving at port before the prime-time broadcast, a Pentagon official admitted, the USS *Abraham Lincoln* made "lazy circles" 30 miles at sea and took 20 hours to cross a distance that could have been covered in an hour or so.[49] (Without the stagecraft, in other words, Bush could have *walked* aboard, rather than flown.) During his speech, commanders gauged the wind and glided along at precisely the right speed so sea breezes would not blow across the ship and create unwanted noise. When the wind shifted during the speech, the ship changed course.[50]

Similar attention went into the staging of Bush's surprise visit to Baghdad on Thanksgiving 2003 to share turkey with the troops. Although Bush was shown on camera cradling a huge platter laden with a golden-brown turkey, the object in his hands was actually a decoration. "A contractor had roasted and primped the turkey to adorn the buffet line, while the 600 soldiers were served from cafeteria-style steam trays," reported the *Washington Post*.[51] The soldiers who cheered Bush were prescreened for his arrival, while others showing up for turkey were turned away.[52] In a letter to *Stars and Stripes*, the Pentagon-authorized newspaper for the U.S. military, Sgt. Loren Russell complained that the soldiers under his command in Iraq had actually been denied their expected evening meal, because the facility where they usually ate had been reserved for Bush's appearance. "I'm lucky enough to be with soldiers who often complain among themselves, but all they expect are good leadership and three square meals a day," Russell wrote. He added, "Imagine their dismay when they walked 15 minutes to the Bob Hope Dining Facility, only to find that they were turned away from their evening meal because they were in the wrong unit. . . . And all of this happened on Thanksgiving, the best meal of the year when soldiers get a taste of home cooking."[53]

The point to these exercises in politics as theater is that they enable symbolism and style to substitute for substance. The speech aboard the aircraft carrier sent a message that "the war is over," even if Bush didn't use those precise words. The turkey hoisted in his arms on Thanksgiving sent a message that he cared enough about the troops to serve them their food in person. Imagery substitutes so thoroughly for substance that the Bush administration's photo opportunities have often directly contradicted his actual policies:

- In March 2001, Bush visited Egleston Children's Hospital in Atlanta, Georgia. "This is a hospital, but it's also—it's a place full of love," he said, adding, "There's a lot of talk about budgets right now, and I'm here to talk about the budget. My job as the president is to submit a budget to the Congress and to set priorities, and one of the priorities that we've talked about is making sure the health-care systems are funded."[54] Yet Bush's first budget proposal actually proposed *cutting* grants to children's hospitals (including the "place full of love" in Egleston) by $35 million, or 15 percent.[55]

● A year later, Bush gave speeches before groups of "first responders" (police, rescue workers and firefighters). "We're dealing with first-time responders to make sure they've got what's needed to be able to respond," he said, standing before a large backdrop that featured a huge, blown-up photo of a 9/11 rescue worker.[56] Yet Bush actually opposed requests from fire chiefs for funding to help communities hire additional firefighters. According to the International Association of Fire Chiefs (IAFC) and the International Association of Fire Fighters (IAFF), fire departments throughout the country were vastly understaffed and unprepared to cope with a terrorist attack. To fill this gap, they called for a federal grant program that would help hire 75,000 new firefighters, at a cost of $7.6 billion. Bush responded with a proposal for less than half that amount, most of which was allocated for equipment and training rather than personnel.[57] The gap between pretty poses and actual money prompted the IAFF to vote unanimously in August 2002 to boycott Bush's planned national tribute to firefighters who died on September 11. "Don't lionize our fallen brothers in one breath, and then stab us in the back by eliminating funding for our members to fight terrorism and stay safe," said IAFF president Harold Schaitberger. "President Bush, you are either with us or against us. You can't have it both ways."[58]

● In June 2002, Bush toured a housing project supported by a HOPE VI grant from the U.S. Department of Housing and Urban Development (HUD). He was photographed standing alongside happy home dwellers who had obtained assistance from the program, which was set up in 1992 to pay for rehabilitation, new construction and other housing improvements in America's most distressed public housing. "Part of being a secure America is to encourage home ownership," Bush said as he toured the project, adding, "All you've got to do is shake their hand and listen to their stories and watch the pride that they exhibit when they show you the kitchen and the stairs."[59] In his 2004 proposed budget, Bush eliminated funding for HOPE VI.[60]

- In January 2003, Bush gave a speech at a St. Louis warehouse announcing his new tax plan. He stood in front of what appeared to be a backdrop of cardboard boxes stamped "Made in U.S.A." The backdrop, however, was actually a façade painted on canvas. The warehouse where he gave his speech did contain cardboard boxes, but the real boxes were all stamped "Made in China." To minimize the possibility that anyone would notice the difference between reality and the painted façade, a Bush aide had carefully taped white labels over all of the actual boxes, obscuring the words "Made in China."[61]

The Last Action Hero

Of course, Republicans are not the only political players who have adapted to the political environment created by television. Many of the antics of the hippies and yippies in the 1960s—"levitating the Pentagon," running a pig for president—were deliberate theater. Abbie Hoffman declared that the yippies were created "to manipulate the media." In fact, they tried to *be* the media. "We are living TV ads, movies," he wrote. Following the Chicago demonstrations in 1968, Hoffman declared, "We were an advertisement for revolution."[62] Citizen groups ranging from Greenpeace to Mothers Against Drunk Driving to Pro-Life America have all learned the impact of sound bites and celebrity endorsements. Among Democratic Party politicians, the most skilled practitioner of this art has undoubtedly been Bill Clinton. But yippies and other activists have never really *succeeded* at "being the media." At most, they have managed to occasionally use the media opportunistically. To "be" the media requires ownership or some other way of exerting actual power, and even Democrats, who are certainly more powerful than yippies, have found that they are often helpless to control the way their image is represented. Consider, for example, the treatment of Massachusetts Senator John Kerry, one of the party's candidates in the campaign for the 2004 presidential nomination.

Three months after Arnold Schwarzenegger announced his candidacy on *The Tonight Show*, Kerry made his own appearance with Jay Leno, hoping to jump-start his campaign. The plan, agreed upon in advance with Leno's people, was for Kerry, a motorcycle fan, to roar onstage on a Harley, dressed in denim and jeans, for some good-natured banter. Leno, also a motorcycle fan, had expressed his admiration for Kerry and had scheduled the appearance for Veterans Day, which Kerry's people hoped would highlight their candidate's background as a Vietnam veteran.[63]

For Kerry, though, things did not go exactly as hoped. To begin with, Leno gave him second billing. As he straddled his hog and waited to ride onstage, Kerry had to wait while his appearance was upstaged and ridiculed by "Triumph the Insult Comic Dog."

"Triumph" is a plastic, talking hand puppet that looks like a Rottweiler and appeared for years on another NBC talk show, *Late Night with Conan O'Brien*. The running joke with Triumph is his potty mouth and his insulting manner. He insults people and makes jokes about "pooping" on them. And Leno didn't just give Triumph top billing. He gave the comic insult dog twice as much airtime as the senator, much of which was spent mocking the Kerry campaign.

"What's going on with this show?" Triumph said. "Yes, the Terminator can take over the show, but John Kerry, a war veteran, has to follow a friggin' dog puppet. What's going on in America? What is wrong with America? I hope you clean the chair for him, at least."

"Yes, we will," said Leno.

"What do you think, he's got no shot?" asked the hand puppet.

"Is that the problem?" said Leno.

"Come on folks," Triumph said. "Who's giving who the poop? Jay, the poop I made in your dressing room has more heat than John Kerry."

The rule for a politician, of course, is that he is never supposed to show weakness, anger or frustration, even when a talking dog puppet has just compared him to a pile of steaming feces. When Kerry's turn came, he dutifully rode his Harley onstage and chatted amiably with Leno, throwing in a joke to the effect that Triumph might make a good vice-presidential running mate. This rather lame attempt at humor did little to soften the blow. Although Kerry's own campaign weblog gushed about how "cool" their candidate looked in his motorcycle duds, it was the run-in with Triumph that dominated the newspapers the following day. On the radio, Matt Drudge—filling in for Rush Limbaugh, who was in drug rehab—recounted the Triumph-Kerry encounter and crowed that Kerry's campaign was dead in the water. In Kerry's home state of Massachusetts, the *Boston Globe* interviewed the director of a Washington, D.C., political think tank, who predicted that Kerry's Leno appearance could become the campaign's defining moment. "Michael Dukakis had the tank picture, and Kerry's going to have Triumph," said Matthew T. Felling, media director for the Center for Media and Public Affairs.[64]

The New Republic's Michael Crowley was one of the few pundits who considered the appearance a success for the Kerry campaign, giving the candidate a "B" grade for his "general likeability." "To my surprise," he wrote, "Kerry actually came off well. . . . Kerry handled this small humiliation with a self-deprecating humor and no trace of self-importance. Kerry, I was reminded, is at his best when his craggy face flashes a big, genuine smile."[65]

As silly as this episode may have seemed at the time, there is something serious at stake in it. John Kerry's encounter with a rubber dog puppet is significant precisely *because* it was so ridiculous, and because this sort of ridiculousness has come to influence something as important to the future of America as our presidential elections. Even Crowley, Kerry's defender, accepted the absurd rules of discourse. What mattered wasn't whether Kerry's economic policies made sense, or his foreign policy, or his views on abortion or AIDS or the environment. What mattered was that his "craggy face" was capable of a "big, genuine smile."

Observers agreed that the 2004 election was likely to be a defining moment for the future of the United States. After four years of nearly uncontested power, the Republican Party under the leadership of President George W. Bush hoped to consolidate its newly won control over every branch of the U.S. government—

the presidency, both houses of Congress, and the judiciary. If it succeeded, its supporters pledged to continue an aggressive foreign policy that had already generated unprecedented hostility toward the United States throughout much of the rest of the world. At home, the Republicans expected to continue their planned rollbacks of environmental protection and labor rights, even as their tax breaks to the wealthy created unprecedented budget deficits that economists feared would further undermine the country's unsteady economy.

On most of these matters, significant policy differences separated the Bush administration from its Democratic challengers. Moreover, opinion polls showed that the public's policy preferences aligned more closely on most issues with the Democrats than with Republicans. Paradoxically, however, the Democratic presidential candidates seemed to have a hard time bringing their issues to the forefront of discussion, let alone achieving presidential stature in the eyes of the public. Of course, it is difficult to achieve presidential stature from the back of a motorcycle, especially if your running mate is Triumph the Insult Comic Dog.

CHAPTER FIVE

Block the Vote

All the Republican razzle-dazzle in the world has been unable to win the support of African-American voters for the party that, until the mid-20th century, was still associated with Abraham Lincoln. In recent elections, 85 to 90 percent of blacks have consistently voted for Democratic candidates. In 1998, conservative movement strategist David Horowitz commented on the habits of black voters with a column in Salon.com titled "Baa Baa Black Sheep," in which he complained that blacks "vote like the populations of Communist countries, who lack the ability to exercise free choice."[1] Of course, a key difference that Horowitz ignored is that in Communist countries, voters went unanimously for a single party because there were no other options. In the United States, black voters can vote for Republicans if they want to, but most of them *prefer* Democrats.

In the face of overwhelming rejection from African-American and other minority voters, Republicans have adopted a two-tiered strategy: token efforts at symbolic inclusion (aimed primarily at soothing the conscience of white voters, many of whom want to see themselves as supporters of a racially inclusive party), combined with a variety of strategies for minimizing the number and influence of black votes. For years, Democrats supported and Republicans opposed the National Voter Registration Act (known as the Motor-Voter Law), which made voter registration available at driver-license bureaus, libraries, welfare agencies, military recruitment centers and other public facilities. Motor-Voter, which was expected to increase the registration of low-income and minority voters, was approved by Congress and the Senate in 1992 but vetoed by George H. W. Bush. Following Bill Clinton's election to the White House, the Senate overcame two GOP filibusters—one blocking initial discussion of the bill and one blocking the floor vote on it—before Clinton finally signed the Act into law in 1993. When the law took effect in 1995, six Republican members of Congress introduced measures to repeal or weaken it. Seven GOP-led states challenged Motor-Voter in the courts, and a challenge by Republican Governor Pete Wilson of California went as far as the U.S. Supreme Court.[2] "I can't think of anyone in America who wants this bill," claimed Republican senator Bob Dole,[3] but an estimated 11 million people registered to vote in the 15 months after it went into effect—a much greater response than Motor-Voter proponents had hoped for.

Following the 1992 elections, Republican political consultant Ed Rollins openly boasted of his success at "voter suppression" during a journalists' breakfast. Rollins said he had bribed Democratic campaign workers during the New Jersey governor's race between Democrat Jim Florio and Rollins's client, Christine Todd Whitman. According to Rollins, workers who had been hired to help get out the Democratic vote were told, "How much have they paid you to do your normal duty? . . . We'll match it. Go home, sit, and watch television." In addition, Rollins said, "We went into black churches and we basically said to ministers who had endorsed Florio, 'Do you have a special project?' And they said, 'We've already endorsed Florio.' And we said, 'That's fine, don't get up on the Sunday pulpit and preach. . . . Don't get up there and say it's your moral obligation that you go out on Tuesday and vote for Jim Florio.'" Ministers who cooperated, Rollins said, received contributions to their "favorite charities." As a result, Rollins said, "I think, to a certain extent, we suppressed their vote."[4]

Rollins's comments, which amounted to an admission of illegal behavior, prompted a brief scandal and a Democratic lawsuit, forcing Rollins to backpedal swiftly. Under grilling by Democratic attorneys, Rollins claimed that his boast to journalists had been an empty lie, part of a "psychological warfare" game he was playing with James Carville, the campaign manager for Whitman's opponent.[5] A few days previously, though, Carl Golden, Whitman's campaign spokesman, had already made much the same admission as Rollins, telling a reporter, "Sometimes vote suppression is as important in this business as vote getting." Dan Todd, the candidate's brother who had served as her manager before Rollins took over the campaign, also made similar remarks during a post-election symposium at Princeton University's Woodrow Wilson School for Public and International Affairs. Todd told the symposium that the Whitman campaign had worked at "getting out the vote on one side and vote sup— . . . and keeping the vote light in others." Although Todd caught himself before uttering the taboo word "suppression," his meaning was clear.[6]

Voter suppression was also an issue in New Hampshire's November 2002 election. The state Republican Party paid $15,600 to GOP Marketplace, an out-of-state firm, supposedly for the purpose of making get-out-the-vote calls. Instead, the firm's subcontractor made repeated five-second hang-up calls on Election Day, jamming the phone lines of a get-out-the-vote operation staffed by volunteers from the city's firefighters union and the state Democratic Party. Democratic officials said the two-hour phone jam "lasted long enough to undermine their efforts to reach people who needed rides to the polls."[7]

Republicans have also attempted to suppress black votes by running negative campaign ads that accuse Democrats of racism. If they can't persuade blacks to vote Republican, the goal is to make them cynical enough that they won't bother to vote at all. In Missouri and Kansas, the Republican political action committee GOPAC paid for an infamous radio ad that accused white Democrats of using Social Security to take money away from black Americans. "You've heard about reparations. You know, where whites compensate blacks for enslaving us?" the ad began. "Well, guess what we've got now? Reverse reparations. Under Social Security today, blacks receive twenty-one thousand dollars less in retirement benefits than whites of similar income and marital status. . . . One-third of the brothers die before retirement and receive nothing. . . . So the next time some Democrat says he won't touch Social Security, ask why he thinks blacks owe reparations to whites."[8]

A similar effort to suppress the black vote has been linked to black preacher Al Sharpton's campaign in the 2004 Democratic presidential primary. Sharpton postured as a radical firebrand, accusing other Democratic candidates such as Howard Dean of racial bias. The *Village Voice* reported in February 2004 that "Roger Stone, the longtime Republican dirty-tricks operative who led the mob that shut down the Miami–Dade County recount and helped make George W. Bush president in 2000, is financing, staffing, and orchestrating the presidential campaign of Reverend Al Sharpton. . . . Sharpton has a little-noticed history of Republican machinations inconsistent with his fiery rhetoric. . . . [A]ny Sharpton-connected outrage against the party could either lower black turnout in several key close states, or move votes to Bush."[9] Stone conceded to the *New York Times* that he had been behind several of Sharpton's most visible campaign tactics, including scrutiny of Dean's record of minority appointees when he was governor of Vermont.[10]

Some efforts to minimize black voting have involved deception and intimidation. During the closely fought campaign of North Carolina Senator Jesse Helms in 1990, the Helms campaign sent out a pre-election mailing of postcards to 120,000 black voters, falsely threatening that they could be sent to jail if they had moved within the past month and attempted to vote.[11] Black voters who visited the polls anyway encountered openly hostile Republican "ballot security teams" that showed up at more than a dozen heavily black precincts in the guise of poll-watchers. During the 2002 election, a flyer was circulated anonymously in predominantly black neighborhoods in Baltimore, Maryland, giving the wrong election date and falsely insinuating that voters would be turned away at the polls if they had any outstanding parking tickets, were late in paying their rent, or had any outstanding warrants.[12] In Pine Bluff, Arkansas, reports Laughlin McDonald, director of the Voting Rights Project of the American Civil Liberties Union, "Democrats accused Republican poll watchers of driving away voters in predominantly black precincts by taking photos of them and demanding identification during pre-election day balloting."[13] During the hotly contested 2003 governor's race in Kentucky, NAACP president Kweisi Mfume expressed alarm at GOP plans to place "challengers"—party loyalists responsible for questioning the credentials of individual voters—at predominantly African-American precincts. "The use of challengers at majority African-American precincts amounts to nothing but blatant voter intimidation by the Republican Party," Mfume said.[14]

The Florida Disaster

Perhaps the most striking recent example of voter suppression came in the 2000 presidential election, where a slim margin of 537 votes in Florida gave George W. Bush the votes in the electoral college that he needed to claim victory over Al Gore. (Nationwide, Gore won the popular vote by 543,614 votes.)

What most people remember from Florida, of course, is the "butterfly ballots" in Palm Beach County, the lengthy voter recount, hanging chads and legal filings on behalf of candidates Al Gore and George Bush. There were other disturbing events connected with the 2000 presidential election, such as a report that General Electric chairman Jack Welch visited the studio of NBC News (which is owned by GE) on election night, where he cheered when Bush was ahead and at one point reportedly asked a staffer, "What would I have to give you to call the race for Bush?"[15] At Fox News, the election-night "decision desk" was headed by John Ellis, a first cousin of Bush who was instrumental in the network's decision to call the race for Bush before any of the other networks.[16] It was also disturbing to see the supposedly spontaneous "Brooks Brothers riot" (so nicknamed because of participants' upscale clothing) staged by GOP staffers and activists that helped stop the Miami recount,[17] after which the "rioters" and other GOP anti-recount organizers received plum positions within the Bush administration.[18]

Another disturbing aspect of the Florida election was the double standard used by Republicans regarding the counting of absentee ballots, including votes by overseas military. After the Supreme Court's decision, the *New York Times* conducted an exhaustive investigation into the handling of absentee ballots, some of which were received after election day but included in the Florida total nevertheless. "With the presidency hanging on the outcome in Florida, the Bush team quickly grasped that the best hope of ensuring victory was the trove of ballots still arriving in the mail from Florida residents living abroad," reported David Barstow and Don Van Natta, Jr. "Over the next 18 days, the Republicans mounted a legal and public relations campaign to persuade canvassing boards in Bush strongholds to waive the state's election laws when counting overseas absentee ballots. Their goal was simple: to count the maximum number of overseas ballots in counties won by Mr. Bush, particularly those with a high concentration of military voters, while seeking to disqualify overseas ballots in counties won by Vice President Al Gore." In counties

where Bush had strong majorities, the GOP team successfully persuaded canvassing boards to accept flawed votes that "included ballots without postmarks, ballots postmarked after the election, ballots
without witness signatures, ballots mailed from towns and cities
within the United States and even ballots from voters who voted
twice. All would have been disqualified had the state's election
laws been strictly enforced." In Gore strongholds, by contrast, "Bush
lawyers questioned scores of ballots, almost always from civilian
Democrats but occasionally from members of the military. They
objected to the slightest of flaws, including partial addresses of witnesses, illegible witness signatures and slight variations in voter signatures." Correcting this disparity alone might have been enough
to tip the balance in Gore's favor, they noted, since "without the
overseas absentee ballots counted after election day, Mr. Gore
would have won Florida by 202 votes, and thus the White House.
But no one knew that until the 36 days were over; by then, it was a
historical footnote."[19]

Other scenarios are possible, of course. Following the election,
a consortium of eight leading U.S. news organizations commis-
sioned the National Opinion Research Center (NORC) at the
University of Chicago to compile a comprehensive study of the
2000 election in Florida, in which trained investigators closely ex-
amined every rejected ballot in the state. They created a database
detailing the condition of each ballot—whether it had a hanging
chad, dimpled ballot, double vote or any of the other characteris-
tics that were bones of contention when the Bush and Gore teams
quarreled over the recount rules. This in turn made it possible to
predict how the election would have turned out under a variety of
different scenarios based on different recount rules. Under six of

the nine scenarios that they considered, Gore would have emerged as the winner—although, ironically, the recount procedure that Gore's team advocated was one of the scenarios that would have still left Bush ahead.[20] These results left sufficient room for interpretation for CNN to declare, "Bush Still Wins,"[21] while other news organizations reported vindication for Gore. But none of these recount scenarios considered the separate role that race played in shaping the election outcome.

In the end, racial disparities in treatment of voters may have been the worst scandal of the Florida 2000 election. Five months before the election, Florida Secretary of State Katherine Harris, acting under the direction of Governor Jeb Bush, sent local election boards a list of 42,389 "probable" and "possible" felons, with instructions that the list should be used to exclude ineligible voters. The scrub list was compiled by a private company hired by the state called Database Technologies, a division of a national database company called ChoicePoint. To compile the list, ChoicePointDBT had compared the state's list of registered voters against lists of known felons and also removed duplicate listings and deceased residents.[22] As journalist Greg Palast and others have noted, the purged names were disproportionately black—54 percent of the names on the ChoicePointDBT list, although only 14.6 percent of the state's residents were black in 2000.[23] ChoicePoint's system for purging names accomplished this in part by purging black people from the voter rolls if their names were the same as or similar to convicted felons, while keeping white people with names similar to convicted felons.[24]

"They were supposed to use their extensive databases to check credit cards, bank information, addresses and phone numbers, in addition to names, ages, and social security numbers. But they didn't," says Palast, who has written extensively about the Florida balloting in his book *The Best Democracy Money Can Buy*. "They didn't use one of their 1,200 databases to verify personal information, nor did they make a single phone call to verify the identity of scrubbed names." Instead, ChoicePoint compiled its list of felons by downloading names from other states' Internet sites. "They scrubbed Florida voters whose names were similar to out-of-state felons," Palast explains. "An Illinois felon named John Michaels could knock off Florida voter John, Johnny, Jonathan or Jon R. Michaels, or even J.R. Michaelson. DBT matched for race and gender, but names only had to be similar to a certain degree. Names could be reversed, and suffixes (Jr., Sr.) were ignored, but aliases were included. So the felon John 'Buddy' Michaels could knock non-felon Michael Johns or Bud Johnson, Jr., off the voter rolls. This happened again and again. Although DBT didn't get names, birthdays or social security numbers right, they were very careful to match for race. A black felon named Mr. Green would only knock off a black Mr. Green, but not a single white Mr. Green."[25]

In addition to kicking out innocent people as felons, Florida committed a number of other irregularities that disadvantaged blacks and elderly voters (who also tend to vote Democrat). "In a presidential race decided by 537 votes, Florida simply *did not count* 179,855 ballots," Palast states.[26] Many votes went uncounted due to inferior voting-machine models and suboptimal machine settings. In counties across the state, Palast reports, racial demographics correlated closely with the proportion of uncounted ballots. Gadsden County, for example, had 52 percent African-American residents and a 12 percent ballot rejection rate, while Citrus

County, with only 2 percent black residents, had only 1 percent of their ballots rejected.[27] When *USA Today* compiled a statewide database correlating race and other factors to rejected ballots, it found that blacks were four times as likely as whites to have their votes go uncounted.[28]

Palast believes that racial factors alone were sufficient to throw the election to Bush, which is certainly plausible given the closeness of the result. Here too, of course, not everyone agrees. The *Palm Beach Post* conducted its own investigation and found "at least 1,100 eligible voters wrongly purged" due to the Choice-PointDBT list—a smaller number than Palast alleges. According to the *Post*, "these voters—some wrongly identified as felons, and many more wrongly turned away based on felony convictions in other states—could have swayed the election had they been allowed to vote."[29] It also noted, however, that ChoicePointDBT's list was so unreliable that elections supervisors in 20 counties ignored it altogether, thereby allowing thousands of *ineligible* felons to vote—a report that has been cited by Republicans as evidence that it was Gore, not Bush, who benefited from the scrub list. However, Florida is one of only 12 states—most of them in the South—that bar felons from voting after their prison term has ended, and there is no question that the law disproportionately bars blacks, who account for 49 percent of felons in the state.[30]

After a lengthy investigation, the U.S. Commission on Civil Rights (USCCR) produced a report in June 2001 titled "Voting Irregularities in Florida During the 2000 Presidential Election." The report concluded, "Despite the closeness of the election, it was widespread voter disenfranchisement, not the dead-heat contest, that was the extraordinary feature in the Florida election. The disenfranchisement was not isolated or episodic." The USCCR found that African-American voters were at least ten times more likely to have their ballots rejected than other voters and that 83 of the 100 precincts with the most disqualified ballots had black majorities.[31] The Florida governor's office responded by dismissing the USCCR report as "biased and sloppy" and "riddled with baseless allegations, faulty reasoning and unsupported conclusions."[32]

The National Association for the Advancement of Colored People (NAACP) disagreed. From the time the polls opened until they closed on election day, the NAACP's national office in Baltimore had received scores of telephone calls from Floridians throughout the state complaining of voter irregularities and intimidation. Following the election, the NAACP convened its own hearings and compiled 300 pages of testimony, based on which it filed a class-action lawsuit against the state of Florida. In September 2002, just days before the lawsuit was scheduled to go before a judge, the state finally agreed to a settlement that included reinstating the voters who had been wrongly disenfranchised as felons. Conveniently for Jeb Bush, who was in the middle of a race for reelection as governor, the settlement came too late to get them reinstated in time for that year's fall elections.[33]

And Florida was not the only state whose elections had racially tinged inequities. Following the 2000 elections, the American Civil Liberties Union filed voting-rights lawsuits in Georgia, California, Illinois and Missouri, in addition to Florida. These suits, filed on behalf of African-Americans who said their votes went uncounted due to systematic irregularities in the voting process, called for improvements in voting systems and technology. A series of newspaper advertisements run around the same time as part of the ACLU's Voting Rights Campaign began: "There was a day in American history when black people counted less than white people. November 7, 2000."[34]

50 Ways to Draw Your District

Another way to minimize the influence of minority voters is through gerrymandering, nowadays termed "redistricting" in polite circles. It was a Republican, in fact, who invented gerrymandering. The term originated in 1811, when Massachusetts governor Elbridge Gerry endorsed a redistricting plan aimed at giving his party an advantage over its Federalist opponents. One district was drawn so oddly that it looked like a salamander, prompting one of the Federalists to quip, "Why not call it a Gerry-mander?"

The basic principle of redistricting is simple. By packing as many members of the opposing party into as few districts as possible, the party that controls redistricting can ensure that it will dominate elections in most of the other districts. Pennsylvania, for example, is a state where 48 percent of voters are registered Democrats and only 42 percent are Republicans, but the GOP nevertheless managed to win control of the state House of Representatives, Senate and governor's mansion in 2002 and promptly redrew the state's voting districts into torturously drawn shapes— one of which was said to resemble a "supine seahorse," another an "upside-down Chinese dragon."[35] Before redistricting, Pennsylvania had 21 seats in the U.S. House of Representatives, 11 in the hands of Republicans and 10 in the hands of Democrats. Afterward, the state had 19 seats, 12 apportioned to Republicans and 7 to Democrats.[36] In Michigan, Republican redistricting gave Republicans a 9-to-6 edge in the 2002 congressional elections, even though 49 percent of voters in the state pulled the lever for Democrats compared to 48 percent for Republicans. In Florida, they expanded their majority from 15-to-8 to 18-to-7—"entirely due to redistricting," according to Rob Richie of the Center for Voting and Democracy, a nonprofit organization founded in 1992 by leading scholars, civic leaders and former elected officials such as John Anderson (the former Illinois congressman who ran for president as an independent in 1980).[37]

For a simplified model of how this works, imagine that you have 200 voters, half of whom are Republicans and half Democrats, divided equally into ten voting districts, as follows:

District	# of Democrats	# of Republicans
1	10	10
2	10	10
3	10	10
4	10	10
5	10	10
6	10	10
7	10	10
8	10	10
9	10	10
10	10	10
TOTAL	**100**	**100**

Under these circumstances, each race would be very close. It would be impossible to predict in advance which party would win a majority of the ten electoral seats, and probably each party would win close to the same number. By redrawing the districts as follows, however, you could give Republicans an obvious advantage:

District	# of Democrats	# of Republicans
1	19	1
2	9	11
3	9	11
4	9	11
5	9	11
6	9	11
7	9	11
8	9	11
9	9	11
10	9	11
TOTAL	**100**	**100**

This new scheme would give Democrats an overwhelming majority and a clear lock on victory in the first district, but the Republicans would have a 55 percent majority in the remaining nine and would expect to win all of those. Although this is a simplified model, we didn't just pull the figure 55 percent out of the air. Political scientists define elections where the victor wins with less than that percent of the vote as "competitive."[38] Districts where the incumbent's majority is 55 percent or more are generally considered "safe," meaning that the winning party there can usually count on retaking that seat in the next election, even if the incumbent does not run for re-election.

Historically, both parties have used gerrymandering to maximize their advantage wherever they have enough power to pull it off. Following completion of the U.S. Census once every ten years, whichever party is in control of a state takes full advantage of the opportunity to redraw the congressional district map to benefit that party's candidates. Texas Democratic Congresswoman Bernice Johnson, who presided over redistricting there in 1991, said the process "is not one of kindness. It is not one of sharing. It is a power grab."[39] Supreme Court Justice and former Arizona state Senator Sandra Day O'Connor once said that any official who failed to protect their party's interest in redistricting "ought to be impeached."[40]

The close alignment of African-American and other minority voters with the Democratic Party, combined with the historic dominance of whites within the party in southern states, has added a racial element to the politics of gerrymandering. In the late 1980s, Republican Party chairman Lee Atwater was able to use this to Republican advantage. "When the civil-rights movement started, you had a lot of white Democrats in power in the South," explained Bobby Scott, an African-American Democratic congressman from Virginia who was first elected in 1992. "And, when these white Democrats started redistricting, they wanted to keep African-American percentages at around thirty-five or forty percent. That was enough for the white Democrats to keep winning in these districts, but not enough to elect any black Democrats. The white Democrats called these 'influence' districts, where we could have a say in who won."[41]

"I began working at the RNC in 1989, and Lee Atwater's first words to me were, 'Do something about redistricting,'" said Benjamin Ginsberg, a Washington attorney who was the party's chief counsel at the time. "We began looking at the data, and we saw that white southern Democrats had dominated the redistricting process literally since the Civil War, and that had created under-representation for two groups—Republicans and minority voters. It was evident, especially to blacks and Republicans, that there was an alliance to build in the state legislatures that were going to be handling redistricting."[42]

The Republicans, Scott says, "came to us and said, We want these districts to be sixty percent black. And blacks liked that idea, because it meant we elected some of our own for the first time. That's where the 'unholy alliance' came in."[43]

The resulting concentration of overwhelmingly Democratic-leaning African-Americans in fewer congressional districts has helped more Republicans get elected to office. Some analysts even believe that racial redistricting contributed significantly to the congressional "Republican revolution" of 1994.[44] In the South, it has also had the effect of further polarizing the two major parties along racial lines, making Republicans the "white party" and Democrats the "black party." Almost all of the new majority-black districts drawn following the 1990 census were in the South.[45] And there has been evidence of white voter backlash; in Mississippi, exit polls indicated that white GOP candidate Haley Barbour won 77 percent of the white vote in his successful November 2003 run for governor.[46]

The availability of sophisticated computer programs has also raised the stakes for election redistricting. "There used to be a theory that gerrymandering was self-regulating," says Nathaniel Persily, a redistricting expert and professor of law and political science at the University of Pennsylvania. "The idea was that the more greedy you are in maximizing the number of districts your party can control, the more likely it is that a small shift of votes will lead you to lose a lot of districts. But it's not self-regulating anymore. The software is too good, and the partisanship is too strong."[47] In the past, the redistricting process increased election day competition, at least for the first few years after the districts were redrawn. In 1992, the first elections to follow the 1990 census saw 84 competitive congressional races in which the incumbent won by less than 10 percent of the vote. By 2000, after incumbents had several years to settle into their new districts, there were only 42 competitive races. Rather than making races *more* competitive, redistricting following the 2000 census actually left only 38 competitive House races in 2002. With the outcome virtually inevitable in all of the other races, it is hardly surprising that voter interest also waned, as turnout dwindled from 52 percent in 1992 to just over 38 percent in 2002.[48]

Republicans liked redistricting so much that in 2003 they took the unprecedented step of *re*-redistricting—redrawing election boundaries more than once in the same decade. Traditionally, redistricting occurs following each decade's U.S. Census, but then the boundaries stay in place until the next census ten years later. According to Tim Storey, a redistricting analyst for the National Conference of State Legislatures, there hasn't been "any case in the last 100 years of mid-decade redistricting without a court order." (Courts can order mid-decade redistricting if they find that the original redistricting violated fair election laws.) In 2003, however, Republicans set out to redraw districts in both Colorado and Texas, even though districts had already been redrawn by their state courts just two years earlier.

After gaining control of Colorado's state government in the 2002 elections, Republican legislators redrew the district map again and pushed it through in the final days of the 2003 legislative session, in what became known as the "midnight gerrymander." Colorado's redistricting action was overruled, however, by the state's supreme court, which found that redistricting more than once in a decade violated the state's constitution. "There is no language empowering the General Assembly to redistrict more frequently or at any other time," the court ruled.[49]

The re-redistricting battle was even more partisan and bitter in Texas. In 2001, the state's Senate was controlled by Republicans while Democrats controlled the state House of Representatives. As in Colorado, their inability to agree on a plan threw redistricting to a panel of federal judges, who drew up a compromise plan that maintained 17 Democrat and 13 Republican districts.[50] After Republicans won control of the house in 2002, however, they drew up a new plan that all concerned agreed would likely give Republicans an additional seven seats in the U.S. House of Representatives. In a desperate attempt to stop it from being adopted, 52 Democratic state representatives actually fled the state in May 2003, chartering two buses so they could secretly leave the state and check into a hotel in Oklahoma in the hope of denying Republicans the quorum of 100 legislators needed to vote on the controversial plan.[51] Texas Congressman Tom DeLay responded by asking the U.S. Justice Department for help tracking down the fugitive legislators, a request that was dismissed as "wacko" by a senior department official.[52] The fugitives managed to remain out of state until the expiration of the special legislative session that Republican Governor Rick Perry had declared for the purpose of redistricting. In July, a dozen state senators fled to New Mexico, again successfully thwarting a vote on the new district map. In October, however, Perry called a third special session, and the

Republicans finally had their way. Despite a legal challenge by Democrats, a federal court ruled that redistricting more than once per decade is permissible under Texas state law, even though it had never previously been done.[53] Re-redistricting in Texas has also been ruled acceptable by the office of U.S. Attorney General John Ashcroft, notwithstanding opposition from the state's major civil rights groups, including the NAACP, the Mexican-American Legal Defense and Educational Fund, the League of United Latin American Citizens and the American GI Forum.[54]

CHAPTER SIX

Traitor Baiters

America was born in rebellion, through acts of civil disobedience such as the Boston Tea Party and overt efforts to overthrow British rule. Not surprisingly, therefore, the founding fathers who wrote the United States Constitution had the good sense to define the crime of treason in very careful and limited terms, thereby ensuring that parties in power could not use it as a weapon against their political opponents. As James Madison wrote in the Federalist Papers in 1788, "new-fangled and artificial treasons have been the great engines, by which violent factions . . . have usually wrecked their alternate malignity on each other."[1] Similar observations came from James Wilson, who also played a major role in drafting the U.S. Constitution and was one of the first judges appointed by George Washington to the Supreme Court.

The accusation of treason, Wilson warned in 1791, "furnishes an opportunity to unprincipled courtiers, and to demagogues equally unprincipled, to harass the independent citizen, and the faithful subject, by treasons, and by prosecutions for treasons, constructive, capricious, and oppressive."[2]

As defined by the Constitution, treason consists of two types of crimes, both of which constitute intentional acts of betraying the nation. "Treason against the United States," it declares, "shall consist only in levying war against them, or, adhering to their Enemies, giving them Aid and Comfort." Recognizing the serious nature of such a charge, U.S. courts have rarely sought to use it as the basis for criminal prosecutions. In the entire history of the country, there have been fewer than 40 federal trials for treason and even fewer convictions.

Following the terrorist attacks of September 11, however, the rhetoric of the conservative movement marked an abandonment of this tolerant tradition. The charge of treason has been bandied about routinely against liberals in general and especially against critics of the Bush administration's invasion of Iraq. Examples include:

- After correspondent Peter Arnett gave an interview with Iraqi state television during the war in Iraq, Kentucky Senator Jim Bunning called for Arnett to be "brought back and tried as a traitor to the United States of America, for his aiding and abetting the Iraqi government during a war." Even after Arnett apologized for his remarks and was fired by MSNBC, Bunning declared in a speech on the Senate floor that "that's not enough for me. . . . I think Mr. Arnett should be met at the border and arrested should he come back to America."[3]

- Shortly after September 11, David Horowitz published a column calling anti-war professor Noam Chomsky "the most treacherous intellect in America. . . . Disruption in this country is what the terrorists want, and what the terrorists need, and what the followers of Noam Chomsky intend to give them."[4] A year later, Horowitz commented on a speech that Chomsky gave in Texas: "If the word 'traitor' has any meaning at all, Noam Chomsky is an American traitor, and in fact the leading advocate of the call for all progressive citizens of America to betray their country."[5]

- In April 2003, Tennessee State Senator Tim Burchett drew cheers when he called for the deportation of war critics. "That's treason, not patriotism," Burchett said. "They ought to be run out of our country and not allowed back."[6]

- After a number of celebrities joined other prominent Americans in opposing the war in Iraq, the ProBush.com website urged visitors to "boycott Hollywood" and created a "traitor list" including entertainers such as George Clooney, Sheryl Crow, Johnny Depp, Danny Glover, Mike Farrell, Janeane Garofalo, Whoopi Goldberg, Madonna, Sean Penn, Julia Roberts, Susan Sarandon, Martin Sheen and Barbra Streisand.[7]

- The Clear Channel radio network pulled the Dixie Chicks from their playlists after the group's lead singer, Natalie Maines, told fans in London that they were ashamed to be from the same state as President Bush. Only a few days previously, Clear Channel Entertainment, the company's concert tour promotional arm, had been enthusiastically promoting its co-sponsorship of

26 upcoming concerts in the Chicks' upcoming "Top of the World Tour."[8] In Colorado Springs, two disk jockeys were suspended from Clear Channel affiliate KKCS for defying the ban.[9]

Variations on the theme of treason have also become a reliable catch phrase in the titles of recent bestselling books by right-wing authors:

- Mona Charen's *Useful Idiots: How Liberals Got It Wrong in the Cold War and Still Blame America First*, features cover photos of Phil Donahue, Peter Jennings, Al Gore, Hillary Clinton and Jimmy Carter and recounts a litany of alleged liberal betrayals in places like Cuba, Vietnam and Nicaragua.

- *Off with Their Heads: Traitors, Crooks and Obstructionists in American Politics, Media and Business*, by former Clinton campaign adviser turned Fox News commentator Dick Morris, compares the "liberal media" to Radio Moscow, accuses it of undermining the Bush administration's war on terror and declares, "All our terrorist problems were born during the Clinton years." (This is the same Dick Morris who resigned in disgrace after his trysts with prostitute Sherry Rowlands were exposed, along with the fact that he had tried to impress her by having her listen in on his phone conversations with the president. Fortunately, Rowlands was not a terrorist.)

- Sean Hannity's *Deliver Us from Evil: Defeating Terrorism, Liberalism, and Despotism*, "reveals how the disgraceful history of appeasement has reached forward from the days of Neville Chamberlain and Jimmy Carter to corrupt the unrepentant leftists of the modern Democratic Party—from Howard Dean and John Kerry to Bill and Hillary Clinton."

- Daniel J. Flynn's *Why the Left Hates America: Exposing the Lies That Have Obscured Our Nation's Greatness*, promises to "punch a hole right through the thin veneer of political correctness that has long protected these anti-Americans—exposing their rotting, vacuous core. . . . And what may be most shocking is that many of these anti-Americans are at the same time teachers, professors, journalists, news reporters, and even judges and politicians."

- Michael Savage's *The Enemy Within: Saving America from the Liberal Assault on Our Schools, Faith, and Military*, compares Supreme Court Justice Ruth Bader Ginsburg to "the general counsel of the Ku Klux Klan" and declares that liberalism is "either treason or insanity."

- Laura Ingraham's *Shut Up and Sing: How Elites from Hollywood, Politics, and the UN Are Subverting America*, declares that the "elites" who "think all freedom-loving Americans are stupid" include environmentalists, anti-war protesters ("moral morons"), academics ("snotty, sanctimonious dolts"), internationalists ("want to murder America") and entertainers ("shut up and sing").

In one way or another, all of these popular books equate liberals with hating America, providing aid and comfort to Saddam Hussein or Osama bin Laden and in general betraying the nation. Conservative pundit Ann Coulter's *Treason: Liberal Treachery from the Cold War to the War on Terrorism* has perhaps gone further in this direction than any of the others. Her book derides Democrats as "the Treason Party," stating, "Liberals have a preternatural gift for striking a position on the side of treason. You could be talking about Scrabble and they would instantly leap to the anti-American position. Everyone says liberals love America, too. No they don't. Whenever the nation is under attack, from within or without, liberals side with the enemy. This is their essence."[10] Coulter claims that liberals have been conspiring to destroy the nation for the past half century, beginning with the Cold War when "Democrats opposed anything opposed by their cherished Soviet Union."[11] In contrast with the Constitution, which declares that treason must be *intentional*, Coulter insists that it *doesn't even matter* whether liberals know they are betraying the nation. "They are either traitors or idiots," she writes, and "the difference is irrelevant."[12]

Even former president Jimmy Carter's acceptance of a Nobel Prize makes him a traitor in Coulter's eyes. Why? Because the prize was awarded in December 2002, both to honor Carter for his "decades of untiring effort to find peaceful solutions to international conflicts" and—in the words of Nobel committee chair Gunnar Berge—as an implicit "criticism of the line that the current administration has taken."[13] By accepting the Nobel at a time when Bush was preparing for war with Iraq, Coulter declares, Carter betrayed the country: "For any American to accept this award on the ground offered," she writes, "does sound terribly like 'adhering to their enemies, giving them aid and comfort.'"[14]

It is tempting to imagine that Coulter and her admirers don't literally believe the words that come out of her mouth. Maybe she is being satirical, exaggerating for effect, or attempting to exploit the nation's post-9/11 mood of war fever and intolerance for alternate views. Whatever the reasons, though, her book spent more than two months on the *New York Times* bestseller list, and she insists that she is serious, so it seems fair to take her at her word and to see her hyperbole as a reflection of beliefs that many conservatives currently hold. Coulter is not alone in charging her fellow Americans with acts of terror, treason and betrayal. The conservative movement has been doing this for years, applying these labels broadly to every movement and belief that falls outside its own political worldview.

A Lean, Mean, Green-Fighting Machine

To judge from the rhetoric emanating from the right, you would think that environmental groups like the Sierra Club are one of the greatest current threats to America's national security. More than 1,000 conservative publications and websites, for example, published Michelle Malkin's 2003 blast at the environmental movement as "terrorists with tofu breath . . . bomb-throwing Birkenstock brats. Wolves in hemp clothing. Enemies of scientific progress. Inveterate haters of humanity."[15]

Even before 9/11, corporate think tanks and the conservative movement regularly demonized environmental and other activist groups by associating them with terrorism. In 1991, the Ketchum PR firm was embarrassed when one of its memos leaked to the press, outlining contingency plans to protect the image of its client, Clorox, by launching an ad campaign with the slogan, "Stop Environmental Terrorism." The Center for the Defense of Free Enterprise, an organization run by anti-environmentalist crusader Ron Arnold, has been tossing around the term "eco-terrorism" for years, defining it as "any crime committed in the name of saving nature," which "includes but is not limited to crimes officially designated as 'terrorism' by the Federal Bureau of Investigation." This definition of "eco-terrorism" is so broad that it even includes activities such as sit-ins and other forms of peaceful civil disobedience.

When they use the term "eco-terrorism," Arnold and other conservatives highlight the actions of groups like the Earth Liberation Front (ELF) and the Animal Liberation Front (ALF), which have engaged in property destruction and other illegal acts. ELF and ALF have claimed responsibility for millions of dollars of property damage. Although they have targeted property rather than people, their willingness to commit acts such as arson certainly reflects a reckless disregard for human safety. Leading environmental groups have clearly condemned such acts as criminal, pointing to the difference between these attacks and the activities—public education, advocacy, letter-writing campaigns and peaceful protests—through which the environmental movement works to mobilize support for its goals. The conservative movement, however, has habitually and deliberately broadened the definition of terrorism to mean anything that might arouse any kind of fear or apprehension—including traditionally legitimate efforts to inform the public of potential health hazards such as unsafe foods or products.

The American Council on Science and Health (ACSH), which derives a large share of its funding from the chemical and food industries, routinely uses the word "terror" to stigmatize food safety advocates, environmental activists and even scientists. In ACSH director Elizabeth Whelan's 1993 book, *Toxic Terror: The Truth Behind the Cancer Scare*, she attacked "the bad news syndrome" regarding pesticides and chemical contaminations of food and the environment. Whelan has also coined the phrase "mouse terrorism" to ridicule animal tests used to assess product safety, calling such tests a "philosophy of 'mouse terrorism,' which sees a human health threat in any substance that causes cancer in rodents at extremely high doses."[16]

Michael Fumento, another prolific conservative commentator, coined the term "tampon terrorism" to attack women's groups that have raised concern about dioxin in chlorine-bleached tampons.[17] At the libertarian *Reason* magazine, tobacco industry apologist Jacob Sullum has used the term "tobacco terror."[18] Sam Waltz, the former chairman of the Public Relations Society of America, has even coined the term "ethical terrorism." Waltz, who served in Vietnam-era army counterintelligence before going to work as a public relations executive for DuPont, uses the term "to describe the actions of those who raise questions about the motivation and integrity of an individual, company, or other entity, in order to gain the upper hand."[19]

Eric Dezenhall of the Nichols-Dezenhall PR firm refers to people who use the Internet to say negative things about his clients as "cyberterrorists" and advocates an aggressive response. "Despite its sexy sheen, the real power of animal rights remains in terror," Dezenhall stated in his 1999 book, *Nail 'em! Confronting High-Profile Attacks on Celebrities and Businesses.* In a section of the book titled "Victims Groups as Cultural Terrorists," Dezenhall lashed out at "attackers . . . who use nonviolent terror to accomplish their goals." What is "nonviolent terror"? Dezenhall was referring to people with multiple chemical sensitivity (MCS) who "intimidate doctors and research institutions that won't diagnose MCS and other boutique disabilities."[20] Dezenhall's partner, Nick

Nichols, offered similar thoughts in his own book, titled *Rules for Corporate Warriors*. Nichols has advised corporations to use "attack technologies" against activists, whom he accused of playing on the public's sympathies for "vulnerable" people such as children, the elderly, consumers, animals or nature and the earth itself. Quoted in *Feedstuffs*, a meat-industry trade publication, Nichols said companies should "gather information about attackers, move quickly with both defensive and offensive strategies, deploy globally, fight like guerrillas and 'take no prisoners.'" To emphasize his point, he quoted the wisdom of Chicago gangster Al Capone, who reportedly said: "You can get more with kind words and a smile and a gun than you get with kind words and a smile."[21]

Frontiers of Freedom, an anti-environmental group whose funders include the timber industry, ExxonMobil and conservative foundations including Scaife, Bradley and Olin, petitioned the Internal Revenue Service to rescind tax-exempt nonprofit status for the Rainforest Action Network (RAN), a San Francisco–based environmental group. RAN needed to be taken down, according to a Frontiers news release, because of its protests against the Boise Cascade company's logging activities in old-growth forests.[22] Frontiers also sponsored a website attacking attorney John Banzhaf, one of the trial lawyers hated by industry because he has successfully sued the tobacco industry on behalf of clients with lung cancer. According to the BanzhafWatch.com website, this made Banzhaf "an enemy" and a "legal terrorist."[23] Apparently the folks at Frontiers haven't figured out yet that terrorists are people who do *illegal* and *violent* things.

Beware of Grannies in Tennis Shoes

Self-proclaimed "junk science" critic Steven Milloy, another conservative pundit and defender of the tobacco and chemical industries, has routinely used the label of terrorist to attack environmental groups and scientists who raise concerns about health and environmental problems. In September 2000, he used the terms "taco terrorism" and "biotechnology terrorists" to describe anti-biotech activists who publicized the fact that Taco Bell taco shells contained genetically engineered Starlink corn, which has not been approved for human consumption.[24] That same month, he joined other conservative commentators at a Frontiers of Freedom conference titled "Environmental Extremism and Eco-Terrorism: The Costs Imposed on Americans." Milloy told the conference that the Environmental Protection Agency and scientists involved in the study of endocrine-disrupting chemicals are "eco-terrorists" who "have corrupted our laws with junk science."[25]

Speaking at the same conference, Edward Badolato of the Counterterrorism and Security Education and Research Foundation (funded by Carthage and Scaife) used an even broader definition of terrorism. The "northwest corner of the United States," he said, was full of "different types of weirdos and environmental wackos, as some people call them—some of whom are involved in these terrible acts of domestic terrorism. With that in mind, it is important to note that in the past we were worried because terrorists around the world were just a plane ride away. Now it could be that nice little college kid down the street or that nice grandmother in tennis shoes, who may be part of or financially supporting one of these radical groups involved directly or indirectly in domestic eco-radical terrorism."[26]

R. J. Smith of the Competitive Enterprise Institute also spoke at the conference and argued that terrorism was ingrained in the very philosophy of the environmental movement, which sees "man as somehow being alien in nature, a threat to the natural order. That is why one hears environmentalists saying man is a cancer on the planet, a sort of invading virus that needs to be eliminated. This is a philosophical stream that runs through the leadership of most of the environmental organizations in America today."[27]

Just four days before the terrorist attacks of 9/11, KREM-TV reporter Jeff Humphrey in Spokane, Washington, produced a report titled "Cracking Down on Eco-Terrorism" in which he noted that Washington Congressman George Nethercutt "is even talking about the death penalty as punishment" for "eco-terrorists who kill their victims."[28] With this kind of rhetoric running rampant in conservative circles, it is not surprising that Republican Congressman Don Young of Alaska responded to 9/11 by speculating publicly that environmental wackos might be the real killers. "If you watched what happened [at past protests] in Genoa, in Italy, and even in Seattle, there's some expertise in that field," Young said. "I'm not sure they're that dedicated, but eco-terrorists—which are really based in Seattle—there's a strong possibility that could be one of the groups."[29]

The day following the September 11 attacks, the "Reagan Information Interchange," a website run by Ronald Reagan's son Michael, published an analysis by its editor, Mary Mostert, who opined that Osama bin Laden was "just a minor player" in the terror attacks. "Supporters of bin Laden say he doesn't have the ability to pull off such an attack," Mostert argued. "Who would want to, and could, destroy the World Trade Center? Does bin Laden have the ability to orchestrate the hijacking of four domestic airliners at about the same time from several airports and pilot them into the middle of the World Trade Center in New York and the Pentagon in Washington, D.C., from his bat cave headquarters deep in the mountains of Afghanistan?"

Instead of foreigners, Mostert argued, the culprits would probably be "other Americans"—specifically, "environmentalist and anti-globalist groups . . . the radicals on the left" who were planning to protest economic globalization during upcoming meetings in Washington of the International Monetary Fund and the World Bank. "It sure looks to me as if the 'Battle of Washington' was begun yesterday with the bombing of the Pentagon and the World Trade Center," she wrote. "In a world with a population of 8 billion people, 100,000 well-trained, dedicated terrorists with the technical ability and the money to plan, coordinate and execute an attack like we saw yesterday can make a lot of trouble, especially when they are pictured in a supportive media as mere 'protestors' and the police are labeled as the monsters."[30]

Even after it became clear that Islamist fundamentalists were behind the attacks on the World Trade Center and the Pentagon, conservative attacks on other straw men have continued. Tom Randall of the National Center for Public Policy Research—the conservative advocacy group that we described in Chapter Two, "The Echo Chamber"—used 9/11 as a pretext for demanding action to stop "domestic terrorists" such as the ELF and ALF. "While these terrorists are small-time compared to the terrorists who struck the World Trade Center and the Pentagon and are not known to have killed anyone as yet, they appear to be intent on expanding their violence and putting American lives at risk," Randall wrote.[31] On October 7, the *Washington Times* published an editorial calling for "war against eco-terrorists," describing ELF and ALF as "key links in the web of violent environmental groups—an eco-al-Qaeda" with "a fanatical ideology and a twisted morality."[32]

One striking indicator of the right wing's misguided preoccupation with environmentalists is the fact that Congressman Scott McInnis (R–Colorado) had scheduled congressional hearings on "eco-terrorism" to be held on September 12, 2001, one day after Washington and New York experienced an attack by *real* terrorists. The 9/11 attacks forced McInnis to temporarily postpone his plans, rescheduling his hearings to February 2002.[33] His agenda, however, remained unchanged. Testimony at the February hearings came from figures like Rick Berman, a Washington lobbyist for the tobacco, restaurant and alcohol industries who specializes in attacking activist groups as diverse as Action on Smoking and Health, the Center for Food Safety, the Center for Science in the Public Interest, Greenpeace, Mothers Against Drunk Driving, the Organic Consumers Association, People for the Ethical Treatment of Animals (PETA) and the Rainforest Action Network (RAN). In his testimony, Berman singled out PETA and RAN as examples of activist groups that have become a "breeding ground for environmental criminals . . . groups that have helped to fund—directly or indirectly—these domestic terrorists."[34] Interviewed by ABC News, Berman said he wanted Congress "to look at the tax-exempt status of groups like PETA. I don't see this being any different from George Bush being able to shut down foundations funneling money to al Qaeda."[35]

In May 2002, the National Center for Public Policy Research (NCPPR) launched a new website, EnviroTruth.org, to attack what it called the "jihad" that environmental activists are waging against corporations. "For too long, environmental groups have seized the world stage and the public's attention by distorting facts, bending the truth and even committing acts of terrorism against innocent citizens," said NCPPR President Amy Ridenour. "EnviroTruth.org sheds light on the environmentalist movement, offering information about their tactics, terrorist acts and fund-raising machines."[36] Ridenour's reference to "terrorism" was particularly ironic since NCPPR itself was founded in the 1980s to support the Contra guerrillas in Nicaragua, who were notorious for targeting civilians and were therefore considered terrorists by leading human rights groups.[37]

Kill Them Before They Drink Latte Again

Of course, environmentalists are not the only targets of rightist wrath. Repeatedly and relentlessly, conservatives have hammered away at the theme that liberals, Democrats and anyone else with whom they disagree are conscious traitors engaged in fifth-column subversion within the United States. "Even fanatical Muslim terrorists don't hate America like liberals do," declared Ann Coulter at the February 2002 annual conference of the Conservative Political Action Committee. Speaking before an audience of 3,500 that included luminaries such as Lynne Cheney, Bill Bennett and Health and Human Services Secretary Tommy Thompson, Coulter drew applause when she commented on the recent capture of

John Walker Lindh, an American citizen who fought alongside the Taliban in Afghanistan. "In contemplating college liberals," Coulter said, "you really regret, once again, that John Walker is not getting the death penalty. We need to execute people like John Walker in order to physically intimidate liberals by making them realize that they could be killed, too."[38] (Actually, John Walker Lindh himself is not a liberal. Like Coulter, he is a fundamentalist.)

The post-9/11 political climate made it easier for voices within the White House and the conservative movement to accuse their ideological opponents of treason. In speeches criticizing the Senate's hesitation to pass a bill creating the Homeland Security Department, Bush repeatedly characterized Democratic opponents of the bill as "interested in special interests in Washington and not interested in the security of the American people."[39] Conservative pundit Andrew Sullivan inveighed against "the enemy within the West itself—a paralyzing, pseudo-clever, morally nihilist fifth column that will surely ramp up its hatred in the days and months ahead."[40] Journalist Michael Kelly declared that opponents of war in Afghanistan were "on the side of future mass murders of Americans. They are objectively pro-terrorist. . . . That is the pacifists' position, and it is evil."[41]

After television personality Bill Maher made remarks that were perceived as critical of previous U.S. military campaigns, White House Press Secretary Ari Fleischer told journalists that Americans "need to watch what they say, what they do. This is not a time for remarks like this; there never is."[42] William Bennett, Reagan's former education secretary, authored a book titled *Why We Fight: Moral Clarity and the War on Terrorism*. Through his organization, Empower America, he launched Americans for Victory over

Terrorism (AVOT), a group of well-connected Republicans including L. Paul Bremer, Jack Kemp, Jeane Kirkpatrick and Trent Lott. According to AVOT, the threats that America faces today "are both external and internal: external in that there are groups and states that want to attack the United States; internal in that there are those who are attempting to use this opportunity to promulgate their agenda of 'blame America first.' Both threats stem from either a hatred for the American ideals of freedom and equality or a misunderstanding of those ideals and their practice."[43]

Attorney General John Ashcroft used similar rhetoric in support of the USA Patriot Act, legislation approved by Congress in October 2001 that gives the Justice Department new powers to spy on U.S. citizens. Critics objected that the act expands the ability of police to spy on telephone and Internet correspondence in anti-terrorism investigations and even in routine criminal investigations unrelated to terrorism, makes the payment of membership dues to suspect political organizations a deportable offense and creates a broad new definition of "domestic terrorism" that could target people who engage in acts of political protest and subject them to wiretapping and enhanced penalties. "To those who scare peace-loving people with phantoms of lost liberty," Ashcroft responded, "my message is this: Your tactics only aid terrorists—for they erode our national unity and diminish our resolve. They give ammunition to America's enemies, and pause to America's friends."[44]

In May 2002, controversy erupted when the Bush administration was forced to admit that it had received a general warning of possible airplane hijackings by terrorists prior to 9/11. Vice President Dick Cheney responded by accusing Democrats of "incendiary suggestions," adding that "such commentary is thoroughly irresponsible and totally unworthy of national leaders in a time of war."[45] White House Communications Director Dan Bartlett charged that Democratic comments "are exactly what our opponents, our enemies, want us to do."[46] Mississippi Senator Trent Lott said Democrats were "talking like our enemy is George W. Bush and not Osama bin Laden."[47] According to Fox News commentator Fred Barnes, Democrats "looked like not a loyal opposition but a disloyal opposition, encouraging . . . conspiracy theories about how President Bush might have known about the terrorist attacks prior to September 11 and didn't do anything about them."[48]

In December 2002, White House spokesman Ari Fleischer used traitor-baiting to dismiss criticisms of Bush by the Democratic Party's presidential contenders. "Any candidate who suggests that when the enemy attacks, the blame lies with the United States and not with the enemy does so at great peril to their own political future," he said. (None of the candidates had actually said that.)[49]

Standing Up to the Little Guy

You might be tempted to shrug off this rhetoric as the normal, if mean-spirited, posturing of one side in a two-sided, rough-and-tumble political debate. At present, however, Republican dominance of America's governmental institutions has turned this rhetoric into the language of the powerful against the powerless. As the conservative movement understands perfectly well, ideas have consequences, and the ideas expressed by Bill Bennett and Ann Coulter affect the lives and freedom of everyday citizens.

When Fox News commentator Bill O'Reilly declares that Americans who don't support the war in Iraq should "just shut up" or "be considered enemies of the state,"[50] millions of viewers hear his ideas and start looking for ways to put them into practice:

- In Houston, the owner of an art gallery received a visit from two FBI agents after the agency received an anonymous complaint that "anti-American" ideas lurked in a gallery exhibit titled "Secret Wars," which featured paintings inspired by U.S. covert operations and government secrets.[51] In North Carolina, two Secret Service agents interrogated a college student about the "un-American material" in her apartment—which, in this case, turned out to be a poster criticizing Bush for his support of the death penalty. San Franciscan Barry Reingold, a 60-year-old retired phone company worker, received an FBI visit after someone at the gym where he exercises reported that he had described President Bush as "a servant of the big oil companies."[52] When asked about these visits, an FBI spokesperson responded that the agency was simply following up on every lead in its pursuit of terrorists.

- Ed Gernon, the producer of a CBS miniseries about Adolf Hitler, learned firsthand about the price of freedom in America when he made the mistake of talking freely to *TV Guide*. Gernon was interviewed in April 2003 prior to the broadcast of his docudrama, *Hitler: The Rise of Evil*. He told *TV Guide* that the story "basically boils down to an entire nation gripped by fear, who ultimately chose to give up their civil rights and plunged the whole world into war. I can't think of a better time to examine this history than now." These innocuous remarks—in which Gernon made no mention whatsoever of George W. Bush— were then attacked in Rupert Murdoch's *New York Post,* which ran an item in its gossip column that described Gernon's comment as a sign of "Hollywood's anti-Americanism" and an attempt to "look at the Bush White House through the prism of Germany's genocidal psychopath."[53] A separate column in the *Post* by John Podhoretz called the miniseries "an act of slander against the president of the United States—and by extension, toward the United States itself."[54] Gernon was fired two days later.[55]

● In New Mexico, high school teacher Bill Nevins was suspended from his job and told that his contract would not be renewed after a student on his poetry team read an anti-war poem over the school's closed-circuit TV system. The poetry club was also disbanded. Several other high school teachers in the state were also suspended or fired after refusing to enforce pro-war views in their classrooms. Geoff Barrett, a teacher at Albuquerque's Highland High School, was suspended after refusing to remove student-made artwork expressing views on the war in Iraq. The artwork included both pro- and anti-war views, but Barrett says he was told that the pro-war posters were not "pro-war enough."[56]

● Even soldiers stationed in Iraq have come under pressure to stifle themselves. With frustration mounting and morale dropping over their lengthening deployment, *Stars and Stripes* magazine reported that "soldiers are smacking head-on into limits on their public speech." Troops interviewed in Germany and Iraq said they had been briefed to refer questions to a public-affairs specialist and that soldiers were getting in trouble for speaking out. "I'm not comfortable telling you what I really think, and I'm not going to lie to you, so it's better if I just don't say anything," said one soldier. Another commented, "I find it absurd that these same people we put our lives on the line for can punish us for having our own opinions."[57] Shortly after soldiers with the Third Infantry Division criticized President Bush and Donald Rumsfeld, many reporters embedded with the division were expelled, and the troops were forbidden to talk to the media without prior approval. Back home, their families also received an e-mail message from a rear-detachment commander warning against contacting the press "in a negative manner regarding the military and this deployment."[58]

• In September 2002, police used mass arrests of the innocent to subdue demonstrators who had gathered in Washington, D.C., to protest a meeting of the World Bank and International Monetary Fund. The arrests, observed George Washington University law professor Jonathan Turley, "had one common element: All the students were arrested while trying to comply with the law. The D.C. and National Park Service police had used the same technique in each instance: Surround the crowd. Tell its members to disperse or face arrest. And then, as people try to disperse, block their escape with rows of officers in riot gear and arrest them." In addition to protesters, journalists were also swept up in the arrests, and one student photographer was clubbed by police while taking pictures.[59]

Miami Blues

In November 2003, police attacks on demonstrators in Miami, Florida, drew criticism from the human rights organization Amnesty International, which said it was "deeply concerned" by "reports of the indiscriminate and inappropriate use of non-lethal weapons on non-violent protestors resulting in scores of injuries; the obstruction of those providing medical treatment; multiple and random arrests, including of legal observers and journalists, and the denial of the right to freedom of expression and association. There have also been unconfirmed reports of ill-treatment of some of those arrested while they were detained."[60]

An estimated ten to twenty thousand people participated in the November demonstrations, which coincided with the multilateral trade negotiations connected to the Free Trade Area of the Americas (FTAA), an extension of the North American Free Trade Agreement (NAFTA). The demonstrators were a diverse mix of trade unionists, environmentalists, retirees and student activists, and even individuals like Stephen O. Starr, who calls himself a "registered Republican, pro-life, pro-gun, ex-military in favor of kicking Muslim butts and letting Allah sort them out."[61] Although Starr considered himself "in opposition to the vast majority of participants in the protest," he agreed with their opposition to the FTAA. "I came to the protest expecting to find throngs of purple-haired, nose-ringed and tattooed radical revolutionaries," Starr stated. "What I found was a bunch of kids that could be my children, old people, union people and an incredible amount of media. There were legal observers, and even field medical personnel. It was not at all what I expected."[62]

"While I was there, the demonstrations were peaceful—and more surreal, fun and fascinating than photos or TV images conveyed," says Ina Paiva Cordle, who reported on the protests for the *Miami Herald*. "Covering both an AFL–CIO Workers Forum on Wednesday and the rally at Bayfront Park Amphitheater was a lesson in seeing an issue through others' eyes. At the forum, I heard workers from Mexico, Colombia and Nicaragua describe unfair labor conditions. And a former Maytag employee talked about the difficulties he and others in Galesburg, Ill., have endured since the company decided to close a plant there. Most significantly, all week, everyone I approached—whether a water quality activist from Wisconsin, a steelworker from Kentucky, an auto assembler from Canada or a family counselor from Ohio—had a specific, personal reason for coming to Miami to oppose the FTAA."[63]

The peace was broken, however, by the substantial, combined effort from local, state and federal law-enforcement officials, whose actions went far beyond crowd-control techniques used at similar previous demonstrations. Al Crespo, a 61-year-old Miami photojournalist, said the Miami police took up positions and started firing rubber bullets and tear gas at demonstrators. "It looked like a re-enactment of a Civil War battle," he said. As protesters retreated from the attack, the police "proceeded to march down the street and chase these people, chase them for blocks. These were people trying to get away, and they kept marching and shooting."[64]

- Cheri Hoggan, the 44-year-old wife of a retired steelworker "verbally protested what she considered the abusive treatment of a student activist. . . . She was slammed to the ground face down by police and a gun was aimed point blank at the back of her head."[65] "I'm just bruised up and down," she said. "It was a pretty scary ordeal."[66]

- Orlando Mendez, interviewed by a reporter while still bleeding from a rubber-bullet wound to his chest, said the police were shooting without provocation: "I was just taking pictures, and they fired at me."[67]

- Nikki Hartman, interviewed while bleeding from the head, said the police also fired rubber bullets at her without cause or warning: "They shot me in the back."[68]

- A medical doctor on the scene reported treating one victim for a rubber-bullet wound to the head, even as the police shot the person again in the back. The doctor "was also shot himself, once in the arm and once in the leg despite clearly displaying the red cross symbol. He also reported having medical equipment confiscated whilst helping the injured."[69]

- A small contingency of "seniors, union members, young people" and others who separated themselves from the main protest in order to avoid the melee were rushed by police officers: "The cops came up the hill, tear-gassed us and shot people with rubber bullets," said Stewart Acuff, the AFL–CIO's organizing director. "They pepper-sprayed a senior citizen in his seventies who was sitting in a chair completely away from any kind of problem, without provocation."[70]

"This was a paramilitary assault," said Naomi Archer of the group South Floridians for Fair Trade and Global Justice.[71]

"The Miami Police Department disgraced itself with an outrageous use of force," said Thea Lee, chief international economist with the AFL–CIO.[72]

A Korean War veteran remarked, "This is like we're being attacked by another country."[73]

The architect of the police strategy was Miami Police Chief John Timoney, who had previously overseen aggressive police tactics against demonstrators as Philadelphia's police chief during the 2000 Republican National Convention. Taking a page from the Iraq War PR handbook, Timoney "embedded" local television reporters, outfitting them with flak jackets and riot helmets as they accompanied police squads.[74] He characterized the FTAA protesters as "outsiders coming to terrorize and vandalize our city."[75]

After the trade talks and demonstrations had ended, Miami Mayor Manny Diaz proudly claimed that the FTAA police operations stood as "a model for homeland security."[76] He may be correct. FBI agents, Department of Homeland Security officials and law-enforcement leaders from Georgia and New York traveled to Miami to observe cutting-edge crowd-control tactics in action.

If the "Miami model" takes hold, however, we can expect more examples of violent harassment aimed at peaceful dissent. Coky Michel, a retired Miami-area schoolteacher who participated in the FTAA protests, recalled the smell of tear gas and police who shouted contradictory orders and threats while pointing guns at her and her husband as they tried to obey a command to disperse. "I made it home safely," she said, "but I will never feel the same about the police, especially in Miami. Protesters were constantly intimidated and harassed as we walked to and from the demonstration, and the police officers themselves seemed puzzled and disorganized when handling the nonviolent crowd. Not once in this ordeal did I feel that the officers were there to protect me. Chief Timoney and Mayor Diaz looked pleased and proud on television: Their thousands of officers, armed to the teeth, had won a heroic battle against a few young and possibly violent trouble-makers. The majority of the protesters, however—peaceful and law-abiding citizens like me, who should have had the right to express our views without fear or intimidation—went home with sore feet and a bad taste in our mouths."[77]

CONCLUSION

The Three-Banana Problem

In the slang of engineers and computer programmers, simple tasks are said to be "so easy that a monkey could do them." Monkeys, of course, get paid in bananas, so a "one-banana problem" is especially trivial, whereas a three-banana problem is actually fairly difficult. Solving the problems that we have posed in this book will take at least three bananas, if not more.

Partly due to the post-9/11 political climate and partly due to the conservative movement's own organizing strengths, the Republican right has succeeded in moving the United States in directions that would have seemed unthinkable a few years ago. In addition to embroiling the nation in costly overseas military adventures, the Bush administration has presided over massive budget deficits, increasing political polarization at home and an alarming growth of anti-American sentiment abroad. In the long run, these trends are not likely to be sustainable, and pressures to change course will mount.

It has taken more than half a century for the right wing to achieve the power that it now enjoys in American politics, and it is unrealistic to imagine that its successes can be quickly reversed. There is no reason, however, to expect that turning the tide will take another half century. Information and events move quickly today, and people possess tools for organizing that did not exist in the past, such as the Internet. Solutions often do not become clear until after the fact, but hopefully some lessons can be drawn from studying how the right has organized itself.

Fruitful Organizing

To begin with, progressives should emulate the right's planful discipline. Consider something as basic as the weekly Wednesday meeting that Grover Norquist holds in the office of Americans for Tax Reform, which we discussed in the introduction. The idea is simple, inexpensive and obviously effective. In 2001—nine years after Norquist began holding his weekly meeting—House Democratic leader Richard Gephardt attempted to do the same thing for Democrats, organizing his own weekly meeting to facilitate networking among labor leaders, environmentalists, abortion-rights groups and other Democratic-leaning activists.[1] Note the difference, however. Americans for Tax Reform is a conservative organization that is closely linked to the Republican Party, but Norquist is not a party representative or elected official, which gives him the freedom to be a passionate, *radical* conservative without worrying that he might lose an election. Gephardt's attempt to emulate Norquist in fact ended a year after it started, when Nancy Pelosi replaced him as House minority leader.

Conservatives have been shrewd about simultaneously organizing a grassroots movement *outside* the Republican Party at the same time that they work to get people *within* the party elected. A similar strategy has defined the conservative movement's approach to the media. They have created their own, unabashedly conservative media, while simultaneously working to advance the careers and visibility of conservative journalists *within* the mainstream. This dual strategy gives them the ability to constantly push forward ideas that are on the conservative margins, promoting radically conservative ideas while simultaneously appealing to the center. Grover Norquist is one of the radicals, but he describes his movement as a *"center*-right" coalition. "It's like this," he explained. "Some of us in the movement want to get to St. Louis, and some of us to Utah, and some to Los Angeles, and some of us want to go all the way to Japan. Bush wants to get to St. Louis. Is there any reason to argue with him about the need to get to LA? Or to get really flaky and say we need to go all the way to Japan? Of course not."[2]

Liberal activists could adopt this dual strategy, but they haven't. Instead, the Democratic Party's centrist faction has tried to exclude or marginalize factions that are seen as "too far to the left." For their part, some of those factions have become outside spoilers rather than participants in the Democratic coalition. Moreover, the pattern of conservatives pushing from the right versus Democrats moving toward the center has had the effect over time of steadily redefining the "center" further and further to the right.

The conservative movement actually learned some of its strategy from the left. The labor, civil rights and anti-war movements all honed the techniques of grassroots organizing. For inspiration, they turned to the ideas of Mohandas Gandhi and Martin Luther King or to books like Saul Alinsky's *Rules for Radicals,* a 1972 guidebook for organizers.[3] Alinsky saw politics as a struggle between "haves" and "have-nots" and saw grassroots organizing— strength in numbers—as the crucial asset that everyday people could turn to their advantage as they sought to counter the entrenched power of wealth and privilege.

Subsequently, however, corporations and other wealthy interests learned to adapt these organizing techniques for their own purposes, creating their own grassroots institutions such as Ralph Reed's Christian Coalition or the anti-environmental "wise use" movement. In 1995, Edward Grefe, a former vice president of public affairs for the Philip Morris tobacco company, joined Republican Party organizer Martin Linsky to author their own book, titled *The New Corporate Activism: Harnessing the Power of Grassroots Tactics for Your Organization.* "The heirs of Saul Alinsky can be on both sides of the equation," they declared, chronicling the rise of a "new breed of guerrilla warriors" who were proving that the "haves" could also use Alinsky's grassroots tactics. "The essence of this new way," Grefe and Linsky argued, "is to marry 1990s communication and information technology with 1960s grassroots organizing techniques."[4] This is precisely what the right has done.

The reality behind the conservative movement's success is that—thanks in part to the lessons it borrowed from the left—it has simply done a better job of organizing from the grassroots up. This was brought home forcefully to us when we recently interviewed Felice Pace, an environmental activist from Oregon, where the "wise use" movement has successfully built a core of committed, passionate activists. "When you went down to the parking lot where the rallies were held," he said, "the grassroots guys who came out weren't folks with a lot of money. If you looked at their rigs with the bumper stickers all over them, you could tell that they're not rich folks. They're like retired mill work-ers and stuff. I was there a lot, and I'd go down onto the grounds and talk to people, and it seemed to be truly grassroots to me. It didn't seem to be directed from anywhere else.... I've known some of the people who were involved personally for twenty-five years. I saw no evidence that somebody was pulling the strings from somewhere else."[5]

Death and Taxes

To understand why the left is disorganized while the right is as-cendant, let's compare how each side has dealt with the issues of health care and taxation. No one likes to pay taxes, of course, and groups like Americans for Tax Reform have successfully leveraged their anti-tax campaign into a popular cause that helps conserva-tives in general. Their rhetoric on the issue is stark, visceral and dramatic. To push the repeal of the estate tax—which affects only the estates of multimillionaires—Republicans have successfully renamed it "the death tax."[6] In 2004, Grover Norquist even equated the estate tax with the Nazi Holocaust, apartheid in South Africa and the former Communist regime of East Germany. When National Public Radio interviewer Terry Gross pointed out that the estate tax affects only the wealthiest 2 percent of the population, Norquist responded, "No, the morality that says it's okay to do something to a group because they're a small percentage of the population is the morality that says the Holocaust is okay because they didn't target everybody, just a small percentage."[7]

But no one has actually *died* from the estate tax, whereas according to a recent study by the Institute of Health of the National Academies of Science, lack of health insurance causes roughly 18,000 unnecessary deaths every year in the United States.[8] More than 43 million Americans lack health insurance — 15 percent of the population, not just 2 percent. Even for those who can obtain insurance, costs are spiraling rapidly out of control. Concern about the country's failing health system is strong enough that individual Democratic politicians, such as Bill Clinton, have successfully capitalized on the issue to win elections. The left could be using the issue to build a political movement comparable in power to the right's campaign against taxes.

The possibility that the left might use the health care issue to win power has been acknowledged by Norquist himself. In a 1997 interview with the libertarian *Reason* magazine, he said that he was motivated in the early 1990s to organize his conservative coalition by "sheer terror of Clinton's health care plan. The goal was to stop the government seizure of the health care industry. Had the Democrats taken over health care, I think we would have become a social democracy and we could have never undone it. We wouldn't have won in '94, and even if we did, it wouldn't matter because 50 percent of the population would be on the take. The government has your kids' education, your health care, your parents' health care, and your pension. You want to argue with that government? There isn't an anti-government party in Germany, Sweden, or France.... There's not an anti-government conservatism as a functioning, competing political party that might win an election, because everybody agrees that the government is going to run your health care. Even Margaret Thatcher was really pissy at anybody who wanted to talk about doing something with the National Health Service."[9]

For the past half century, opinion surveys have consistently demonstrated that the majority of Americans support establishing a tax-financed universal health care program in the United States.[10] Moreover, the need for health reform regularly leads the list of priorities expressed by Americans, most of whom believe that the country's health care system is currently in crisis and needs reform.[11] As a recent Harris pollster noted, "A visitor from outer space who looked at these numbers might conclude that most Americans would be strongly supportive of much higher taxation to spend on health care, education and defense. This visitor would be puzzled by the popularity of politicians who favor tax cuts."[12]

Why, then, have liberals failed to capitalize on this issue? For one thing, they have not built the same infrastructure of think tanks, pundits and grassroots advocates with which to market their cause. As we saw in Chapter One, "The Marketplace of Ideas," this failure is not due to lack of money or other resources with which to build such an infrastructure; the problem is that progressive funders have devoted themselves primarily to supporting service programs or academic research, while failing to adequately support the *public promotion* of progressive ideas. As a result, the most visible organizations that talk about health reform have been conservative or industry-backed organizations such as the Coalition for Health Insurance Choices or the Council for Affordable

Health Insurance, both of which were created by the insurance and HMO industries to *oppose* universal health coverage.

During the 2004 Democratic primary, several of the candidates offered proposals that would have extended health coverage to a larger percentage of the population, but the reality of Republican majorities in both the Senate and the House of Representatives meant that none of the Democratic candidates were likely to succeed in getting their plan passed, even if elected. The reality is that health reform cannot be achieved simply by electing a liberal Democrat as president; an entire political movement is necessary first, beginning at the grassroots.

"The movement toward universal health care in Canada started in 1916 (depending on when you start counting), and took until 1962 for passage of both hospital and doctor care in a single province," says Karen Palmer, a Canadian-born nurse who works with Physicians for a National Health Program, a U.S. organization that advocates for universal coverage. "It took another decade for the rest of the country to catch on. That is about 50 years all together. It wasn't like we sat down over afternoon tea and crumpets and said please pass the health care bill so we can sign it and get on with the day. We fought, we threatened, the doctors went on strike, refused patients, people held rallies and signed petitions for and against it, burned effigies of government leaders, hissed, jeered, and booed at the doctors or the Premier depending on whose side they were on. In a nutshell, we weren't the stereotypical nice polite Canadians. Although there was plenty of resistance, now you could more easily take away Christmas than health care."[13]

Media Matters

Another reason for the right's success has been its ability to take advantage of emerging innovations in information technology. During most of the 20th century, the dominant technologies were radio, television and print journalism. These technologies gave a communications and organizing advantage to the ideologically disciplined conservative movement as it allied itself with the wealth and power of large corporations. These technologies lend themselves to top-down control because, by their very nature, they are "one-to-many" technologies in which a relatively small number of people participate in shaping and producing messages that are then transmitted to millions of largely passive recipients. The power that you have over your television is limited. You can turn it on or off or change channels, but you can't rewrite the script to make Gilligan, Jerry Springer or Bill O'Reilly smarter. You have a little more power over your newspaper, but not much.

Not all technologies fit this description, however. The telephone is a system that is best suited for "one-to-one" communication (or "one-to-two" if your spouse or sibling picks up the other line). The values of democracy are most compatible with "many-to-many" or "many-to-one" communications. An election can be seen as an example of many-to-one communication, in which the votes of many people determine a single decision. Many-to-many examples might include town meetings or public hearings.

The Internet can be used to disseminate one-to-many messages, but what makes it especially interesting with regard to the future of democracy is that it also makes many-to-many and

many-to-one communications technologies available and affordable. The political potential of this new information environment
has yet to be fully realized, but there are a number of interesting
developments that give cause for optimism—a fact that has certainly been noticed by corporate communicators.

One of the people who has noticed this potential is public relations specialist Edward Grefe, one of the authors of *The New Corporate Activism*. In 1995, as we described previously, Grefe was
excited about the potential for a corporate-managed marriage of
"1990s communication and information technology with 1960s
grassroots organizing techniques." By 1998, however, he began to
worry that the Internet was actually a threat to the interests of his
clients. "Do not ask for whom the web tolls. It may be your company," he wrote in the September 1998 issue of *Impact*, a public
relations industry trade publication. As an example of the trend
that concerned him, Grefe cited the recent success of an international treaty to ban land mines. "From beginning to end," he
wrote, "that globe-spanning campaign, coordinated by a Vermon-
ter, was a movement started by people who had no power base,
only a mission and a keen awareness of the rallying power of the
Internet. . . . Most politicians around the world wished the campaign would fade away. It succeeded because it appealed to
people at the grassroots in other countries who then pressed their
leaders to act." The result, he warned, is that "We are being
trumped. In nations around the world, grassroots movements are
being formed that will spread fast and far beyond borders. . . . I
would like to be able to assure you that the United States Congress—that Washington itself—is still the dominant player in handling world issues. That would be reassuring to those spending
millions of dollars in this country to defeat agendas being driven

by millions of people in other countries. I cannot, however, offer such assurance."[14]

Here are some examples of ways that the Internet has changed politics already:

- South Korea's traditionally authoritarian political system has been transformed within the space of a few years from conservative to liberal—"all seemingly overnight," the *New York Times* reported in March 2003. According to many observers, it noted, "the most important agent of change has been the Internet. . . . In the last year, as the elections were approaching, more and more people were getting their information and political analysis from spunky news services on the Internet instead or from the country's overwhelmingly conservative newspapers. Most influential by far has been a feisty three-year-old startup with the unusual name of OhmyNews."[15] Founded by Oh Yeon Ho, OhmyNews takes its name from the idea that the news should be stories that make the reader exclaim, "Oh, my!" It has used the Internet to merge traditional reporting with grassroots news gathering. It has a staff of several dozen full-time reporters and editors, but most of its news comes from more than 20,000 "citizen reporters" who write for the site, contributing about 200 stories per day. This army of citizen reporters has enabled OhmyNews to explore stories that the mainstream media in Korea previously ignored. According to *San Jose Mercury News* tech columnist Dan Gillmor, "OhmyNews is transforming the 20th century's journalism-as-lecture model—where organizations tell the audience what the news is and the audience either buys it or doesn't—into something vastly more bottom-up, interactive and democratic."[16]

● In the Philippines—a relatively poor country with a large technology gap—opponents of President Joseph Estrada used web-linked mobile phones and Internet mass mailings in 2000 and 2001 to expose corruption and bring down his government. *Christian Science Monitor* reporter Ilene Prusher noted that Estrada's rapid downfall contrasted with the country's uprising against dictator Ferdinand Marcos 14 years previously, which took years to organize using ham-radio broadcasts and mimeographed fliers. The opponents of Estrada, she noted, "are putting tens of thousands of people into the streets of Manila in a matter of minutes. Call it 'spam democracy' or 'instant protesting,' but the pace of events in this society offers a cautionary tale for government leaders everywhere."[17]

● During the run-up to war with Iraq, opponents of the war—ourselves included—felt frustrated at the peace movement's inability to prevent the war from occurring. However, this frustration should be balanced against some appreciation of the speed with which the anti-war movement was able to mobilize itself. Within the space of only a few months, organizers pulled together demonstrations on February 15, 2003, that involved an estimated 11 million people worldwide—unprecedented numbers to protest a war that at that point had not even begun. *New York Times* writer George Packer called the protests "an instantaneous movement. . . . During the past three months it has gathered the numbers that took three years to build during Vietnam. It may be the fastest-growing protest movement in American history. . . . Internet democracy allows citizens to find one another directly, without phone trees or meetings of chapter organizations, and it amplifies their voices in the electronic storms or 'smart mobs' (masses summoned electroni-cally) that it seems able to generate in a few hours. With cell phones and instant messaging, the time frame of protest might soon be the nanosecond."[18]

- MoveOn.org, which was originally launched by Silicon Valley entrepreneurs Wes Boyd and Joan Blades to oppose the im-peachment of Bill Clinton, has emerged as a major player in the Democratic Party, raising millions of dollars and becoming the backbone of Howard Dean's early success in fund-raising and name recognition during the Democratic primary. "The site is organized in ways traditional political consultants might not stomach," reported CNN in January 2004. "Any member can propose priorities and strategies to which others can re-spond, and the most-supported ideas rise to the top. That means ceding control over much of the content to motivated online participants, producing interactivity that adds grassroots credibility."[19] In January 2004, MoveOn provided an interest-ing example of the way that the new technology might be able to transform the 30-second television campaign advertisement that has become one of the standard weapons of modern elec-tion campaigning. Historically, campaign ads have operated according to the rules of top-down, one-to-many propaganda. They have been expensive to produce and have been the work of small cliques of paid political professionals who possessed the creative and technical skills and the expensive equipment needed to script, shoot and edit the ads. MoveOn's innovation was to create an online contest, inviting visitors to submit their own TV spots critiquing the performance of President Bush. More than 1,500 people produced and submitted ads to the contest, and more than 100,000 people helped vote to select the winner, which MoveOn promised to broadcast. Even before the ads appeared on television, the contest itself and "word-of-mouse" viral marketing had already given them considerable exposure.[20] Perhaps this experiment is merely a curiosity, but it demonstrates the potential for new information technologies to break down the propaganda divide between political advertisers and their audiences.

The MoveOn spots also highlighted, however, one of the ways that progressives should *not* try to emulate the conservative organizing model. Two of the ads submitted by contestants consisted of attempts to compare George W. Bush to Adolf Hitler, and were instantly attacked by Republican pundits as examples of "political hate speech." The MoveOn organizers quickly removed the Hitler-comparison ads from their website and issued a statement distancing themselves from the sentiments, but the ensuing media flap put more stink on MoveOn than on their intended target. Of course, there was more than a dab of hypocrisy in the Republican protest against MoveOn's reductio ad Hitlerum rhetoric. Conservative pundits have been using similar rhetoric against Democrats for years—Rush Limbaugh's repeated dismissals of feminists as "femi-Nazis" and references to "Hitlery Clinton," Grover Norquist's comparison of estate taxes to the Nazi Holocaust, comparisons of anti-war protesters to "apologists for Hitler."[21] The point, though, is that facile comparisons of political adversaries to Hitler or Stalin or other hated historical figures are unhelpful and unconvincing.

In a similar vein, we were disappointed when BuzzFlash.com, a popular liberal website, launched a weekly radio feature called the "GOP Hypocrite of the Week." Here's a sample of what they had to say about Utah Senator Orrin Hatch:

> Orrin Hatch is a creepy guy. Very creepy.
>
> Like Bush, he hides behind the cover of being a devout religious man. This is supposed to forgive this guy from the sin of being a smug, sanctimonious liar. I mean, he gets away with rank hypocrisy, lying, and his tolerance and condoning of all sorts of Republican Party hanky panky. . . . This guy will piss on your head in the morning and claim it's raining. Then he'll run ahead of you into the washroom, steal the last stall before you can get to it, cut off the plumbing so you can't wash your hands, and trip you as you leave the john. . . .
>
> Hatch just oozes hypocrisy, like a festering pustule.[33]

Blather like this is a fairly transparent attempt to mimic the style of Fox News or conservative talk radio, but it is unlikely to help liberals win power—and even if it did succeed, it would do so at the price of undermining the values of fairness and civility that liberals should seek to champion.

The Big Picture

For the left, the triumph of the right has been a frustrating experience, but it should be seen in context. The United States and the world today are in general more democratic, more tolerant and more prosperous than they were a generation ago. Human progress has always been uneven and full of setbacks, but progress happens nonetheless. The recent successes of the right have not

eliminated America's long-standing traditions of political tolerance, diversity and respect for individual freedom—traditions that
reflect generations of debate and political struggle. The United
States has not always honored its democratic principles, but it
has honored them well enough to serve often as an inspiration to
others.

Throughout the world, democracy is on the rise. In June 2003,
the Pew Research Center for the People and the Press published
the results of an international survey that found wide international support for the principles of democracy—freedom of expression, freedom of the press, multiparty systems and equal
treatment under the law.[23] And those values are not merely ideas.
During the past century, they have transformed the societies of
many countries, from Japan to India to the states of the former Soviet Union. Europe, which until the mid-20th century was the
world's cockpit of war, has become a stable and generally progressive island of peace.

Strikingly, however, Pew's surveys also showed that recent U.S.
actions—the war in Iraq especially, but also incidents like the
Florida election debacle and domestic measures such as the Patriot Act—have dramatically diminished America's standing in
world public opinion.[24] On the second anniversary of the 9/11 terror attacks, the *New York Times* surveyed opinions in places from
Africa to Europe to Southeast Asia and found "a widespread and
fashionable view . . . that the United States is a classically imperi-
alist power bent on controlling global oil supplies and on military
domination. That mood has been expressed in different ways by
different people, from the hockey fans in Montreal who boo the
American national anthem to the high school students in Switzer-

land who do not want to go to the United States as exchange students because America is not 'in.'"[25]

The world wants democracy, but—at least for the present—it no longer sees the United States as a democratic leader. This is the real challenge facing the United States. Will it live up to its own traditions and become once again a leader and inspiration to others? Or will the conservative movement's vision of "politics as war" undermine those traditions for a generation to come?

Now, as in the past, democratic renewal in the best American tradition will have to emerge from the initiatives of numerous individual citizens acting separately and yet inspired by common goals. Is it possible for such a democratic movement to emerge? Was it ever possible in the past? It didn't look easy then, either. The answer depends on you and millions of others like you. In a democracy, that's how it should be.

Notes

Although most of the sources cited for this book are traditional books, newspapers and similar print documents, we have tried whenever possible to supply an Internet URL so that interested readers can find the full text of the document cited. Unless otherwise indicated, all Internet URLs listed below were visited between the dates of November 1, 2003, and February 15, 2004. Some URLs are bound to become obsolete over time, but many deleted web pages can still be found on the Internet Archive, <http://www.archive.org>.

Introduction: The War at Home

1. David Horowitz, "I'm a Uniter, Not a Divider," Salon.com, May 6, 1999, <http://www.salon.com/news/feature/1999/05/06/bush/>.
2. "The 2004 Political Landscape: Evenly Divided and Increasingly Polarized," Pew Research Center for the People and the Press, November 5, 2003, <http://people-press.org/reports/display.php3?ReportID=196>.
3. Scott Sherman, "David Horowitz's Long March," The Nation, June 15, 2000, <http://www.thenation.com/doc.mhtml%3Fi=20000703&s=sherman&c=1>.
4. David Horowitz, The Art of Political War and Other Radical Pursuits (Dallas, TX: Spence Publishing Company, 2000), pp. 10–11. We have chosen this book, in which

Notes

Horowitz expands on his original pamphlet, as our source for quotes from this essay because the book is more readily available than the original pamphlet. Versions of "The Art of Political War" have also been published in several other places and with different titles, such as "Full-Contact Politics," *The American Enterprise*, April/ May 2000, <http://www.taemag.com/issues/articleid.17180/article_detail.asp>. Although the wording varies slightly between versions, the essence of Horowitz's arguments remains the same.

5. Hanna Rosin, "The Seeds of a Philosophy," *Washington Post*, July 23, 2000, p. A1, <http://www.dke.org/bushpost722.html>.
6. John J. Miller, "Campaign 2000: Bush's League," *National Review*, December 21, 1998.
7. Horowitz, *The Art of Political War*, p. 24.
8. Robert Dreyfuss, "Grover Norquist: 'Field Marshal' of the Bush Plan," *The Nation*, May 14, 2001, <http://www.thenation.com/docprint.mhtml?i=20010514&s=dreyfuss>.
9. Ibid.
10. Susan Page, "Norquist's Power High, Profile Low," *USA Today*, June 1, 2001, <http://www.usatoday.com/news/washington/2001-06-01-grover.htm>.
11. John Aloysius Farrell, "Right Where He Belongs," *Boston Globe*, April 17, 2001, p. F1, <http://www.atr.org/atrnews/041702bg.html>.
12. John Berlau, "Grover Norquist Takes on the Tyranny of Federal Taxation," *Insight on the News*, January 26, 1998, <http://www.findarticles.com/cf_dls/m1571/n3_v14/20174381/p1/article.jhtml>.
13. Ibid.
14. Page.
15. Dreyfuss.
16. Elizabeth Drew, "The Real Struggle for Political Power in America," Ninth Annual John S. Knight Distinguished Lecture, Stanford University, May 5, 1997, <http://knight.stanford.edu/lectures/knight/1997>.
17. Stanley B. Greenberg, *The Two Americas: Our Current Political Deadlock and How to Break It* (New York, NY: Thomas Dunne Books, 2004), pp. 21, 34.
18. Ibid., pp. 2, 5.
19. John B. Judis and Ruy Texeira, *The Emerging Democratic Majority* (New York, NY: Lisa Drew/Scribner, 2002), p. 177.
20. NBC News/*Wall Street Journal* polls conducted periodically, beginning in July 1990, with the latest survey on November 2003, <http://www.pollingreport.com/abortion.htm>.
21. Harris Poll, September 19–23, 2002, <http://www.pollingreport.com/enviro.htm>.
22. Gallup Poll, March 4–7, 2002, <http://www.pollingreport.com/enviro.htm>.
23. Gallup Poll, March 5–7, 2001, <http://www.pollingreport.com/enviro.htm>.
24. International Social Survey Program: Role of Government I, II and III (ICPSR #s 2808, 6010, 8909), cited in Miriam Laugesen and Susan A. Banducci, "Support for Health Care in the Welfare State: Australia, Britain, Canada, New Zealand and the United States," paper prepared for the Western Political Science Association Annual Meeting, March 25–27, 2000, San Jose, CA, <http://www.banducci.com/papers/wpsa2000_health.pdf>. See also Lawrence R. Jacobs, Robert Shapiro and Eli C. Schulman, "Poll Trends: Medical Care in the United States—an Update,"

Public Opinion Quarterly, vol. 57, no. 3, Fall 1993, p. 394; and Louis Harris, "Poll on popular satisfaction with health care," June 1992. Cited in Gene Costain, "Canada/ United States Healthcare" (student term paper), University of Tennessee, Knoxville, Fall 1996, <http://excellent.com.utk.edu/~mmmiller/jpr525/costain.html>.

25. John Aloysius Farrell, "Rancor Becomes Top D.C. Export: GOP Leads Charge in Ideological War," *Denver Post,* May 26, 2003, p. A1.

26. Ibid.

27. Nebraska is included in our list of Republican-controlled legislatures, although its system is somewhat different from that of the other states. Instead of a bicameral system with a separate senate and house of representatives, Nebraska has a unicameral state legislature whose candidates run in non-partisan elections. As of 2003, however, Republicans held two-thirds of the state's legislative seats. See "Table of Partisan Control of State Legislatures, 1938–2003," National Conference of State Legislatures, <http://www.ncsl.org/programs/legman/elect/hstptyct.htm>. See also Scott Bauer, "Legislature's Conservative Nature More Apparent," Associated Press, January 12, 2003, <http://www.yorknewstimes.com/stories/011303/neb_0113030004.shtml>.

28. Bruce Walker, "The Dying Democrats," November 24, 2002, ConservativeTruth. org, <http://www.conservativetruth.org/archives/brucewalker/11-24-02.shtml>.

29. Grover Norquist, "Step-by-Step Tax Reform," *Washington Post,* June 9, 2003, p. A21, <http://www.washingtonpost.com/ac2/wp-dyn/A32629-2003Jun8>.

30. Adam Nagourney, "Bush, Looking to His Right to Shore Up '04 Support," *New York Times,* June 30, 2003, p. A14.

31. "Tobacco Contributions," Center for Responsive Politics, <http://www.opensecrets. org/news/tobacco/tobacco.htm>.

32. "The Big Picture," Center for Responsive Politics, <http://www.opensecrets.org/ bigpicture/sectors.asp?Cycle=1990&Bkdn=DemRep&Sortby=Sector> and <http:// www.opensecrets.org/bigpicture/sectors.asp?Cycle=2002&Bkdn=DemRep&Sortby= Sector>.

33. John Leo, "A Surprising Jog to the Right," *U.S. News & World Report,* vol. 135, no. 18, November 24, 2003, p. 64, <http://www.townhall.com/columnists/johnleo/ jl20031117.shtml>.

34. Lynn Elber, "Lyndon B. Johnson Aides Call Conspiracy Documentary a Smear," Associated Press, November 19, 2003.

35. Carl von Clausewitz, *On War* (New York, NY: Everyman's Library, 1993), pp. 99, 700, 732. In some translations, including this one, Clausewitz's famous dictum is translated as "war is merely the continuation of *policy* by other means." However, "politics" is also commonly used.

36. Robert Novak, "GOP Pulled No Punches in Struggle for Medicare Bill," *Chicago Sun-Times,* November 27, 2003, <http://www.independent-media.tv/item.cfm? fmedia_id=4025&fcategory_desc=Health>.

37. William M. Welch and Andrea Stone, "Dems Want Inquiry into Reports of Medicare Bribe," *USA Today,* December 5, 2003, <http://www.usatoday.com/news/ washington/2003-12-04-dem-inquiry-bribe_x.htm>. See also "Mr. Smith Limps Home," *New York Times,* December 16, 2003, p. A34, <http://www.nytimes.com/ 2003/12/16/opinion/16TUE2.html>.

Chapter One: The Marketplace of Ideas

1. Ralph K. M. Haurwitz and Jeff Nesmith, "I mean, it was like hell had opened up," *Austin American-Statesman*, July 23, 2001, p. A1, <http://www.statesman.com/specialreports/content/specialreports/pipelines/23pipelively.html>. For video news footage from the disaster (from which some of our account is taken), visit the website of the Danielle Dawn Smalley Foundation, <http://www.smalleyfnd.org/danielle/accident.html>.

2. Michael Saul, "Mission of Grief," *Dallas Morning News*, December 28, 1996, p. 31A.

3. Haurwitz and Nesmith.

4. Ibid.

5. H. Josef Hebert, "EPA Fines Pipeline Firm $35 Million," Associated Press, January 13, 2000.

6. "Koch Industries Indicted for Environmental Crimes at Refinery," U.S. Department of Justice news release, September 28, 2000, <http://www.usdoj.gov/usao/txs/releases/september/000929-koch.html>. See also Jeremy Schwartz, "Documents: Koch Covered Up Its Violations," *Corpus Christi Caller-Times*, September 30, 2000, p. A1.

7. "Records Say Koch Met with Cheney," *Wichita Eagle*, March 2, 2002, p. 7B.

8. Dan Eggen, "Oil Company Agrees to Pay $20 Million in Fines," *Washington Post*, April 10, 2001, p. A3.

9. Oil & Gas Contributions, 1991–2000, Center for Responsive Politics, <http://www.opensecrets.org/news/oil/oil.htm>.

10. "The Forbes 400," *Forbes*, September 18, 2003, <http://www.forbes.com/richlist2003/rich400land.html>.

11. Curtis Moore, "Rethinking the Think Tanks," *Sierra* magazine, July 2002, <http://www.sierraclub.org/sierra/200207/thinktank.asp>.

12. "Koch Family Foundations," MediaTransparency.org, <http://www.mediatransparency.org/funders/koch_family_foundations.htm>.

13. Karen Rothmyer, "The Man Behind the Mask," Salon.com, April 7, 1998, <http://www.salon.com/news/1998/04/07news.html>.

14. Phil Kuntz, "Citizen Scaife: Heir Turned Publisher Uses Financial Largess to Fuel Conservatism," *Wall Street Journal*, October 12, 1995, p. A5.

15. "Scaife—Funding Father of the Right," *Washington Post* special report, May 2–3, 1999, <http://www.washingtonpost.com/wp-srv/politics/special/clinton/stories/scaife050299.htm>.

16. Sarah Scaife Foundation, 2002 Annual Report, <http://www.scaife.com/sarah02.pdf>; Allegheny Foundation, 2002 Annual Report, <http://www.scaife.com/allegh02.pdf>; Carthage Foundation, 2002 Annual Report, <http://www.scaife.com/cartha02.pdf>.

17. Bradley Foundation, 2002 Financial Statement, <http://www.bradleyfdn.org/02ar/FinStmt2002.pdf>.

18. "Buying a Movement: Right-Wing Foundations and American Politics" (Washington, D.C.: People for the American Way, 1996), <http://www.pfaw.org/pfaw/dfiles/file_33.pdf>.

19. James Piereson, "The Insider's Guide to Spend Down," *Philanthropy* magazine (Philanthropy Roundtable), March/April 2002, <http://www.philanthropyroundtable. org/magazines/2002/march/piereson.html>.

20. Bruce Mirken, "Coors Courts Gays," *Mother Jones*, July 13, 2001, <http://www. motherjones.com/news/feature/2001/07/coors.html>.

21. Susan Goldsmith, "Beer Brawl," *New Times* (Los Angeles, CA), June 4, 1998.

22. Heidi Przybyla, "DC Firm Will Help Coors Tap More of Gay Market," *Business Dateline*, vol. 17, no. 22, October 9, 1998, p. 6.

23. "Castle Rock Foundation," MediaTransparency.org, <http://www.mediatransparency. org/funders/castle_rock.htm>.

24. Castle Rock Foundation, 2002 Annual Report, <http://www.castlerockfoundation. org/CR2002AR.pdf>.

25. Robert Kuttner, "Philanthropy and Movements," *The American Prospect*, July 15, 2002, <http://www.prospect.org/print/V13/13/kuttner-r.html>.

26. Ibid.

27. Ibid.

28. "Moving a Public Policy Agenda: The Strategic Philanthropy of Conservative Foundations," National Committee for Responsive Philanthropy, July 1997, <http://www.ncrp.org>.

29. "Buying a Movement."

30. David Ozonoff, "The Political Economy of Cancer Research," *Science and Nature*, no. 2 (1979), p. 13.

31. "Buying a Movement."

32. Jon Wiener, "Olin Money Tree: Dollars for Neocon Scholars," *The Nation*, vol. 250, no. 1, January 1, 1990, p. 12.

33. David Von Drehle, "Liberals Get a Think Tank of Their Own," *Washington Post*, October 23, 2003, p. A29, <http://www.washingtonpost.com/wp-dyn/articles/ A2623-2003Oct22.html>.

34. Figures for the Hoover Institution were taken from the Hoover Institution brochure: Finances, <http://www-hoover.stanford.edu/Main/brochure/finances.html>. All other figures were taken from the latest financial reports (2001 or later) available on the GuideStar database of nonprofit organizations, <http://www.guidestar.org>.

35. James A. Smith, *The Idea Brokers: Think Tanks and the Rise of the New Policy Elite* (New York, NY: The Free Press, 1991), pp. 24–27.

36. Ibid., pp. 39–40.

37. Ibid., p. 18.

38. Larry Hatfield and Dexter Waugh, "Right Wing's Smart Bombs," *San Francisco Examiner*, May 24, 1992.

39. With respect to gay rights, for example, Heritage opposed President Clinton's "don't ask, don't tell" policy, supporting instead a full ban on gay and lesbians in the military. It also opposed the Legal Services Corporation, which provides legal aid to poor people, for giving legal assistance to gay and lesbian couples seeking to adopt children, and strongly criticizing the U.S. Supreme Court for striking down Colorado's anti-gay "Amendment 2." See John Luddy, "The Military Gay Ban: Why Don't Ask, Don't Tell Don't Work," Heritage Foundation executive memorandum #359, July 1, 1993, <http://www.heritage.org/Research/NationalSecurity/

EM359.cfm>; Kenneth F. Boehm and Peter T. Flaherty, "Why the Legal Services Corporation Must Be Abolished," Heritage Foundation backgrounder #1057, October 18, 1995, <http://www.heritage.org/Research/LegalIssues/BG1057. cfm>; and Edwin Meese III and Rhett DeHart, "The Imperial Judiciary . . . and What Congress Can Do About It," *Policy Review*, no. 81, January-February 1997, <http://www.policyreview.org/jan97/meese.html>.

40. Douglas Burton, "To Win the Battle of Ideas, Send in the Think Tanks," *Insight*, March 6, 1995, pp. 16–17.

41. Philip J. Garcia, "Meese to Join Heritage Foundation," United Press International, July 14, 1988; William J. Bennett, "The War Over Culture in Education," Heritage Foundation, 1991.

42. Sharon Beder, *Global Spin* (White River Junction, VT: Chelsea Green Publishing Co., 1998), p. 78.

43. Heritage Foundation website: "Taxes," <http://www.heritage.org/Research/Taxes>; "Candidate's Briefing Book," <http://www.heritage.org/About/Bookstore/issues2002. cfm>; "Public Policy Experts," <http://www.policyexperts.org>; "Job Bank," <http://www.heritage.org/About/JobBank/index.cfm>.

44. Robert Parry, "D(OIL)E: What Wouldn't Bob Do for Koch Oil?" *The Nation*, August 26, 1996, <http://www.mediatransparency.org/reprints/bobdolekoch.htm>.

45. Cato Institute Timeline, 1977–2002, <http://www.cato.org//about/timeline.html>.

46. Richard Morin, "Free Radical," *Washington Post*, May 9, 2002, p. C1, <http://www.cato.org/dailys/01-01-03.html>.

47. Ibid.

48. Biographic listing of Michael Gough, the Cato Institute's director of science and risk studies, "Directory of Experts on Junk Science and Technophobia," FreeMarket.net, <http://www.free-market.net/directorybytopic/myths/C3/>.

49. Cato Institute Policy Analysis No. 223, "Polluting Our Principles," April 20, 1995, <http://www.cato.org/pubs/pas/pa-223.html>.

50. Wallace Kaufman, "No Turning Back: Dismantling the Fantasies of Environmental Thinking," *Cato Journal*, vol. 15, no. 2–3, <http://www.cato.org/pubs/journal/cj15n2-3-13.html>.

51. Morin.

52. Citizens for a Sound Economy mission statement, <http://www.cse.org/know/mission.php>.

53. Dan Morgan, "Think Tanks: Corporations' Quiet Weapon," *Washington Post*, January 29, 2000, p. A1, <http://www.washingtonpost.com/ac2/wp-dyn/A46598-2000Jan28>.

54. Moore.

55. Morgan.

56. Ibid.

57. "Buying a Movement."

58. This figure is taken from ALEC's IRS Form 990 for 2002, available on the Guidestar database of nonprofit organizations, <http://www.guidestar.org>.

59. "Burgeoning Conservative Think Tanks: The Madison Group: Heritage Offshoots Seek to Influence State Legislation," *Responsive Philanthropy*, June 1991, pp. 1, 12, 20. See also Nick Penniman, "Outing ALEC," *The American Prospect*, July 1,

2002, <http://www.prospect.org/print/V13/12/penniman-n.html>. A list of ALEC's foundation funders can be found on the MediaTransparency website, <http://www.mediatransparency.org>. See also John Nichols, "ALEC Meets Its Match," *The Nation*, May 29, 2003, <http://www.acorn.org/campaigns/pc.hph?p=2403>.

60. M. Asif Ismail, "A Most Favored Corporation," Center for Public Integrity, January 6, 2003, <http://www.public-i.org/dtaweb/report.asp?ReportID=487> and <http://www.public-i.org/dtaweb/report.asp?ReportID=491>.

61. Joe Stephens, "Hard Money, Strong Arms and 'Matrix,'" *Washington Post*, February 10, 2002, p. A1, <http://www.washingtonpost.com/ac2/wp-dyn/A51802-2002Feb9>.

62. Ibid.

63. "Enron Total Contributions to Federal Candidates and Parties, 1989–2001," Center for Responsive Politics, <http://www.opensecrets.org/alerts/v6/enron_totals.asp>.

64. Howard Kurtz, "Life in the Post-Enron World," *Washington Post*, January 28, 2002, <http://www.washingtonpost.com/ac2/wp-dyn/A48411-2002Jan28>.

65. Robert W. Hahn, "The False Promise of 'Full Disclosure,'" *Policy Review*, Hoover Institution, October 2002, <http://www.policyreview.org/OCT02/hahn.html>.

66. Hollinger International news release, November 17, 2003.

67. "Hollinger International Files Complaint Against Conrad M. Black, F. David Radler, Hollinger Inc., the Ravelston Corporation Limited, and Ravelston Management Inc.," Hollinger International news release, January 17, 2004.

68. Jacques Steinberg and Geraldine Fabrikant, "Friendship and Business Blur in the World of a Media Baron," *New York Times*, December 22, 2003, p. A1.

69. Ibid.

70. Ibid.

71. Ibid.

72. Ibid.

Chapter Two: The Echo Chamber

1. White House press briefing by George Stephanopolous, May 20, 1993, <http://www.ibiblio.org/pub/archives/whitehouse-papers/1993/May/Press-Briefing-by-George-Stephanopolous-52093>.

2. Thomas L. Friedman, "Haircut Grounded Clinton While the Price Took Off," *New York Times*, May 21, 1993, p. A10.

3. "Commuter Headache," *Journal of Commerce*, May 21, 1993, p. 6A.

4. See for example, "Scissor-gate," *The Hotline*, May 21, 1993.

5. White House press briefing by George Stephanopolous, May 20, 1993.

6. White House press briefing by Dee Dee Myers, May 20, 1993, <http://www.ibiblio.org/pub/academic/political-science/whitehouse-papers/1993/ May/Press-Briefing-by-Dee-Dee-Myers228----May-20-1993-AM>.

7. CNN's *Crossfire* (transcript #838), May 21, 1993.

8. Ibid.

9. Jill Dougherty, "Clinton Has Bad Hair Day Aboard 'Hair Force One,'" CNN, May 20, 1993.

10. "Cash and Coif: Kerry Haircut Costs $150," *Drudge Report*, December 2, 2002, <http://www.drudgereport.com/kerry.htm>.

11. Bill Whalen, "Hair Today, Gone Tomorrow?" *National Review*, December 5, 2002, <http://www.nationalreview.com/comment/comment-whalen120502.asp>.

12. "Report: Haircut Caused No Delays," *Dallas Morning News*, July 1, 1993, p. 12A.

13. Paul Richter and Greg Krikorian, "Sartorial Splendor May Cut into Clinton's Image," *Los Angeles Times*, May 21, 1993, p. A1.

14. "Cash and Coif."

15. "Maybe I'm Amazed," Urban Legends Reference Pages, <http://www.snopes.com/history/american/bushscan.htm>.

16. Sara Diamond, *Spiritual Warfare* (Boston, MA: South End Press, 1989), p. 41.

17. Edward E. Plowman, "Campus Crusade into All the World," *Christianity Today*, June 9, 1972, p. 38, <http://www.christianitytoday.com/ct/2003/129/14.0.html>.

18. Diamond, p. 39.

19. For an account of the relationship between the Birchers, Buckley and Young Americans for Freedom, see William A. Rusher, *The Rise of the Right* (New York, NY: William Morrow, 1984), pp. 115–116.

20. Diamond.

21. Dom Bonafede, "Part Science, Part Art, Part Hokum, Direct Mail Now a Key Campaign Tool," *National Journal*, vol. 14, no. 31, July 31, 1982, p. 1332.

22. William Claiborne, "Little in 'New Right' War Chest Finding Its Way to Candidates," *Washington Post*, March 20, 1978, p. A1.

23. Richard A. Viguerie, *The New Right: We're Ready to Lead* (Falls Church, VA: The Viguerie Company, 1981), pp. 3–5, 78, 90–98.

24. Bonafede.

25. Kent Jenkins, Jr., "North's Consultants Turn Junk Mail into Gold Mine of Financial Support," *Washington Post*, July 31, 1994, p. B1.

26. John Persinos, "Ollie, Inc.," *Campaigns & Elections*, June 1995.

27. Jim Drinkard, "Postal Inspectors Investigate Seniors Group's Mailings," Associated Press, September 29, 1995.

28. Diana Walsh, "The Fear Merchants," *San Francisco Examiner*, February 8, 1998, p. A1.

29. Ibid.

30. Ibid.

31. National Center for Public Policy Research, IRS Form 990 for 2001, taken from the Guidestar database, <http://www.guidestar.org>.

32. John Diamond, "POW Panel Grills Fund-Raisers," Associated Press, December 2, 1992.

33. John Diamond, "Stockdale Doubts POWs Were Left Behind in Vietnam," Associated Press, December 3, 1992.

34. Martin Tolchin, "Direct-Mail Schemes Aimed at Kin of POW's Condemned as Deceit," *New York Times*, December 3, 1992, p. A5.

35. Charles Doe, "Senate Panel Grills MIA Hunters, Refers One Case to FBI," United Press International, December 3, 1992.

36. Bonafede.
37. Michael Shain and Anthony Scaduto, "Inside New York," *Newsday*, July 25, 1994, p. A10.
38. Ralph Z. Hallow, "North Knows No Equal as Fundraiser," *Washington Times*, April 1, 1994, p. A1.
39. Bonafede.
40. George Lardner, Jr., "Outlays for Reagan Avoid Federal Ceiling," *Washington Post*, November 4, 1984, p. A8.
41. Jenkins.
42. "Bruce W. Eberle & Associates—About the Company" (company website), <http://www.bruceeberle.com/About.shtml>.
43. Jon Sawyer, "Ashcroft Pushes Contributed Money Back into Nationwide Mail Campaign," *St. Louis Post-Dispatch*, July 22, 1998, p. A6.
44. Deirdre Shesgreen, "Sen. Ashcroft Reconsiders Policy of Selling List of Campaign Contributors," *St. Louis Post-Dispatch*, December 12, 1999, p. A1.
45. "Bruce W. Eberle & Associates—About the Company."
46. Brian Maffly, "Utahns Can Check Out Fund-Raisers Before Donating," *Salt Lake Tribune*, February 22, 1998, p. B5.
47. Shesgreen.
48. "Bruce W. Eberle & Associates—About the Company."
49. Donna St. George, "They're Trying to Shut You Up!" *Detroit Free Press*, October 30, 1994, p. 1F.
50. Ibid.
51. Walsh.
52. "What Is Action E-Mail?" Omega List website, <http://www.omegalist.com/popwin/blanquita2.html>.
53. "What Is Action E-Mail?" Omega List website, <http://www.omegalist.com/popwin/blanquita3.html>, <http://www.omegalist.com/popwin/blanquita6.html>.
54. "Incredible Deals on Wireless Products and Services!" e-mail received by Sheldon Rampton, ConservativeHQ.com, November 30, 2000.
55. "A Win-Win Offer from Rogaine," e-mail received by Sheldon Rampton, ConservativeHQ.com, March 22, 2001.
56. "Sign a thank you card to Jesse Helms," e-mail received by Sheldon Rampton, ConservativeHQ.com, September 4, 2001.
57. "Help the Boy Scouts Against Political Correctness," e-mail received by Sheldon Rampton, BeCounted.com, July 22, 2001.
58. "Celebrate Earth Day By Countering Radical Environmentalist Propaganda," e-mail received by Sheldon Rampton, BeCounted.com, April 23, 2001.
59. Media Transparency website, <http://www.mediatransparency.org/all_in_one_results.php?Message=new+criterion>.
60. Herbert London, "Why I Am a Neocon," *The World and I*, vol. 1, p. 583, September 1986, <http://www.worldandi.com/public/1986/september/mt5.cfm>.
61. Media Transparency website, <http://www.mediatransparency.org/search_results/info_on_any_recipient.php?recipientID=241>.

62. *The Public Interest* website, <http://www.thepublicinterest.com>.
63. Grant Data Matrix, American Spectator Educational Foundation, Media Transparency website, <http://www.mediatransparency.org/search_results/info_on_any_recipient.php?23>.
64. Diamond, pp. 59–60.
65. Thomas Goetz, "I'm Not a Reporter, But I Play One on GOP-TV," *Columbia Journalism Review*, September/October 1994, <http://www.cjr.org/year/94/5/gop.asp>.
66. "New Project" (memorandum), Philip Morris, tobacco industry archives, page 3, Bates Nos. 2046662829-37, <http://legacy.library.ucsf.edu/tid/blz55e00>.
67. Although Weyrich touted NET as a network that reached millions of people, this simply means that millions of subscribers were *able* to get it on their cable network, not that they actually watched it. According to a 1997 profile by David Gann, "So few cable systems carried National Empowerment Television that it reached barely 10 percent of all households." See David Grann, "Robespierre of the Right," *New Republic*, October 27, 1997, p. 20. In a 1994 letter to Philip Morris executive Thomas Borelli, Paul Weyrich cited a Nielsen viewership survey undertaken from March 14–18 of that year, which calculated the rating for NET as 0.2. Weyrich described this as "one-quarter of the actual viewership of a major, heavily-marketed nationwide cable network specializing in sports programming," but noted that a 0.2 rating would translate into a maximum audience of 85,212. See Paul Weyrich, letter to Thomas Borelli, September 23, 1994, <http://legacy.library.ucsf.edu/tid/bsw87d00>.
68. National Empowerment Television, "Changing the Picture" (funding proposal), tobacco industry archives, Bates No. 2046563238-58, September 1994, p. 12, <http://legacy.library.ucsf.edu/tid/xsw87d00>.
69. Lawrence Morahan, "Conservative Icon Weyrich Warns 'Moral Minority' Still Dwindling," Conservative News Service, January 14, 2002, <http://www.conservative-news.org/Politics/archive/200201/POL20020114b.html>.
70. Tim Rutten, "Miles from 'Fair and Balanced,'" *Los Angeles Times*, November 1, 2003, p. E1.
71. Ken Auletta, "Vox Fox," *The New Yorker*, May 26, 2003, p. 58.
72. Matt Gross, "The Right-wing Bias Was Up-front and Obvious," Poynter Forum, October 31, 2003, <http://www.poynter.org/forum/default.asp?id=letters>.
73. Randall Rothenberg, "Planet of the Apers; Proliferation of Television Networks," *Esquire*, no. 1, vol. 126 (July 1996), p. 48.
74. Howard Kurtz, "Crazy Like a Fox," *Washington Post*, March 26, 1999, p. C1.
75. Ibid.
76. Auletta.
77. Ibid.
78. Ibid.
79. Rutten.
80. Charlie Reina, "The Fox News Memo," Poynter Forums, October 31, 2003, <http://poynter.org/forum/?id=thememo>.
81. William A. Rusher, *The Coming Battle for the Media* (New York, NY: William Morrow and Co., Inc., 1988), p. 9.
82. Ibid., p. 94.

83. "Interview with Matt Labash, The Weekly Standard," JournalismJobs.com, May 2003, <http://www.journalismjobs.com/matt_labash.cfm>.

84. Paul Glastris, "Why Can't Democrats Get Tough?" *Washington Monthly*, no. 3, vol. 34 (March 1, 2002), p. 38.

85. Eric Alterman, "What Liberal Media?" *The Nation*, February 6, 2003, <http://www.thenation.com/doc.mhtml?i=20030224&s=alterman2>.

86. Thomas Toch, "Under the Right's Wing," *Washington Monthly*, vol. 28, no. 11, November 1996, p. 22. See also Collegiate Network website, <http://www.collegiatenetwork.org/map.php>

87. Media Transparency website, <http://www.mediatransparency.org/search_results/info_on_any_recipient.php?recipientID=74>.

88. Collegiate Network website, <http://www.collegiatenetwork.org/cn.php?load=alumni>.

89. Joseph A. D'Agostino, "Conservative Spotlight: National Journalism Center," *Human Events*, October 9, 2003, <http://humaneventsonline.com/article.php?id=2028>.

90. National Journalism Center website, "Who We Are," <http://nationaljournalism center.org/whatis.html>.

91. Dudley Clendinen, "Conservative Paper Stirs Dartmouth," *New York Times*, October 13, 1981, p. A18.

92. Ellen Messer-Davidow, "Manufacturing the Attack on Liberalized Higher Education," *Social Text*, Fall 1993, p. 67.

93. Dinesh D'Souza, *The End of Racism: Principles for a Multiracial Society* (New York, NY: The Free Press, 1995), p. 527. Like many modern race-baiters, D'Souza hedges his inflammatory language with just enough caveats to justify apologetics. His reference to the "criminal and irresponsible black underclass" is preceded by the phrase "for many whites." After this passage was criticized by Glenn Loury, D'Souza responded that Loury had "completely lost" this "distinction" between his own views and those of "many whites." (*The End of Racism*, p. 20) In the original passage on page 527, however, D'Souza goes on to declare his essential agreement with the views that he attributes to whites. "If this is true," the passage continues, "the best way to eradicate beliefs in black inferiority is to remove their empirical basis. . . . [I]f blacks as a group can show that they are capable of performing competitively in schools and the work force, and exercising both the rights and responsibilities of American citizenship, then racism will be deprived of its foundation in experience."

94. D'Souza, p. 179.

95. Glenn Loury, "One Scholar Meets . . . Another Man's Poison," *Bostonia*, Winter 1995–96, p. 74.

96. Dinesh D'Souza's website, <http://www.dineshdsouza.com>.

97. Stanley Ridgley, *Start the Presses! A Handbook for Student Journalists* (ISI Books, 2000), p. 95.

98. "A Once-bright Star Dims," *The Nation*, no. 6, vol. 276, February 17, 2003, p. 29.

99. Jason Mattern, "Judy Shepard Indoctrinates RWU," *Hawk's Right Eye*, vol. 8, September 30, 2003, <http://www.rwucr.com/hve/pdf/8.pdf>.

100. "University to Conservative Students: All Ideas Welcome . . . Except Yours" (news

release), Young America's Foundation, October 16, 2003, <http://www.yaf.org/press/10_16_03.asp>.

101. Jason Mattera, "Roger Williams Witchhunt," <http://www.frontpagemag.com/Articles/ReadArticle.asp?ID=10394>; and Jason Mattera, "Censorship on a Rhode Island Campus," Students for Academic Freedom website, <http://students foracademicfreedom.org/archive/2003/JasonMatteraRWU101703.html>.

102. Linda Borg, "Student Newsletter Loses Funds Over Views on Gays," *Providence Journal*, October 24, 2003, <http://www.projo.com/news/content/projo_20031024_repub24.112a2.html>.

103. Jason Mattera, "ER in the Red," *National Review Online*, July 16, 2003, <http://www.nationalreview.com/comment/comment-mattera071603.asp>.

104. David Brock, *Blinded by the Right: The Conscience of an Ex-Conservative* (New York, NY: Three Rivers Press, 2002), p 18.

105. Ibid., p 20–22, 77, 85.

106. Grant Data Matrix, American Spectator Educational Foundation, Media Transparency website, <http://www.mediatransparency.org/search_results/info_on_any_recipient.php?23>.

107. Brock, p. 118.

108. Ibid., pp. 107, 108, 118, 124.

109. Ibid., p. 127–129.

110. Ibid., pp. 142–43.

111. Daniel Wattenberg, "Fortuitous Sex Story Bypass," *Washington Times*, January 21, 1999, p. A17.

112. Ibid., pp. 150, 171.

113. David Brock, "Living with the Clintons," *American Spectator*, January 1994.

114. Brock, *Blinded by the Right*, pp. 164–65.

115. Ibid., p. 168.

116. "'Arkansas Project' Led to Turmoil and Rifts," *Washington Post*, May 2, 1999, p. A24, <http://www.washingtonpost.com/wp-srv/politics/special/clinton/stories/scaifeside 050299.htm>.

117. Brock, *Blinded by the Right*, pp. 213–14.

118. Grant Data Matrix, Federalist Society for Law and Public Policy Studies, Media Transparency website, <http://www.mediatransparency.org/search_results/info_on_any_recipient.php?112>.

119. Ken Rudin, "George Washington Slept Here . . . and Here," *Washington Post*, August 21, 1998, <http://www.washingtonpost.com/wp-srv/politics/campaigns/junkie/archive/junkie082198.htm>. Grover Cleveland never denied fathering a child by Maria Helpin, with whom he admitted having an affair. For details, see his biography at the American President web site, <http://www.americanpresident.org/history/grovercleveland/biography/CampaignsElections.common.shtml>. Warren Harding's several extramarital liaisons and the daughter he fathered by Nan Britton are also mentioned in the *Encyclopedia Americana*, <http://ap.grolier.com/article?assetid=0193620-00>. FDR's affair with Lucy Mercer is discussed on the Franklin D. Roosevelt American Heritage Center website, <http://fdrheritage.com/erbio.htm>.

120. Woody West, "Media Abuzz with Rumors that Clinton Fathered Boy," *Washington Times*, January 6, 1999, p. A1.

121. Andrea Sachs, "Scandal Interruptus," *Time*, January 18, 1999, p. 18.

122. Maggie Haberman, "DNA Shows Bill's Not Boy's Dad," *New York Post*, January 10, 1999, p. 2.

123. David Mastio, "Prime-time Propagandist," Salon.com, February 25, 2000, <http://dir.salon.com/media/feature/2000/02/25/stossel/index.html>.

124. Description of the "Greed" teaching kit from Stossel's "In the Classroom" website, <http://www.intheclassroom.org/stossel/greed.htm>.

125. Description of the "Freeloaders" teaching kit from Stossel's "In the Classroom" website, <http://www.intheclassroom.org/stossel/freeloaders.htm>.

126. Mastio.

127. Ibid.

128. Ted Rose, "Laissez-Faire TV," *Brill's Content*, March 2000.

129. Ibid.

130. Environmental Working Group, "Give Us a Fake," <http://www.ewg.org/reports/GiveMeaFake/stossel.html>.

131. Ibid.

132. Kenneth A. Cook, letter to David Westin, president, ABC News, July 17, 2000, <http://www.ewg.org/reports/GiveMeaFake/westin.html>.

133. Support John Stossel website, <http://www.supportjohnstossel.org>.

134. Message from Allen James to RISE Members Alerts Team, March 27, 2001, <http://www.great-lakes.net/lists/enviro-mich/2001-04/msg00000.html>.

135. "Re: John Borowski," e-mail from Angela Bendorf Jamison to John Borowski, April 23, 2001.

136. Marianne Manilov, "More Underhanded Reporting from ABC News," TomPaine.com, June 26, 2001, <http://www.tompaine.com/feature2.cfm/ID/4393>.

137. "Personal Story: ABC News Correspondent John Stossel Taking Heat Over the Environment," *The O'Reilly Factor*, Fox News, June 27, 2001, transcript #062704cb.256.

138. *TV Guide*, May 10, 2003.

139. Alison Mitchell, "A Sustained GOP Push to Mock Gore's Image," *New York Times*, October 15, 2000, <http://www.nytimes.com/2000/10/15/politics/15REPU.html>.

140. Al Gore, interview on CNN's *Late Edition with Wolf Blitzer*, March 9, 1999, <http://www.cnn.com/ALLPOLITICS/stories/1999/03/09/president.2000/transcript.gore>.

141. Although their role in developing the Internet was important and has been widely honored, in fact there is no single "father" of the Internet, whose development reflects the contributions of multiple individuals. For a succinct history, see Charles L. Jackson, "The Origins of the Internet," *World and I*, no. 10, vol. 16, October 1, 2001, p. 36.

142. Robert Kahn and Vinton Cerf, "Al Gore and the Internet," September 28, 2000, <http://www.politechbot.com/p-01394.html>.

143. Mark Sandalow, "Forbes Makes 2000 Bid from Podium on Web," *San Francisco Chronicle*, March 16, 1999, p. A3.

144. Phil Agre, "Who Invented 'Invented'? Tracing the Real Story of the 'Al Gore Invented the Internet' Hoax," October 17, 2000, <http://lists.essential.org/

pipermail/random-bits/2000-October/000443.html>. The headlines listed here were compiled from the LexisNexis news database.

145. William Powers, "For Gore, It Was No Love Story," *National Journal*, December 20, 1997, p. 2568. See also Melinda Henneberger, "Author of 'Love Story' Disputes a Gore Story," *New York Times*, December 14, 1997, p. 40.

146. Commentary by Tony Snow, Maria Liasson and Brit Hume, *Fox News Sunday*, June 13, 1999.

147. "Al Gore's Mission" (editorial), *Washington Times*, June 17, 1999, p. A20.

148. Bob Somerby, "Tale of Two Hopefuls," *The Daily Howler*, June 21, 1999, <http://www.dailyhowler.com/h062199_1.shtml>.

149. Bob Somerby, "The Love Story Must Go On," *The Daily Howler*, April 1, 1999, <http://www.dailyhowler.com/h040199_1.shtml>.

150. David Yepsen and Jeff Zeleny, "Gore Makes His Candidacy Official," *Des Moines Register*, March 19, 1999, p. 1A.

151. Deborah Orin, "Gore's Daze of Swine and Hoses," *New York Post*, March 18, 1999, p. 18.

152. Fox Special Report with Brit Hume (transcript), Fox News, March 18, 1999.

153. Cal Thomas, "Striving to Reinvent Al Gore," *Washington Times*, March 21, 1999, p. B3.

154. Michael Kelly, "Farmer Al," *Washington Post*, March 24, 1999, p. A27.

155. Bob Zelnick, *Gore: A Political Life* (Washington, D.C.: Regnery Publishing, Inc., 1999).

156. Bill Turque, *Inventing Al Gore* (New York, NY: Houghton Mifflin, 2000). Cited in Bob Somerby, "Farm Team," *The Daily Howler*, May 26, 2000, <http://www.dailyhowler.com/h052600_1.shtml>.

157. Mona Charen, "More Mendacity," Creators Syndicate, October 6, 2000, <http://www.townhall.com/columnists/monacharen/mc2000106.shtml>.

158. Quoted in Robert Parry, "He's No Pinocchio," *Washington Monthly*, April 2000, <http://www.washingtonmonthly.com/features/2000/0004.parry.html>.

159. For a longer discussion of alleged Gore gaffes and actual facts, see Phil Agre, "The New Science of Character Assassination," October 15, 2000, <http://commons.somewhere.com/rre/2000/RRE.The.New.Science.of.C.html>.

160. Parry.

Chapter Three: The One-Party State

1. Alexander Hamilton, James Madison and John Jay, *The Federalist*, Edited by Jacob E. Cooke (Middletown, CT: Wesleyan University Press, 1961), pp. 426–37.

2. Alexis de Tocqueville, one of the first foreign observers to praise American democracy, believed that foreign policy was one of the areas where democratic governments "appear decidedly inferior to others," but subsequent evidence suggests that democracies actually fare better even in wartime than other forms of government. "Since 1815, democracies have won more than three quarters of the wars in which they have participated," note professors Dan Reiter and Allan C. Stam. This can be explained, they say, because "being vulnerable to the will of

the people restrains democratic leaders and helps prevent them from initiating foolhardy or risky wars." Moreover, freedom of dissent makes it easier for democracies to adapt and innovate in wartime, recognizing and correcting errors of strategy that inevitably arise. See Dan Reiter and Allan C. Stam, *Democracies at War* (Princeton, NJ: Princeton University Press, 2002).

3. Sheldon Rampton and John Stauber, *Weapons of Mass Deception: The Uses of Propaganda in Bush's War on Iraq* (New York, NY: Tarcher/Penguin, 2003).

4. Paul Krugman, "Delusions of Power," *New York Times*, March 28, 2003, p. A17.

5. See the "Group Influence" chapter in David G. Myers, *Social Psychology*, 7th edition (New York, NY: McGraw-Hill, 2002).

6. Jim VandeHei, "Bush Policies Ease Transition for Aides into Lobbyist Jobs," *Wall Street Journal*, March 19, 2001, p. A22.

7. Joshua Green, "Ergonomic Enemy," *American Prospect*, vol. 12, no. 16, September 10, 2001, <http://www.prospect.org/print/V12/16/green-j.html>.

8. Elizabeth Shogren, "Bush Environment Jobs Are Skewed to Business," *Los Angeles Times*, June 24, 2001, p. A1.

9. VandeHei.

10. Michael Kinsley, "Influence-peddling on 'K Street,'" *Slate*, September 17, 2003, <http://msnbc.msn.com/id/3080823>.

11. Nicholas Confessore, "Welcome to the Machine," *Washington Monthly*, July/August 2003, <http://www.washingtonmonthly.com/features/20030307.confessore.html>.

12. Jim VandeHei, "GOP Monitoring Lobbyists' Politics," *Washington Post*, June 10, 2002, p. A01, <http://www.washingtonpost.com/ac2/wp-dyn/A22406-2002Jun9>.

13. Confessore.

14. Ibid.

15. Thomas B. Edsall, "Big Business's Funding Shift Boosts GOP," *Washington Post*, Wednesday, November 27, 2002, p. A01.

16. Ibid.

17. "2002 Cycle: Business-Labor-Ideology Split in PAC, Soft & Individual Donations to Candidates and Parties," Center for Responsive Politics, <http://www.opensecrets.org/bigpicture/blio.asp?cycle=2002>.

18. David Brooks, "The Problem with K Street Conservatism," *Weekly Standard*, vol. 7, issue 40, June 24, 2002, p. 11.

19. Confessore.

20. Ibid.

21. "Clinton's Cash Hunt Affirmed," *Detroit Free Press*, January 31, 1997, p. 5A.

22. Frank Greve, "Lincoln Bedroom Becomes Another Soiled Symbol," *Austin American-Statesman*, March 2, 1997, p. J1.

23. Roger Cossack, Greta Van Susteren, Greg LaMotte, "JonBenet Ramsey Update/ Dozing for Dollars?" CNN, February 27, 1997.

24. Robert A. Rankin, "Anatomy of a Scandal," *Florida Times-Union*, March 9, 1997, p. H1.

25. M. Asif Ismail, "Fat Cat Hotel Still Open for Business," Center for Public Integrity, August 22, 2002, <http://www.publicintegrity.org/dtaweb/report.asp?ReportID=460>.

26. "The Power 25: Top Lobbying Companies," *Fortune*, May 28, 2001, <http://www.fortune.com/fortune/power25/lobbyingcompanies>.

27. Leslie Wayne, "An Ex-G.O.P. Chairman Is Comfortable in 2 Hats," *New York Times*, July 23, 2001, p. A14.
28. Ibid.
29. Joshua Micah Marshall, "Talking Points Memo," September 26, 2003, <http://www.talkingpointsmemo.com/archives/002005.html>.
30. Joshua Micah Marshall, "The Bush Crony Full-Employment Act of 2003," *The Hill*, October 1, 2003, <http://www.hillnews.com/marshall/100103.aspx>.
31. "Secret Bids," ABC News, March 22, 2003, <http://abcnews.go.com/sections/wnt/World/iraq_rebuilding_contract030322.html>.
32. "Winning Contractors," Center for Public Integrity, October 30, 2003, <http://www.publicintegrity.org/wow>.
33. Jill Junnola, "Who Funds Whom?" *Energy Compass*, October 4, 2002.
34. Ibid.
35. Robert Dreyfuss, "The Pentagon Muzzles the CIA," *American Prospect*, vol. 13, issue 22, December 16, 2002, <http://www.prospect.org/print-friendly/print/V13/22/dreyfuss-r.html>.
36. George L. Mosse, *Nazi Culture* (New York, NY: Schocken Books, 1981), p. 198.
37. "Politics and Science in the Bush Administration," report prepared for Rep. Henry A. Waxman (D-California), August 2003 (updated November 13, 2003), <http://www.house.gov/reform/min/politicsandscience/method_research.htm> and <http://www.house.gov/reform/min/politicsandscience/pdfs/pdf_politics_and_science_rep.pdf>.
38. Stephanie Simon, "Abortion Foes Seize on Reports of Cancer Link in Ad Campaign," *Los Angeles Times*, March 24, 2002, p. A26.
39. Oliver Burkeman, "Man of Steel," *Guardian* (UK), September 17, 2002, <http://www.guardian.co.uk/g2/story/0,3604,793417,00.html>.
40. Alessandra Stanley, "Nancy Reagan, in a Whisper, Fights Bush Over Stem Cells," *New York Times*, September 29, 2002, section 1, p. 1.
41. USDA, List of Sensitive Issues for ARS Manuscript Review and Approval by National Program Staff — February 2002 (revised) (Feb. 2002).
42. Perry Beeman, "Ag Scientists Feel the Heat," *Des Moines Register*, December 1, 2002, p. 1A.
43. Rick Weiss, "HHS Seeks Science Advice to Match Bush Views," *Washington Post*, September 17, 2002, p. A01, <http://www.washingtonpost.com/ac2/wp-dyn/A26554-2002Sep16>.
44. "Turning Lead into Gold: How the Bush Administration is Poisoning the Lead Advisory Committee at the CDC," report by the staff of Rep. Edward J. Markey (D-Massachusetts), October 8, 2002, <http://www.house.gov/markey/iss_environment_rpt021008.pdf>.
45. Deposition of Dr. William Banner, Jr. (June 13, 2002), in *State of Rhode Island v. Lead Industries Assoc.*, C.A. No. 99-5526 (Sup. Ct. R.I. Apr. 2, 2001).
46. Weiss.
47. David Michaels et al., "Advice Without Dissent," *Science*, no. 5594, vol. 298 (October 25, 2002), p. 703.
48. John Fleck, "UNM Prof Says Politics Moves in on Science," *Albuquerque Journal*, December 20, 2002, p. A1; and Aaron Zitner, "Advisors Put Under a Microscope,"

Los Angeles Times, December 23, 2002, p. 1, <http://www.truthout.org/docs_02/12.25C.microscope.htm>.

49. "Human Impacts on Climate," statement adopted by the American Geophysical Union Council in December 2003, <http://www.agu.org/sci_soc/policy/climate_change_position.html>.

50. "Climate Change Research: Issues for the Atmospheric and Related Sciences," statement adopted by the American Meterological Society Council on February 9, 2003, *Bulletin of the American Meteorological Society,* vol. 84, pp. 508–15, <http://www.ametsoc.org/policy/climatechangeresearch_2003.html>.

51. National Academy of Sciences, Commission on Geosciences, Environment and Resources, *Climate Change Science: An Analysis of Some Key Questions* (Washington, DC: National Academy Press, 2001), <http://www.nap.edu/catalog/10139.html?onpi_webextra6>.

52. "The 2000 Campaign: Second Presidential Debate Between Governor Bush and Vice President Gore" (transcript), *New York Times,* October 12, 2000, p. A22.

53. Robert Novak and Bill Press, "Christine Todd Whitman Discusses the Bush Administration's Environmental Policy" (transcript), CNN's *Crossfire,* February 26, 2001.

54. "Italian Police Block Anti-globalisation Protesters at G8 Meeting," Channel NewsAsia, March 4, 2001.

55. "Clearing the Air" (transcript), *Now with Bill Moyers,* September 19, 2003, <http://www.pbs.org/now/transcript/transcript_clearingtheair.html>.

56. Memo from Randy Randol, ExxonMobil Washington Office, to John Howard, White House Council on Environmental Quality (Feb. 6, 2001) (online at http://www.nrdc.org/media/docs/020403.pdf).

57. Jeff Nesmith, "Global Warming Official Out," *Atlanta Journal-Constitution,* April 20, 2002, p. 9A.

58. Andrew Lawler, "Battle Over IPCC Chair Renews Debate on U.S. Climate Policy," *Science,* no. 5566, vol. 296, April 12, 2002, p. 232.

59. *U.S. Climate Action Report,* U.S. Department of State, May 2002, <http://yosemite.epa.gov/oar/globalwarming.nsf/content/ResourceCenterPublicationsUSClimateActionReport.html>.

60. Myron Ebell, "Phil, Thanks for Calling," e-mail to Phil Cooney, Council on Environmental Quality, White House, June 3, 2002, <http://dynamic.greenpeace.org/smoking-gun/CEImemo.swf>.

61. Tom Doggett, "EPA Chief Was Left in the Dark on U.S. Climate Report," Reuters, June 13, 2002.

62. John Heilprin, "Bush Dismisses Climate Change Study," Associated Press, June 4, 2002.

63. Paul Harris, "Bush Covers Up Climate Research," *Observer* (UK), September 21, 2003, p. 20.

64. "Clearing the Air."

65. Ibid.

66. Harris.

67. Eric Pianin and Guy Gugliotta, "EPA Chief Whitman to Resign," *Washington Post,* May 22, 2003, p. A1, <http://www.washingtonpost.com/ac2/wp-dyn/A23338-2003May21>.

68. Ibid.

69. James Glanz and Andrew C. Revkin, "A Nation Challenged: Haunting Question: Did the Ban on Asbestos Lead to Loss of Life?" *New York Times*, September 18, 2001, p. F2.

70. John Heilprin, "EPA Watchdog Rips White House on NYC Air," Associated Press, August 22, 2003.

71. Monsanto is one of 250 leading corporations—the *Financial Times* of London called them "a who's who of American industry"—that face serious liability claims related to asbestos. See "The Toxic Time-bomb Exploding Throughout the Corporate World," *Financial Times* (London), September 9, 2002, p. 26. In 1997, Monsanto attempted to eliminate its liability for asbestos and other chemicals by creating a subsidiary company, Solutia Inc., which assumed Monsanto's liabilities when it was spun off as an independent corporation. Subsequently, however, Solutia declared bankruptcy and has petitioned to transfer liabilities back to Monsanto, beginning with a $3 million asbestos liability payment that it failed to make in December 2003. See Christopher Carey, "Solutia's Financial Pressures Run Deep," *St. Louis Post-Dispatch*, December 21, 2003, p. G1.

72. *EPA's Response to the World Trade Center Collapse: Challenges, Successes, and Areas for Improvement*, Report No. 2003-P-00012, U.S. Environmental Protection Agency, Office of Inspector General, August 21, 2003, p. 17, <http://www.epa.gov/oigearth/reports/2003/WTC_report_20030821.pdf>.

73. Ibid.

74. "EPA, OSHA Update Asbestos Data, Continue to Reassure Public About Contamination Fears" (news release), U.S. Environmental Protection Agency, September 16, 2001, <http://www.epa.gov/wtc/stories/headline_091601.htm>.

75. "Whitman Details Ongoing Agency Efforts to Monitor Disaster Sites, Contribute to Cleanup Efforts" (news release), U.S. Environmental Protection Agency, September 18, 2001, <http://www.epa.gov/wtc/stories/headline_091801.htm>.

76. Steven Milloy, "Asbestos Could Have Saved WTC Lives," Fox News, September 14, 2001, <http://www.foxnews.com/story/0,2933,34342,00.html>.

77. "Re: Risk," comments on Radsafe Listserv, November 16, 2001, <http://www.vanderbilt.edu/radsafe/0111/msg00258.html>.

78. Susan Q. Stranahan, "Air of Uncertainty," *American Journalism Review*, January/February 2003, <http://www.ajr.org/article.asp?id=2746>.

79. Alyssa Katz, "Toxic Haste," *American Prospect*, February 25, 2002, <http://www.prospect.org/print/V13/4/katz-a.html>.

80. Juan Gonzalez, "A Toxic Nightmare at Disaster Site," *New York Daily News*, October 26, 2001, p. 2.

81. Stranahan.

82. "Church in Crisis; Newsmaker; Aftermath; Toxic Fallout," *NewsHour with Jim Lehrer*, April 16, 2002, transcript #7310.

83. Paul M. Crawzak, "Disappointing EPA Critics, Popular Former EPA Ombudsman Won't Return," Copley News Service, August 29, 2002.

84. Benjamin Shors, "Ombudsman Quits EPA Over Transfer," *Spokesman Review*, April 23, 2002, p. B1.

85. David J. Prezant et al., "Cough and Bronchial Responsiveness in Firefighters at the World Trade Center Site," *New England Journal of Medicine*, vol. 347, no. 11, September 12, 2002, pp. 806–15.

86. Christine Haughney, "Respiratory Ills Plague Ground Zero Workers," *Washington Post*, September 16, 2002, p. A3, <http://www.washingtonpost.com/ac2/wp-dyn/A22212-2002Sep15>.

87. "EPA Report: White House Lied to New Yorkers About Health Hazards Near Ground Zero" (interview transcript), *Democracy Now!*, August 26, 2003, <http://www.democracynow.org/article.pl?sid=03/08/26/145232>.

Chapter Four: Pumping Irony

1. "Schwarzenegger Not Saying No," CBS News, June 27, 2003, <http://www.cbsnews.com/stories/2003/07/17/entertainment/main563728.shtml>.

2. "Arnold Schwarzenegger Auditions for New Role—'Governator,'" NBC4 TV, August 7, 2003, <http://www.nbc4.tv/politics/2385057/detail.html>.

3. Bernard Weinraub, "Hollywood Is All Eyes As One of Its Own Takes a New Stage," *New York Times*, August 8, 2003, <http://www.ajc.com/news/content/news/0803/08hollywood.html>.

4. "Arnold Schwarzenegger Auditions for New Role—'Governator.'"

5. Max Blumenthal, "California Confidential," *American Prospect*, August 13, 2003, <http://www.prospect.org/webfeatures/2003/08/blumenthal-m-08-13.html>.

6. Deno Seder, "Attack Ads: Protecting Against Viewer Backlash," in *Winning Elections: Political Campaign Management, Strategy and Tactics*, edited by Ronald A. Faucheux (New York, NY: M. Evans and Company, Inc., 2003), p. 380.

7. John Connolly, "Arnold the Barbarian," *Premiere*, March 2001.

8. Mark Z. Barabak, "California and the West," *Los Angeles Times*, March 9, 2001, p. 3.

9. Dana Milbank and Mike Allen, "Schwarzenegger Outcome Could Affect Bush in 2004," *Washington Post*, August 14, 2003, p. A05, <http://www.washingtonpost.com/ac2/wp-dyn/A56084-2003Aug13>.

10. Joe Mathews, Jessica Garrison and Mark Z. Barabak, "Schwarzenegger Uses Talk Radio to Start Spelling Out His Views," *Los Angeles Times*, August 28, 2003, <http://www.latimes.com/news/local/politics/cal/la-me-gop28aug28000428,1,5771748.story?coll=la-news-politics-california>.

11. Mathews et al.

12. Joe Mathews, "After a Shaky Opening, a Candidate Is Born," *Los Angeles Times*, October 9, 2003, <http://www.latimes.com/news/politics/la-me-reconstruct9oct09,1,1957250.story>.

13. Anthony York, "Donors Ponied Up Big Bucks Last Month for Possible Schwarzenegger Campaign," *Political Pulse*, July 25, 2003, <http://www.politicalpulse.com/ArchiveFeaturedStory/FS072503.htm>.

14. "Schwarzenegger Staff Pledges Confidentiality," *Los Angeles Times*, September 19, 2003, <http://www.latimes.com/news/custom/showcase/la-me-notebook19sep19.story>.

15. James Sterngold, "Schwarzenegger Met the Press His Way: Celebrity Status Changed Media Landscape," *San Francisco Chronicle*, October 13, 2003, <http://sfgate.com/cgi-bin/article.cgi?file=%2Fc%2Fa%2F2003%2F10%2F13%2FMEDIA.TMP>.

16. Matt Labash, "Arnold Uber Alles," *The Weekly Standard*, vol. 9, no. 6, October 20, 2003, <http://www.weeklystandard.com/Content/Public/Articles/000/000/003/237obvee.asp>.

17. "Arnold Schwarzenegger Auditions for New Role—'Governator.'"

18. Labash.

19. Ibid.

20. Neal Koch, "The Terminator at Work?" *Columbia Journalism Review*, vol. 29, no. 5, January/February 1991, p. 28.

21. Gary Cohn, Carla Hall and Robert W. Welcos, "Women Say Schwarzenegger Groped, Humiliated Them," *Los Angeles Times*, October 2, 2003, <http://www.latimes.com/news/printedition/front/la-me-women2oct02,1,4493659,print.story>; and Gary Cohn, Carla Hall, Jack Leonard and Tracy Weber, "4 More Women Go Public Against Schwarzenegger," *Los Angeles Times*, October 5, 2003, <http://www.latimes.com/news/politics/recall/la-me-women5oct05,1,583359,print.story>.

22. Steve Lopez, "Mud Splashes Back at Governor," *Los Angeles Times*, December 14, 2003, <http://www.latimes.com/news/local/la-me-lopez14dec14,1,3505560.column>.

23. John S. Carroll, "The Story Behind the Story," *Los Angeles Times*, October 12, 2003, <http://www.latimes.com/news/politics/recall/la-oe-carroll12oct12,0,4817752.story>.

24. Sharon Waxman, "The Recall Show with Jay Leno," *Washington Post*, October 9, 2003, p. C1, <http://www.washingtonpost.com/ac2/wp-dyn/A412-2003Oct8>. The fact that Schwarzenegger's appearance was preplanned is evident from the fact that he came with a video clip from his victory celebration, which the show broadcast.

25. Ibid.

26. Ibid.

27. "Long-term Contribution Trends," openSecrets.org, <http://www.opensecrets.org/industries/indus.asp?ind=C1100> and <http://www.opensecrets.org/industries/indus.asp?ind=B02>.

28. "Most Heavily Partisan Industries," openSecrets.org, <http://www.opensecrets.org/bigpicture/partisans.asp?cycle=2002>.

29. Anne Kelly-Saxenmeyer, "Playing the Candidate," Backstage.com, October 6, 2003, <http://www.backstage.com/backstage/features/article_display.jsp?vnu_content_id=1994710>.

30. Greg Mitchell, *The Campaign of the Century: Upton Sinclair's Race for Governor of California and the Birth of Media Politics*, (New York, NY: Random House, 1992).

31. Ian Hargreaves, "Spinning Out of Control," *History Today*, vol. 53, no. 3, March 2003.

32. David Greenberg, "Nixon's Legacy: In Politics, Image is Everything," *Los Angeles Times*, October 6, 2003, p. B11.

33. Paul Keyes, a friend of Nixon and a *Laugh-In* writer, helped arrange Nixon's appearance on the show on September 16, 1968. For details, see Susan King,

"Television; The Bippy Revolution," *Los Angeles Times*, June 29, 2003, Part 5, p. 28.

34. Joe McGinniss, *The Selling of the President* (New York, NY: Penguin Group, 1988 reprint), p. 63.

35. Ibid., p. 103.

36. Ibid., pp. 63–66.

37. Greenberg.

38. Rich Thomaselli, "The Natural: Dusenberry Leaves Imprint on Ad World," *Advertising Age*, May 20, 2003, p. 4.

39. Frank Lovece, "A New Museum Exhibit Chronicles 40 Years of Political Commercials and Other Memorable Campaign Moments on Television," *Newsday*, July 5, 1992, p. 18. See also Kathleen Hall Jamieson, "Our Appalling Politics," *Washington Post*, October 30, 1998, p. C1.

40. Kathleen Hall Jamieson, "Insinuation and Other Pitfalls in Political Ads and News." Originally published as "The Subversive Effects of a Focus on Strategy in News Coverage of Presidential Campaigns," in *1-800 President*, Twentieth Century Fund Task Force on Television and the Campaign of 1992 (New York, NY: Twentieth Century Fund Press, 1993).

41. Mark Crispin Miller, "Political Ads: Decoding Hidden Messages," *Columbia Journalism Review*, January/February 1992, <http://archives.cjr.org/year/92/1/political ads.asp>.

42. Leslie Stahl, *Reporting Live* (New York, NY: Touchstone Books, 2000), p. 210.

43. Ibid.

44. Ibid., p. 211.

45. James Moore and Wayne Slater, *Bush's Brain: How Karl Rove Made George W. Bush Presidential* (Hoboken, NJ: John Wiley & Sons, 2003), p. 273.

46. "President Bush Announces Major Combat Operations in Iraq Have Ended," White House Office of the Press Secretary, May 1, 2003, <http://www.whitehouse. gov/news/releases/2003/05/iraq/20030501-15.html>.

47. Ken Fireman, "Dems: Landing Cost $1M," *Newsday*, May 8, 2003, p. A43.

48. Mike Allen, "Ship Carrying Bush Delayed Return," *Washington Post*, May 8, 2003, p. A29.

49. Ibid.

50. Scott Lindlaw, "Accommodating TV-friendly Presidential Visit Caused a Few Changes in Navy Carrier's Routine," Associated Press, May 2, 2003.

51. Mike Allen, "The Bird Was Perfect but Not for Dinner," *Washington Post*, December 4, 2003, p. A33, <http://www.washingtonpost.com/ac2/wp-dyn/A33090-2003Dec3>.

52. Dana Milbank, "A Baghdad Thanksgiving's Lingering Aftertaste," *Washington Post*, December 12, 2003, p. A35, <http://www.washingtonpost.com/ac2/wp-dyn/A57870-2003Dec11>.

53. Sgt. Loren Russell, "Bush Visit Disrupted Dining," *Stars and Stripes* (European and Mideast editions), December 5, 2003, <http://www.stripes.com/article.asp?section=125&article=19124>.

54. Remarks by the President at Leadership Forum, Egleston Children's Hospital,

Atlanta, Georgia, March 1, 2001, <http://www.whitehouse.gov/news/releases/2001/03/20010301-6.html>.

55. Jeffrey McMurray, "Bush Budget Would Cut Funding for Hospital He Visited," Associated Press, April 10, 2001.

56. "President Rallies First Responders in Georgia," Remarks by the President to Georgia First Responders, Georgia Institute of Technology, Atlanta, GA, White House news release, March 27, 2002, <http://www.whitehouse.gov/news/releases/2002/03/20020327-7.html>.

57. Bill Miller, "White House Resists Pressure from Fire Chiefs," *Washington Post*, October 16, 2002, p. A23.

58. Steve Friess, "Firefighters Vote to Boycott Bush's Sept. 11 Tribute," Reuters, August 14, 2002.

59. "President Calls for Expanding Opportunities to Home Ownership," Remarks by the President on Homeownership, St. Paul AME Church, Atlanta, Georgia, White House news release, June 17, 2002, <http://www.whitehouse.gov/news/releases/2002/06/20020617-2.html>.

60. Dana Milbank and Dan Morgan, "Some Pet Programs Are Targeted for Cuts," *Washington Post*, February 5, 2004, p. A11, <http://www.washingtonpost.com/wp-dyn/articles/A13975-2004Feb4.html>.

61. "'Made in (Deleted)'—Bush's Sales Pitch Has a Gargantuan Cover-up," Associated Press, January 23, 2003, <http://seattlepi.nwsource.com/national/105400_boxes23.shtml>.

62. Abbie Hoffman, *The Best of Abbie Hoffman*, edited by Daniel Simon (New York, NY: Four Walls, Eight Windows, 1989), pp. 44, 51, 75.

63. Patrick Healy, "Biting Remarks on Candidacy by 'Canine' on 'Tonight Show,'" *Boston Globe*, November 12, 2003, p. A3.

64. Joanna Weiss, "Late-Night's Not Always a Laugher for Candidates," *Boston Globe*, November 22, 2003, p. C1.

65. Michael Crowley, "Stayin' Alive," *The New Republic*, November 12, 2003, <http://www.tnr.com/primary/index.mhtml?pid=961>.

Chapter Five: Block the Vote

1. David Horowitz, "Baa Baa Black Sheep," Salon.com, November 9, 1998, <http://dir.salon.com/col/horo/1998/11/nc_09horo.html>.

2. Cathleen Decker, "Motor Voter Law Drives Registration to High Levels," *Los Angeles Times*, March 16, 1996, p. A1.

3. Lawrence Knutson, "Senate Ends GOP Filibuster, Approves Motor Voter Bill," Associated Press, May 11, 1993.

4. Linda Feldmann, "GOP Campaign Tactics Spark New Jersey Furor," *Christian Science Monitor*, November 12, 1993, p. 2.

5. Michelle Ruess and Dunstan McNichol, "Grand Jury Hears Whitman's Kin," *The Record* (Bergen, NJ), November 25, 1993, p. A1.

6. Michelle Ruess, "Whitman Says of Payoffs: Never Happened," *The Record* (Bergen, NJ), November 13, 1993, p. A1.

7. Jim Geraghty, "NH Democrats Say Attorney General Investigating Election Day Phone Jamming," *States News Service*, February 20, 2003.

8. John B. Judis, "Soft Sell," *The New Republic*, November 11, 2002.

9. Wayne Barrett, "Sleeping with the GOP," *Village Voice*, February 5, 2004, <http://www.villagevoice.com/issues/0405/barrett.php>.

10. Michael Slackman, "The 2004 Campaign: The Consultant: Sharpton's Bid Aided by an Unlikely Source," *New York Times*, January 25, 2004, section 1, p. 22.

11. Laughlin McDonald, "The New Poll Tax," *American Prospect*, vol. 13, no. 23, December 30, 2002, <http://www.prospect.org/print-friendly/print/V13/23/mcdonald-l.html>.

12. Sean Wilentz, "Jim Crow, Republican Style: Voter Suppression in 2002," in Andrew Cuomo, ed., *Crossroads* (New York, NY: Random House, 2003), p. 280.

13. McDonald.

14. NAACP press release, "NAACP to Send Election Observers to Kentucky; NAACP Asks the Justice Department to Send Federal Election Monitors," October 31, 2003, <http://www.naacp.org/news/releases/ElecObserKY103103.shtml>.

15. Megan Garvey, "NBC Balks at Sharing Election Night Tapes," *Los Angeles Times*, August 8, 2001, p. A1; and Megan Garvey, "Waxman Renews NBC News Assault," *Los Angeles Times*, September 11, 2001, p. A1.

16. Todd Gitlin, "How TV Killed Democracy on Nov. 7," *Los Angeles Times*, February 14, 2001, p. B11.

17. Robert Parry, "Bush's Conspiracy to Riot," *Consortium News*, August 5, 2002, <http://www.consortiumnews.com/2002/080502a.html>.

18. Carol Rosenberg, "Political Jobs Go to Bush's Recount Warriors; Appointees Fought Gore Bid in Florida," *Miami Herald*, July 14, 2002, p. A1.

19. David Barstow and Don Van Natta, Jr., "How Bush Took Florida: Mining the Overseas Absentee Vote," *New York Times*, July 15, 2001, p. 1.

20. "Gore Wins Under Six of Nine Scenarios," *Palm Beach Post*, November 12, 2001, <http://www.palmbeachpost.com/news/content/news/gore_wins6of9.html>.

21. "Florida Recount Study: Bush Still Wins," CNN special, <http://www.cnn.com/SPECIALS/2001/florida.ballots/stories/main.html>.

22. Scott Hiaasen, Gary Kane and Elliot Jaspin, "Felon Purge Sacrificed Innocent Voters," *Palm Beach Post*, May 27, 2001, p. 1A. The figure of 42,389 cited by Hiaasen et al. differs from the 57,700 cited by Greg Palast in *The Best Democracy Money Can Buy* (New York, NY: Plume, 2002), p. 62.

23. Palast, p. 62. For an online summary of Palast's conclusions, see Gregory Palast, "Florida's Flawed 'Voter-Cleansing' Program," Salon.com, December 4, 2000, <http://dir.salon.com/politics/feature/2000/12/04/voter_file/index.html>. See also Anthony York, "Eliminating Fraud—Or Democrats?" Salon.com, December 8, 2000, <http://archive.salon.com/politics/feature/2000/12/08/integrity/index.html>; and John Nichols, *Jews for Buchanan: Did You Hear the One About the American Presidency?* (New York, NY: New Press, 2001). Nichols, a national political correspondent for *The Nation*, estimates that the Reconstruction-era law disenfranchising felons cost Gore 85,000 votes.

24. The *New York Times*, which declined to publish Palast's reports on voter disenfranchisement when they were first written in 2001, belatedly acknowledged in a 2004

editorial that Florida's "massive purge of eligible voters" showed "how easy it is for registered voters to lose their rights by bureaucratic fiat. . . . Thousands of Florida voters ended up being wrongly purged." See "How America Doesn't Vote," *New York Times*, February 15, 2004, section 4, p. 10, <http://www.nytimes.com/2004/02/15/opinion/15SUN1.html>.

25. Liam Scheff, "Winning the Election the Republican Way: Racism, Theft and Fraud in Florida," *The Weekly Dig* (Boston, MA), April 22, 2003, <http://www.gregpalast.com/detail.cfm?artid=217&row=2>. See also Robert E. Pierre, "Botched Name Purge Denied Some the Right to Vote," *Washington Post*, May 31, 2001, p. A1, <http://www.washingtonpost.com/ac2/wp-dyn/A99749-2001May30>. Pierre says that the problems in Florida may have been "errors" rather than deliberate disenfranchisement. "No one has proven intent to disenfranchise any group of voters," he states. Nevertheless, he acknowledges, "The impact of the botched felon purge fell disproportionately on black Floridians and, by extension, on the Democratic Party."

26. Palast, p. 62.

27. Palast, p. 63.

28. Dennis Cauchon, "Errors Mostly Tied to Ballots, Not Machines," *USA Today*, November 7, 2001, <http://www.usatoday.com/news/washington/nov01/ballots-usat.htm>.

29. Hiaasen et al.

30. Scott Hiaasen, Gary Kane and Elliot Jaspin, "Thousands of Felons Voted Despite Purge," *Palm Beach Post*, May 28, 2001, p. 1A.

31. U.S. Commission on Civil Rights, "Voting Irregularities in Florida During the 2000 Presidential Election," June 2001, <http://www.usccr.gov/pubs/vote2000/report/main.htm>. See also Katharine Q. Seelye, "Divided Civil Rights Panel Approves Election Report," *New York Times*, June 9, 2001, p. A8.

32. Text of letter from Charles T. Canady, General Counsel, Office of Florida Governor Jeb Bush to Edward A. Hailes, Jr., General Counsel, U.S. Commission on Civil Rights, June 6, 2001.

33. Catherine Wilson, "Florida, Counties Settle NAACP Suit Over 2000 Election," Associated Press, September 3, 2002.

34. ACLU, <http://archive.aclu.org/graphics/voting_ad.jpg>.

35. Jeffrey Toobin, "The Great Election Grab," *The New Yorker*, December 12, 2003, <http://www.newyorker.com/fact/content/?031208fa_fact>.

36. Shannon P. Duffy, "Gerrymander: Good Politics or Power Grab?" *Legal Times*, December 15, 2003, p. 8.

37. Sasha Abramsky, "The Redistricting Wars," *The Nation*, vol. 277, no. 22, December 9, 2003, p. 15.

38. "Redistricting, Turnout and Competitiveness," issue brief, Alliance for Better Campaigns, <http://www.bettercampaigns.org/issuebriefs/display.php?BriefID=12>.

39. Rob Richie and Steven Hill, "Re-redistricting Is an Ugly Power Grab," *Houston Chronicle*, June 29, 2003.

40. Toobin.

41. Ibid.

42. Michael Kelly, "Segregation Anxiety," *The New Yorker*, November 20, 1995.

43. Toobin.

44. Ibid.

45. David Lublin, "Racial Redistricting and Southern Realignment in the 1990s," presentation at the Joint Center for Political and Economic Studies' conference "Redistricting 1992–2002: Voting Rights and Minority Representation," May 22, 2002, Washington DC, <http://www.jointcenter.org/whatsnew/redistricting-conference/Lublin.pdf>.

46. Thomas F. Schaller, "A Route for 2004 That Doesn't Go Through Dixie," *Washington Post*, November 16, 2003, <http://www.washingtonpost.com/wp-dyn/articles/A40359-2003Nov14.html>.

47. Toobin.

48. The Center for Voting and Democracy, "Dubious Democracy Report: 2003–2004," <http://www.fairvote.org/dubdem/overview.htm>.

49. "Steven K. Paulson, Colorado Supreme Court Rules Republicans' Redistricting Unconstitutional," Associated Press, December 1, 2003.

50. Toobin.

51. Laylan Copelin, "Catch Us If You Can: How the Killer D's Pulled Off an Improbable Plot to Freeze the House," *Austin American-Statesman*, May 18, 2003, p. A1.

52. Eric Lichtblau, "Justice Department Rejected Idea of Joining Texas Dispute," *New York Times*, August 13, 2003, p. A16.

53. David Pasztor, "Redrawn Districts Pass Test at Justice; Agency Finds No Voting Rights Violation; Map Still Faces Legal Hurdle," *Austin American-Statesman*, December 20, 2003, p. A1.

54. Michael King, "Here We Go Again: The Redistricting Case Resumes, One Battle in a Protracted War," *Austin Chronicle*, December 5, 2003, <http://www.austinchronicle.com/issues/dispatch/2003-12-05/pols_capitol.html>.

Chapter Six: Traitor Baiters

1. James Madison, "The Same Subject Continued (The Powers Conferred by the Constitution Further Considered)," from the Federalist Papers, No. 43, for the Independent Journal, January 23, 1788; in Alexander Hamilton, James Madison and John Jay, *The Federalist*, Edited by Jacob E. Cooke (Middletown, CT: Wesleyan University Press, 1961).

2. James Wilson, "Of Crimes Immediately Against the Community, Lectures on Law," *The Works of James Wilson*, edited by Robert Green McCloskey, (Cambridge, MA: Belknap Press of Harvard University Press, 1967), pp. 663–69.

3. Carl Weiser, "KY Senator Sees TV Reporter's Remarks as Treason," Gannett News Service, April 1, 2003.

4. David Horowitz, "The Sick Mind of Noam Chomsky," *Front Page*, September 26, 2001, <http://www.frontpagemag.com/Articles/ReadArticle.asp?ID=1020>.

5. David Horowitz, "MIT Loon Sounds Off at UT, Gets a Big Audience and an Appreciative Press," David's Blog, October 22, 2002, <http://www.frontpagemag.com/blog/BlogEntry.asp?ID=68>.

6. J. J. Stambaugh, "Tribute to the Troops," *Knoxville News-Sentinel*, April 8, 2003, p. Al.

7. "Traitor List," <http://www.probush.com/traitor.htm>. The ProBush.com website declares that it is a "parody" and that the traitors "are not legal 'traitors' of the United States," but it is hard to see the humor in its straightforward statements deploring critics of the Bush administration. In the call to "boycott Hollywood," for example, the site complains that actress Jessica Lange stated, while in Spain accepting an award, that Bush "stole the election" and that the U.S. people "have been suffering under his leadership." The webmaster responds: "Trashing a president while on foreign soil as she did, with the possibility of a war looming is tantamount to treason." See <http://www.probush.com/boycott_hollywood.htm>.

8. "Dixie Chicks' 'Top of the World Tour' a Great Success" (news release), Clear Channel Entertainment, Inc., March 7, 2003, <http://biz.yahoo.com/bw/030307/75279_1.html>.

9. "DJs Suspended for Playing Dixie Chicks," *Washington Post*, May 6, 2003, <http://www.washingtonpost.com/wp-dyn/articles/A19571-2003May6.html>.

10. Ann Coulter, *Treason: Liberal Treachery from the Cold War to the War on Terrorism* (New York, NY: Crown Forum, 2003), p. 1.

11. Ibid., p. 171.

12. Ibid., p. 16.

13. "A Double-edged Peace Prize," *Guardian* (UK), October 11, 2002, <http://www.guardian.co.uk/international/story/0,3604,810140,00.html>.

14. Coulter, p. 257.

15. Michelle Malkin, "Terrorists with Tofu Breath," *Washington Times*, November 22, 2003, <http://www.townhall.com/columnists/michellemalkin/mm20031119.shtml>.

16. "Delaney: A Welcome Escape from the Mousetrap," *Priorities*, American Council on Science and Health, vol. 8, no. 3, 1996, <http://www.acsh.org/publications/priorities/0803/escape.html>.

17. Michael Fumento, "Tampon Terrorism," *Forbes*, May 17, 1999.

18. Jacob Sullum, "Tobacco Terror," *Reason*, April 8, 1998, <http://reason.com/sullum/040898.shtml> (April 16, 2003).

19. Tina Gasperson, "Ethical Terrorism," <http://www.stormloader.com/tdg/ethical.html> (April 16, 2003).

20. Eric Dezenhall, *Nail 'em!* (Amherst, NY: Prometheus Books, 1999), p. 81.

21. Rod Smith, "Agriculture Told to Fight on Activists' Ground Using 'Attack Technologies' or Face Destruction," *Feedstuffs*, March 26, 2001. Note: With the retirement of Nick Nichols in September 2003, the Nichols-Dezenhall PR firm is now called Dezenhall Resources.

22. Glen Martin, "Attack on Tax Status of Environment Group," *San Francisco Chronicle*, June 21, 2001, <http://www.sfgate.com/cgi-bin/article.cgi?file=/c/a/2001/06/21/MN187865.DTL>.

23. BanzhafWatch.com website, <http://www.banzhafwatch.com>.

24. Steven Milloy, "Taco Terrorism," Cato Institute website, September 28, 2000, <http://www.cato.org/dailys/09-28-00.html>.

25. "Environmental Extremism and Eco-Terrorism," conference monograph, Frontiers

of Freedom Institute, June 13, 2001, <http://www.ff.org/media/PDF/ec_conference.
pdf> (April 16, 2003).

26. Ibid.

27. Ibid.

28. Jeff Humphrey, "Cracking Down on Eco-Terrorism," Northwest Cable News,
September 7, 2001.

29. Ben White, "Will the Environment Become a Casualty of the Terrorist Attacks?"
Grist, September 15, 2001, <http://www.gristmagazine.com/grist/muck/muck
091501.asp?source=daily> (April 16, 2003).

30. Mary Mostert, "Was It Osama bin Laden or Is He Just a Minor Player?" Reagan Information Interchange, September 12, 2001, <http://www.reagan.com/HotTopics.
main/document-9.13.2001.8.html> (September 21, 2001). Archived at <http://
www.bannerofliberty.com/OS9-01MQC/9-12-2001.1.html>.

31. Tom Randall, "As a Nation Struggles, Domestic Terrorists Brag," *National Policy
Analysis*, National Center for Public Policy Research, September 2001, <http://
www.nationalcenter.org/NPA368.html> (April 16, 2001).

32. "War Against Eco-terrorists," *Washington Times*, October 7, 2001, p. B2.

33. "McInnis Presses Forward with 'ELF' Subpoena" (news release), October 2, 2001,
<http://www.house.gov/mcinnis/press/2001/pr011002.htm>.

34. Richard B. Berman, "Ecoterrorism, Its Connections to Animal-Rights Terrorism,
and Their Common Above-Ground Support System," testimony before the U. S.
House of Representatives, Committee on Resources, Subcommittee on Forests
and Forest Health, February 12, 2002, <http://www.cdfe.org/berman.htm>.

35. Dean Schabner, "New Front on Ecoterror?" ABC News, February 26, 2002, <http://
abcnews.go.com/sections/us/DailyNews/ecoterror_support020226.html>. Full disclosure: Berman has also attacked authors Sheldon Rampton and John Stauber as
terrorists, claiming that our 1997 book about mad cow disease was intended to
"scare" people who eat beef.

36. "New Web Site, EnviroTruth.org, Brings Truth to the Environmentalist Movement" (news release), PR Newswire, May 6, 2002, <http://www.findarticles.com/
cf_dls/m4PRN/2002_May_6/85931436/p1/article.jhtml>.

37. *Nicaragua, The Human Rights Record, 1986–1989* (London: Amnesty International,
1989). See also *Violations of the Laws of War By Both Sides in Nicaragua, 1981–
1985* (New York, NY: Americas Watch, March 1985); and "Nicaragua," Human
Rights Watch report, 1989, <http://www.hrw.org/reports/1989/WR89/Nicaragu.htm>.

38. "February: Highlights: Conservative Political Action Committee Conference 2002,"
Right Wing Watch Online (e-mail newsletter), February 26, 2002, <http://
www.pfaw.org/pfaw/general/default.aspx?oid=1625>. See also Jay Bookman, "Liberals, Report to Re-education," *Atlanta Journal-Constitution*, February 14, 2002, p. 18A.

39. White House Press Briefing, September 25, 2002, <http://www.whitehouse.gov/
news/releases/2002/09/20020925-3.html>.

40. Andrew Sullivan weblog, September 18, 2001, <http://www.andrewsullivan.com/
index.php?dish_inc=archives/2001_09_16_dish_archive.html>.

41. Michael Kelly, "Pacifist Claptrap," *Washington Post*, September 26, 2001, p. A25,
<http://www.washingtonpost.com/wp-dyn/articles/A26290-2001Sep26.html>.

42. Press briefing by Ari Fleischer (transcript), White House Office of the Press Secretary, September 26, 2001, <http://www.whitehouse.gov/news/releases/2001/09/20010926-5.html>.

43. William Bennett, open letter, "Week in Review" section, *New York Times*, March 10, 2002.

44. Testimony of Attorney General John Ashcroft, Senate Committee on the Judiciary, December 6, 2001, <http://www.usdoj.gov/ag/testimony/2001/1206transcriptsenate judiciarycommittee.htm>.

45. "Cheney Cautions Democrats Criticizing Bush," Associated Press, May 17, 2002, <http://www.usatoday.com/news/nation/2002/05/17/cheney.htm>.

46. Dan Balz, "Bush and GOP Defend White House Response," *Washington Post*, May 18, 2002; Page A01, <http://www.washingtonpost.com/ac2/wp-dyn/A35718-2002May17>.

47. "Bush, GOP Blast Calls for 9/11 Inquiry," CNN, May 17, 2002, <http://www.cnn.com/2002/ALLPOLITICS/05/16/president.gop.senators>.

48. *The Beltway Boys*, Fox News, transcript #051801cb.257, May 19, 2002.

49. Adam Nagourney, "Eyes on 2004 Vote, Democrats Fault U.S. Terror Defense," *New York Times*, December 26, 2002, p. A1.

50. *The O'Reilly Factor*, Fox News, February 26, 2003, transcript #022601cb.256.

51. Kris Axtman, "Political Dissent Can Bring Federal Agents to the Door," *Christian Science Monitor*, January 8, 2002, <http://www.csmonitor.com/2002/0108/p1s4-usju.html>.

52. Ibid.

53. "Rise of Lunacy at Six," Page Six column, *New York Post*, April 3, 2003, <http://www.pagesix.com/pagesix/33385.htm>.

54. John Podhoretz, "A Hitler Miniseries Meant to Bash Bush," *New York Post*, April 9, 2003.

55. Lisa de Moraes, "Producer Is a Casualty in CBS's 'Hitler' Miniseries," *Washington Post*, April 11, 2003, p. C7.

56. Eric Haas and Jama Fisk, "Speak Out for Academic Freedom," *Albuquerque Tribune*, May 20, 2003, <http://www.abqtrib.com/archives/opinions03/052003_opinions_teachers.shtml>.

57. Steve Liewer, "Servicemembers Speaking Out: A Look at the Policies, Consequences," *Stars and Stripes*, July 22, 2003, <http://www.estripes.com/article.asp?section=104&article=15991&archive=true>.

58. Douglas Quenqua, "Pentagon Makes Moves to Contain Complaints from U.S. Troops in Iraq," *PR Week*, August 4, 2003, <http://www.prweek.com/news/news_story.cfm?ID=186846&site=3>.

59. Jonathan Turley, "Un-American Arrests," *Washington Post*, October 6, 2002, p. B8.

60. Susan Lee, program director, Amnesty International Americas Regional Program, Letter to Governor Jeb Bush, December 16, 2003, <http://www.amnestyusa.org/countries/usa/document.do?id=1E53E2B67703BB0880256E0100479301>.

61. Stephen O. Starr, "Reaction from the Other Side of the Aisle," Indy Media Center FTAA weblog, November 21, 2003, <http://ftaaimc.org/en/2003/11/1459.shtml>.

62. Stephen O. Starr, "Bienvenido a Miami, Scum," Free Republic website, November 23, 2003, <http://www.freerepublic.com/focus/f-news/1027342/posts>.

63. Ina Paiva Cordle, "Reporter's Notebook," *Miami Herald*, November 24, 2003, p. G3.
64. Michelle Goldberg, "This Is Not America," Salon.com, December 16, 2003, <http://salon.com/news/feature/2003/12/16/miami_police/index_np.html>.
65. Leo W. Gerard, International President of the United Steelworkers of America, Letter to the Congressional Leadership, November 24, 2003, <https://www.uswa.org/uswa/program/adminlinks/docs//pdf%20miami%20rights%20letter.pdf>.
66. Mike Schneider, "Protesters Say Police Overreacted During Miami Trade Talks," *Associated Press*, November 21, 2003.
67. Ken Thomas, "Protesters, Police Clash During Free Trade Demonstrations," *Associated Press*, November 20, 2003.
68. Tere Figueras, Sara Olkon and Martin Merzer, "Big Police Presence, Few Clashes," *Miami Herald*, November 21, 2003, p. A1.
69. Lee.
70. Goldberg.
71. Susannah Nesmith, "Police Praise Selves on Absence of Chaos: Police Succeed in Protecting Downtown Miami from a Small Cadre of Violent Protesters, But Activist Groups Complain of Heavy-Handed Tactics," *Miami Herald*, November 22, 2003, p. A1.
72. Ibid.
73. Carlos Hamann, "Protesters, Police Clash as Americas Trade Summit Ends Early," *Agence France-Presse*, November 21, 2003.
74. Cynthia Moothart, "Goons Over Miami: It's the Police, Not the Protesters, Getting Violent," *In These Times*, January 5, 2004, p. 4.
75. Les Kjos, "Analysis: Suits Planned in Miami Protest," *United Press International*, November 24, 2003.
76. Jim Defede, "'Miami Model' of FTAA Security Is Lightning Rod," *Miami Herald*, December 18, 2003, p. B1.
77. Coky Michel, "Chaotic, Forceful Police Muddy Peaceful Gathering," *Miami Herald*, November 25, 2003, p. A21.

Conclusion: The Three-Banana Problem

1. Susan Page, "Norquist's Power High, Profile Low," *USA Today*, June 1, 2001, <http://www.usatoday.com/news/washington/2001-06-01-grover.htm>.
2. Robert Dreyfuss, "Grover Norquist: 'Field Marshal' of the Bush Plan," *The Nation*, May 14, 2001, <http://www.thenation.com/docprint.mhtml?i=20010514&s=dreyfuss>.
3. Saul Alinsky, *Rules for Radicals* (New York, NY: Vintage Books, 1989), inside flap copy.
4. Edward A. Grefe and Martin Linsky, *The New Corporate Activism* (New York, NY: McGraw-Hill, 1995), pp. xi, 2, 9.
5. Sheldon Rampton, "Fish Out of Water: Behind the Wise Use Movement's Victory in Klamath," *PR Watch*, vol. 10, no. 2, second quarter 2003, <http://www.prwatch.org/prwissues/2003Q2/fish.html>.

6. Marta Russell, "Craig Shirley Does the Disabled," *PR Watch*, vol. 8, no. 2, second quarter 2002, <http://www.prwatch.org/prwissues/2001Q2/shirley.html>.

7. Richard Cohen, "Out of Their Anti-tax Minds," *Washington Post*, January 6, 2004, p. A17, <http://www.washingtonpost.com/ac2/wp-dyn/A57436-2004Jan5>.

8. *Insuring America's Health: Principles and Recommendations*, Committee on the Consequences of Uninsurance, Institute of Medicine of the National Academies (Washington, DC: National Academies Press, 2004), p. 8, <http://www.nap.edu/catalog/10874.html>.

9. Rick Henderson and Steven Hayward, "Happy Warrior: An Interview with Grover Norquist," *Reason* magazine, February 1997, <http://reason.com/9702/fe.int.norquist.shtml>.

10. Lawrence R. Jacobs, Robert Shapiro and Eli C. Schulman, "Poll Trends: Medical Care in the United States—an Update," *Public Opinion Quarterly*, vol. 57, no. 3, Fall 1993, p. 394.

11. Louis Harris, "Poll on Popular Satisfaction with Health Care," June 1992. Cited in Gene Costain, "Canada/United States Healthcare" (student term paper), University of Tennessee, Knoxville, Fall 1996, <http://excellent.com.utk.edu/~mmmiller/jpr525/costain.html>.

12. Humphrey Taylor, "As Economy Grows the Public's Priorities for Growth are Health Care, Education and Defense," *The Harris Poll* #33, June 11, 2003, <http://www.harrisinteractive.com/harris_poll/index.asp?PID=382>.

13. Karen S. Palmer, "A Brief History: Universal Health Care Efforts in the U.S.," Physicians for a National Health Program, <http://www.pnhp.org/facts/a_brief_history_universal_health_care_efforts_in_the_us.php>.

14. Edward A. Grefe, "Do Not Ask for Whom the Web Tolls: It May Be for Your Company," *Impact* (Public Affairs Council newsletter), September 1998, p. 1.

15. Howard W. French, "Online Newspaper Shakes Up Korean Politics," *New York Times*, March 6, 2003, p. A3.

16. Dan Gillmor, "A New Brand of Journalism is Taking Root in South Korea," *San Jose Mercury News*, May 18, 2003, <http://www.siliconvalley.com/mld/siliconvalley/business/columnists/5889390.htm>.

17. Ilene R. Prusher, "Hand-held People Power at Web Speed," *Christian Science Monitor*, December 1, 2000, <http://search.csmonitor.com/durable/2000/12/01/fp1s4-csm.shtml>.

18. George Packer, "Smart-Mobbing the War," *New York Times*, March 9, 2003, section 6, p. 46.

19. "MoveOn.org Becomes Anti-Bush Powerhouse," CNN, January 13, 2004, <http://www.cnn.com/2004/TECH/internet/01/12/moveon.org.ap/>.

20. Bush in 30 Seconds website, <http://www.bushin30seconds.org>.

21. For examples, see Al Kamen, "Switching Power: Easier to Pull the Plug," *Washington Post*, June 28, 2000, <http://www.washingtonpost.com/ac2/wp-dyn/A8416-2000Jun27>. See also Ralph Peters, "Dems' Moral Collapse," *New York Post*, September 30, 2003.

22. "GOP Hypocrite of the Week," BuzzFlash.com, November 19, 2003, <http://www.buzzflash.com/editorial/03/11/edi030009.html>.

23. "Views of a Changing World 2003," Pew Research Center for the People and the Press, June 3, 2003, <http://people-press.org/reports/display.php3?ReportID= 185>.

24. "America's Image Further Erodes, Europeans Want Weaker Ties," Pew Research Center for the People and the Press, March 18, 2003, <http://people-press.org/ reports/display.php3?ReportID=175>.

25. Richard Bernstein, "Two Years Later: World Opinion; Foreign Views of U.S. Darken After Sept. 11," *New York Times*, September 11, 2003, p. A1.

Index

About the Authors

Sheldon Rampton and John Stauber both work for the Center for Media and Democracy, a nonprofit organization that Stauber founded in 1993 to monitor and expose deceptive public relations campaigns and other propaganda sponsored by corporations and governments. They write and edit the center's quarterly publication, *PR Watch*. They have co-authored four previous books: *Toxic Sludge Is Good for You: Lies, Damn Lies and the Public Relations Industry* (1995); *Mad Cow U.S.A.: Could the Nightmare Happen Here?* (1997); *Trust Us, We're Experts: How Industry Manipulates Science and Gambles with Your Future* (2001); and *Weapons of Mass Deception: The Uses of Propaganda in Bush's War on Iraq* (2003).

John Stauber is a longtime activist who has worked with public interest, consumer, family-farm, environmental and community organizations at the local, state and national level. Before founding the center, he worked for five years for the Foundation on Economic Trends, a Washington, D.C., nonprofit organization, researching possible health and economic impacts of recombinant bovine growth hormone (rBGH) and organizing concerned citizens and farmers. Born in 1953, he is married and lives in Madison, Wisconsin.

Sheldon Rampton is a graduate of Princeton University who has a diverse background as newspaper reporter, activist and author. In college, he studied writing under Joyce Carol Oates, E. L. Doctorow and John McPhee. In addition to books authored with John Stauber, he is the co-author (with Liz Chilsen) of the 1998 book *Friends In Deed: The Story of US–Nicaragua Sister Cities.* Prior to Joining the Center for Media and Democracy, he worked for the Wisconsin Coordinating Council on Nicaragua (www.wccnica.org) on the NICA Fund, a project that since 1992 has channeled more than $10 million in loans from U.S. investors to support economic development efforts in low-income Central American communities. Born in 1957, he is married and lives in Portage, Wisconsin.

For further information about the authors, including archived copies of PR *Watch*, visit the PR Watch website (www.prwatch.org), or contact:

Center for Media and Democracy
520 University Avenue, Suite 227
Madison, WI 53703
Phone (608) 260-9713